THE BATTLE FOR THE BEGINNING

THE BATTLE
FOR THE BEGINNING

The Bible on Creation and the Fall of Adam

John MacArthur

W PUBLISHING GROUP™

www.wpublishinggroup.com

A Division of Thomas Nelson, Inc.
www.ThomasNelson.com

THE BATTLE FOR THE BEGINNING:
The Bible on Creation and the Fall of Adam

Library of Congress Cataloging-in-Publication Data

MacArthur, John 1939–
The battle for the beginning : the Bible on creation and the fall of Adam /
John F. MacArthur, Jr.
p.   cm.
Includes bibliographical references

ISBN 0-8499-1625-9

1. Creationism. 2. Fall of man. 3. Bible. O.T. Genesis I–III—Criticism, interpretation, etc. I. Title.

BS651.M23   2001
231.7'652–dc21

2001045546

Printed in the United States of America
05 04 03 02 01 BVG 5 4 3

To Bill Zimmer, faithful elder of Grace Community Church and loyal friend, whose lifelong devotion to the Book of Genesis and whose defense of its literal interpretation have been a great example to me.

CONTENTS

ACKNOWLEDGMENTS

THROUGH MORE THAN THREE DECADES of ministry at Grace Community Church, I have had the privilege of presenting expositional sermons almost every Sunday. I have preached systematically through one book of the bible on Sunday mornings and a different book on Sunday evenings. This has produced thousands of messages for which I have extensive original notes as well as taped recordings. It is from that volume of material that all my books are drawn. The number of books I've written could never have been produced without that long-term preparation and preaching ministry.

It would also be impossible for me to publish so many books if it were not for the goodness of the Lord in giving me some exceptional editors who work on the material—most notably Phil Johnson, who for years has faithfully applied his remarkable writing skills to the more critical books such as this one. This volume, like many others, is the product of a friendship and a partnership between us.

Others who assisted in various stages of the editorial process include Mary Hollingsworth and Rhonda Hogan from W Publishing Group, and Gary Knussman from the staff of Grace To You. I also want to say a special thanks to my dear friend and fellow pastor Lance Quinn, who helped by proofreading the final pages.

INTRODUCTION

THANKS TO THE THEORY OF EVOLUTION, naturalism is now the dominant religion of modern society. Less than a century and a half ago, Charles Darwin popularized the credo for this secular religion with his book *The Origin of Species*. Although most of Darwin's theories about the mechanisms of evolution were discarded long ago, the doctrine of evolution itself has managed to achieve the status of a fundamental article of faith in the popular modern mind. Naturalism has now replaced Christianity as the main religion of the Western world, and evolution has become naturalism's principal dogma.

Naturalism is the view that every law and every force operating in the universe is natural rather than moral, spiritual, or supernatural. Naturalism is inherently antitheistic, rejecting the very concept of a personal God. Many assume naturalism therefore has nothing to do with religion. In fact, it is a common misconception that naturalism embodies the very essence of scientific objectivity. Naturalists themselves like to portray their system as a philosophy that stands in opposition to all faith-based world-views, pretending that it is scientifically and intellectually superior precisely because of its supposed non-religious character.

Not so. *Religion* is exactly the right word to describe naturalism. The entire philosophy is built on a faith-based premise. Its basic presupposition—a rejection of everything supernatural—requires a giant leap of faith. And nearly all its supporting theories must be taken by faith as well.[1]

Consider the dogma of evolution, for example. The notion that natural evolutionary processes can account for the origin of all living species has never been and never will be established as fact. Nor is it "scientific" in any true sense of the word. Science deals with what can be observed and reproduced by experimentation. The origin of life can be neither observed nor reproduced in any laboratory. By definition, then, true science can give us no knowledge whatsoever about where we came from or how we got here. Belief in evolutionary theory is a matter of sheer faith. And dogmatic belief in any naturalistic theory is no more "scientific" than any other kind of religious faith.

Modern naturalism is often promulgated with a missionary zeal that has powerful religious overtones. The popular fish symbol many Christians put on their cars now has a naturalist counterpart: a fish with feet and the word *Darwin* embossed into its side. The Internet has become naturalism's busiest mission field, where evangelists for the cause aggressively try to deliver benighted souls who still cling to their theistic presuppositions. Judging from the tenor of some of the material I have read seeking to win converts to naturalism, naturalists are often dedicated to their faith with a devout passion that rivals or easily exceeds the fanaticism of any radical religious zealot. Naturalism is clearly as much a religion as any theistic world-view.

The point is further proved by examining the beliefs of those naturalists who claim to be most unfettered by religious beliefs. Take, for example, the case of Carl Sagan, perhaps the best-known scientific celebrity of the past couple of decades. A renowned astronomer and media figure, Sagan was overtly antagonistic to biblical theism. But he became the chief televangelist for the religion of naturalism. He preached a world-view that was based entirely on naturalistic assumptions. Underlying all he taught was the firm conviction that everything in the universe has a natural cause and a natural explanation. That belief—a matter of faith, not a truly scientific observation—governed and shaped every one of his theories about the universe.

Sagan examined the vastness and complexity of the universe and concluded—as he was bound to do, given his starting point—that there is nothing greater than the universe itself. So he borrowed divine attributes such as infinitude, eternality, and omnipotence, and he made them properties of the universe itself.

"The cosmos is all that is, or ever was, or ever will be" was Sagan's trademark aphorism, repeated on each episode of his highly rated television series, *Cosmos*. The statement itself is clearly a tenet of faith, not a scientific conclusion. (Neither Sagan himself nor all the scientists in the world combined could ever examine "all that is, or ever was, or ever will be" by any scientific method.) Sagan's slogan is perfectly illustrative of how modern naturalism mistakes religious dogma for true science.

Sagan's religion was actually a kind of naturalistic pantheism, and his motto sums it up perfectly. He deified the universe and everything in it—insisting that the cosmos itself is that which was, and is, and is to come (cf. Revelation 4:8). Having examined enough of the cosmos to see evidence of the Creator's infinite power and majesty, he imputed that omnipotence and glory to creation itself—precisely the error the apostle Paul describes in Romans 1:20–22:

> For since the creation of the world His invisible attributes are clearly seen, being understood by the things that are made, even His eternal power and Godhead, so that they are without excuse, because, although they knew God, they did not glorify Him as God, nor were thankful, but became futile in their thoughts, and their foolish hearts were darkened. Professing to be wise, they became fools.

Exactly like the idolaters Paul was describing, Sagan put creation in the Creator's rightful place.

Carl Sagan looked at the universe, saw its greatness, and concluded nothing could possibly be greater. His religious presuppositions forced him to deny that the universe was the result of intelligent design. In fact, as a devoted naturalist, he had to deny that it was created at all. Therefore he saw the universe as eternal and infinite, so it naturally took the place of God in his thinking.

The religious character of the philosophy that shaped Sagan's world-view is evident in much of what he wrote and said. His novel *Contact* (made into a major motion picture in 1997) is loaded with religious metaphors and imagery. It's about the discovery of extraterrestrial life, which occurs in December 1999, at the dawn of a new millennium, when the world is rife with Messianic expectations and apocalyptic fears. In Sagan's imagination, the discovery of intelligent life elsewhere in the universe becomes the "revelation" that affords a basis for the fusing of science and religion into a worldview that perfectly mirrors Sagan's own belief system—with the cosmos as God and scientists as the new priesthood.

Sagan's religion included the belief that the human race is nothing special. Given the incomprehensible vastness of the universe and the impersonality of it all, how could humanity possibly be important? Sagan concluded that our race is not significant at all. In December 1996, less than three weeks before Sagan died, he was interviewed by Ted Koppel on *Nightline*. Sagan knew he was dying, and Koppel asked him, "Dr. Sagan, do you have any pearls of wisdom that you would like to give to the human race?"

Sagan replied:

> We live on a hunk of rock and metal that circles a humdrum star that is one of 400 billion other stars that make up the Milky Way Galaxy, which is one of billions of other galaxies, which make up a universe, which may be one of a very large number—perhaps an infinite number—of other universes. That is a perspective on human life and our culture that is well worth pondering.[2]

In a book published near the end of his life, Sagan wrote, "Our planet is a lonely speck in the great enveloping cosmic dark. In our obscurity, in all this vastness, there is no hint that help will come from elsewhere to save us from ourselves."[3]

Although Sagan resolutely tried to maintain a semblance of optimism to the bitter end, his religion led where all naturalism inevitably leads: to a sense of utter insignificance and despair. According to his world-view, humanity occupies a tiny outpost—a pale blue speck in a vast sea of galaxies. As far as we know, we are unnoticed by the rest of the universe, accountable to no one, and petty and irrelevant in a cosmos so expansive. It is fatuous to talk of outside help or redemption for the human race. No help is forthcoming. It would be nice if we somehow managed to solve some of our problems, but whether we do or not will ultimately be a forgotten bit of cosmic trivia. That, said Sagan, is a perspective well worth pondering.

All of this underscores the spiritual barrenness of naturalism. The naturalist's religion erases all moral and ethical accountability, and it ultimately abandons all hope for humanity. If the impersonal cosmos is all there is, all there ever was, and all there ever will be, then morality is ultimately moot. If there is no personal Creator to whom humanity is accountable and if the survival of the fittest is the governing law of the universe, all the moral principles that normally regulate the human conscience are ultimately groundless—and possibly even deleterious to the survival of our species.

Indeed, the rise of naturalism has meant moral catastrophe for modern society. The most damaging ideologies of the nineteenth and twentieth centuries were all rooted in Darwinism. One of Darwin's earliest champions, Thomas Huxley, gave a lecture in 1893 in which he argued that evolution and ethics are incompatible. He wrote that "the practice of that which is ethically best—what we call goodness or virtue—involves a course of conduct which, in all respects, is opposed to that which leads to success in the cosmic struggle for existence."[4]

Philosophers who incorporated Darwin's ideas were quick to see Huxley's point, conceiving new philosophies that set the stage for the amorality and genocide that characterized so much of the twentieth century.

Karl Marx, for example, self-consciously followed Darwin in the devising of his economic and social theories. He inscribed a copy of his book *Das Kapital* to Darwin, "from a devoted admirer." He referred to Darwin's *The Origin of Species* as "the book which contains the basis in natural history for our view."[5]

Herbert Spencer's philosophy of "Social Darwinism" applied the doctrines of evolution and the survival of the fittest to human societies. Spencer argued that if nature itself has determined that the strong survive and the weak perish, this rule should govern society as well. Racial and class distinctions simply reflect nature's way. There is therefore no transcendent moral reason to be sympathetic to the struggle of the disadvantaged classes. It is, after all, part of the natural evolutionary process and society will actually be improved by recognizing the superiority of the dominant classes and encouraging their ascendancy. The racialism of such writers as Ernst Haeckel (who believed that the African races were incapable of culture or higher mental development) was also rooted in Darwinism.

Friedrich Nietzsche's whole philosophy was based on the doctrine of evolution. Nietzsche was bitterly hostile to religion, and particularly to Christianity. Christian morality embodied the essence of everything Nietzsche hated; he believed Christ's teachings glorified human weakness and were detrimental to the development of the human race. He scoffed at Christian moral values such as humility, mercy, modesty, meekness, compassion for the powerless, and service to one another. He believed such ideals had bred weakness in society. Nietzsche saw two types of people: the "master-class," an enlightened, dominant minority; and the "herd," sheeplike followers who were easily led. And he concluded that the only hope for humanity would be when the master-class evolved into a race of *Übermenschen* (supermen), unencumbered by religious or social mores, who would take power and bring humanity to the next stage of its evolution.

It's not surprising that Nietzsche's philosophy laid the foundation for the Nazi movement in Germany. What is surprising is that at the dawn of the twenty-first century, Nietzsche's reputation has been rehabilitated by philosophical spin-doctors, and his writings are once again trendy in the academic world. Indeed, his philosophy—or something very nearly like it—is what naturalism must inevitably return to.

All of these philosophies are based on notions that are diametrically opposed to a biblical view of the nature of man, because they all start by embracing a Darwinian view of the origin of humanity. They are rooted in anti-Christian theories about human origins and the origin of the cosmos, and therefore it is no wonder that they stand in opposition to biblical principles at every level.

The simple fact of the matter is that all the philosophical fruits of Darwinism have been negative, ignoble, and destructive to the very fabric of society. Not one of the major twentieth-century revolutions led by post-Darwinian philosophies ever improved or ennobled any society. Instead, the chief social and political legacy of Darwinian thought is a full spectrum of evil tyranny with Marx-inspired communism at one extreme and Nietzsche-inspired fascism at the other. The moral catastrophe that has disfigured modern Western society is also directly traceable to Darwinism and the rejection of the early chapters of Genesis.

At this moment in history, even though most of modern society is already fully committed to an evolutionary and naturalistic world-view, our society still benefits from the collective memory of a biblical world-view. People in general still believe human life is special. They still hold remnants of biblical morality, such as the notion that love is the greatest virtue (1 Corinthians 13:13), service to one another is better than fighting for personal dominion (Matthew 20:25–27), and humility and submission are superior to arrogance and rebellion (1 Peter 5:5). But to whatever degree secular society still holds those virtues in esteem, it does so entirely without any philosophical foundation. Having already rejected the God revealed in Scripture and embraced instead pure naturalistic materialism, the modern mind has no grounds whatsoever for holding to any ethical standard, no reason whatsoever for esteeming "virtue" over "vice," and no justification whatsoever for regarding human life as more valuable than any other form of life. Modern society has already abandoned its moral foundation.

As humanity enters the twenty-first century, an even more frightening prospect looms. Now even the church seems to be losing the will to defend what Scripture teaches about human origins. Many in the church are too intimidated or too embarrassed to affirm the literal truth of the biblical account of creation. They are confused by a chorus of authoritative-sounding voices who insist that it is possible—and even pragmatically necessary—to reconcile Scripture with the latest theories of the naturalists.

Of course, theological liberals have long espoused theistic evolution. They have never been reluctant to deny the literal truth of Scripture on any issue. The new trend has also influenced some evangelicals who contend that it is possible to harmonize Genesis 1—3 with the theories of modern naturalism without doing violence to any essential doctrine of Christianity. They affirm evangelical statements of faith. They teach in evangelical institutions. They insist they believe the Bible is inerrant and authoritative. But they are willing to reinterpret Genesis to accommodate evolutionary theory. They express shock and surprise that anyone would question their approach to Scripture. And they sometimes employ the same sort of ridicule and intimidation religious liberals and atheistic skeptics have always leveled against believers: "You don't seriously think the universe is less than a billion years old, do you?"

The result is that over the past couple of decades, large numbers of evangelicals have shown a surprising willingness to take a completely non-evangelical approach to interpreting the early chapters of Genesis. More and more are embracing the view known as "old-earth creationism," which blends some of the principles of biblical creationism with naturalistic and evolutionary theories, seeking to reconcile two opposing world-views. And in order to accomplish this, old-earth creationists end up explaining away rather than honestly exegeting the biblical creation account.

A handful of scientists who profess Christianity are among those who have led the way in this revisionism—most of them lacking any skill whatsoever in biblical interpretation. But they are setting forth a major reinterpretation of Genesis 1–3 designed specifically to accommodate the current trends of naturalist theory. In their view, the six days of creation in Genesis 1 are long ages, the chronological order of creation is flexible, and most of the details about creation given in Scripture can be written off as poetic or symbolic figures of speech.

Many who should know better—pastors and Christian leaders who defend the faith against false teachings regularly—have been tempted to give up the battle for the opening chapters of Genesis. An evangelical pastor recently approached me after I preached. He was confused and intimidated by several books he had read—all written by ostensibly evangelical authors—yet all arguing that the earth is billions of years old. These authors treat most of the evolutionists' theories as indisputable scientific fact. And in some cases they wield scientific or academic credentials that intimidate readers into thinking their views are the result of superior expertise, rather than naturalistic presuppositions they have brought to the biblical text. This pastor asked if I believed it possible that the first three chapters of Genesis might really be just a series of literary devices—a poetic saga giving the "spiritual" meaning of what actually occurred through billions of years of evolution.

I answered unapologetically, *No, I do not.* I am convinced that Genesis 1–3 ought to be taken at face value—as the divinely revealed history of creation. Nothing about the Genesis text itself suggests that the biblical creation account is merely symbolic, poetic, allegorical, or mythical. The main thrust of the passage simply cannot be reconciled with the notion that creation occurred via natural evolutionary processes over long periods of time. And I don't believe a faithful handling of the biblical text, by any acceptable principles of hermeneutics, can possibly reconcile these chapters with the theory of evolution or any of the other allegedly scientific theories about the origin of the universe.

Furthermore, much like the philosophical and moral chaos that results from naturalism, all sorts of theological mischief ensues when we reject or compromise the literal truth of the biblical account of creation and the fall of Adam.

I realize, of course, that some old-earth creationists do hold to the literal creation of Adam and affirm that Adam was a historical figure. But their decision to accept the creation of Adam as literal involves an arbitrary hermeneutical shift at Genesis 1:26–27 and then again at Genesis 2:7. If everything around these verses is handled allegorically or symbolically, it is unjustifiable to take those verses in a literal and historical sense. Therefore, the old-earth creationists' method of interpreting the Genesis text actually undermines the historicity of Adam. Having already decided to treat the creation account itself as myth or allegory, they have no grounds to insist (suddenly and arbitrarily, it seems) that the creation of Adam is literal history. Their belief in a historical Adam is simply inconsistent with their own exegesis of the rest of the text.

But it is a necessary inconsistency if one is to affirm an old earth and remain evangelical. Because if Adam was not the literal ancestor of the entire human race, then the Bible's explanation of how sin entered the world makes no sense. Moreover, if we didn't fall in Adam, we cannot be redeemed in Christ, because Christ's position as the Head of the redeemed race exactly parallels Adam's position as the head of the fallen race: "For as in Adam all die, even so in Christ all shall be made alive" (1 Corinthians 15:22). "Therefore, as through one man's offense judgment came to all men, resulting in condemnation, even so through one Man's righteous act the free gift came to all men, resulting in justification of life. For as by one man's disobedience many were made sinners, so also by one Man's obedience many will be made righteous" (Romans 5:18–19). "And so it is written, 'The first man Adam became a living being.' The last Adam became a life-giving spirit" (1 Corinthians 15:45; cf. 1 Timothy 2:13–14; Jude 14).

So in an important sense, everything Scripture says about our salvation through Jesus Christ hinges on the literal truth of what Genesis 1–3 teaches about Adam's creation and fall. There is no more pivotal passage of Scripture.

What old-earth creationists (including, to a large degree, even the evangelical ones) are doing with Genesis 1–3 is precisely what religious liberals have always done with all of Scripture—spiritualizing and reinterpreting the text allegorically to make it mean what they want it to mean. It is a dangerous way to handle Scripture. And it involves a perilous and unnecessary capitulation to the religious presuppositions of naturalism—not to mention a serious dishonor to God.

Evangelicals who accept an old-earth interpretation of Genesis have embraced a hermeneutic that is hostile to a high view of Scripture. They are bringing to the opening chapters of Scripture a method of biblical interpretation that has built-in antievangelical presuppositions. Those who adopt this approach have already embarked on a process that invariably overthrows faith. Churches and colleges that embrace this view will not remain evangelical long.

One popular view held by many old-earth advocates is known as the "framework hypothesis." This is the belief that the "days" of creation are not even distinct eras, but overlapping stages of a long evolutionary process. According to this view, the six days described in Genesis 1 do not set forth a chronology of any kind, but rather a metaphorical "framework" by which the creative process is described for our finite human minds.

This view was apparently first set forth by liberal German theologians in the nineteenth century, but it has been adopted and propagated in recent years by some leading evangelicals, most notably Dr. Meredith G. Kline of Westminster Theological Seminary.

The framework hypothesis starts with the view that the "days" of creation in Genesis 1 are symbolic expressions that have nothing to do with time. Framework advocates note the obvious parallelism between days one and four (the creation of light and the placing of lights in the firmament), days two and five (the separation of air and water and the creation of fish and birds to inhabit air and water), and days three and six (the emergence of the dry land and the creation of land animals), and they suggest that such parallelism is a clue that the structure of the chapter is merely poetic. Thus, according to this theory, the sequence of creation may essentially be disregarded, as if a literary form in the passage nullified its literal meaning.

Naturally, advocates of this view accept the modern scientific theory that the formation of the earth required several billion years. They claim the biblical account is nothing more than a metaphorical framework that should overlay our scientific understanding of creation. The language and details of Genesis 1 are unimportant, they say; the only truth this passage aims to teach us is that the hand of divine Providence guided the evolutionary process. The Genesis creation account is thus reduced to a literary device—an extended metaphor that is not to be accepted at face value.

But if the Lord wanted to teach us that creation took place in six literal days, how could He have stated it more plainly than Genesis does? The length of the days is defined by periods of day and night that are governed after day four by the sun and moon. The week itself defines the pattern of human labor and rest. The days are marked by the passage of morning and evening. How could these not signify the chronological progression of God's creative work?

The problem with the framework hypothesis is that it employs a destructive method of interpretation. If the plain meaning of Genesis 1 may be written off and the language treated as nothing more than a literary device, why not do the same with Genesis 3? Indeed, most theological liberals do insist that the talking serpent in chapter 3 signals a fable or a metaphor, and therefore they reject that passage as a literal and historical record of how humanity fell into sin. Where does metaphor ultimately end and history begin? After the Flood? After the Tower of Babel? And why there? Why not regard all the biblical miracles as literary devices? Why could not the Resurrection itself be dismissed as a mere allegory? In the words of E. J. Young, "If the 'framework' hypothesis were applied to the narratives of the Virgin Birth or the Resurrection or Romans 5:12 ff., it could as effectively serve to minimize the importance of the content of those passages as it now does the content of the first chapter of Genesis."[6]

Young points out the fallacy of the framework hypothesis:

> The question must be raised, "If a nonchronological view of the days be admitted, what is the purpose of mentioning six days?" For, once we reject the chronological sequence which Genesis gives, we are brought to the point where we can really say very little about the content of Genesis one. It is impossible to hold that there are two trios of days, each paralleling the

other. Day four . . . speaks of God's placing the light-bearers in the firmament. The firmament, however, had been made on the second day. If the fourth and the first days are two aspects of the same thing, then the second day also (which speaks of the firmament) must precede days one and four. If this procedure be allowed, with its wholesale disregard of grammar, why may we not be consistent and equate all four of these days with the first verse of Genesis? There is no defense against such a procedure, once we abandon the clear language of the text. In all seriousness it must be asked, Can we believe that the first chapter of Genesis intends to teach that day two preceded days one and four? To ask that question is to answer it.[7]

The simple, rather obvious fact is that no one would ever think the time-frame for creation was anything other than a normal week of seven days from reading the Bible and allowing it to interpret itself. The Fourth Commandment makes no sense whatsoever apart from an understanding that the days of God's creative work parallel a normal human work week.

The framework hypothesis is the direct result of making modern scientific theory a hermeneutical guideline by which to interpret Scripture. The basic presupposition behind the framework hypothesis is the notion that science speaks with more authority about origins and the age of the earth than Scripture does. Those who embrace such a view have in effect made science an authority over Scripture. They are permitting scientific hypotheses—mere human opinions that have no divine authority whatsoever—to be the hermeneutical rule by which Scripture is interpreted.

There is no warrant for that. Modern scientific opinion is not a valid hermeneutic for interpreting Genesis (or any other portion of Scripture, for that matter). Scripture is God-breathed (2 Timothy 3:16)—inspired truth from God. "[Scripture] never came by the will of man, but holy men of God spoke as they were moved by the Holy Spirit" (2 Peter 1:21). Jesus summed the point up perfectly when He said, "Thy word is truth" (John 17:17 KJV). The Bible is supreme truth, and therefore it is the standard by which scientific theory should be evaluated, not vice versa.

And Scripture always speaks with absolute authority. It is as authoritative when it instructs us as it is when it commands us. It is as true when it tells the future as it is when it records the past. Although it is not a textbook on science, wherever it intersects with scientific data, it speaks with the same authority as when it gives us moral precepts. Although many have tried to set science against Scripture, science never has disproved one jot or tittle of the Bible and it never will.

It is therefore a serious mistake to imagine that modern scientists can speak more authoritatively than Scripture on the subject of origins. Scripture is God's own eyewitness account of what happened in the beginning. When it deals with the origin of the universe, all science can offer is conjecture. Science has proven nothing that negates the Genesis record. In fact, the Genesis record answers the mysteries of science.

A clear pattern for interpreting Genesis is given to us in the New Testament. If the language of early Genesis were meant to be interpreted figuratively, we could expect to see Genesis interpreted in the New Testament in a figurative sense. After all, the New Testament is itself inspired Scripture, so it is the Creator's own commentary on the Genesis record.

What do we find in the New Testament? In every New Testament reference to Genesis, the events recorded by Moses are treated as historical events. And in particular, the first three chapters of Genesis are consistently treated as a literal record of historical events. The New Testament affirms, for example, the creation of Adam in the image of God (James 3:9).

Paul wrote to Timothy, "Adam was formed first, then Eve. And Adam was not deceived, but the woman being deceived, fell into transgression" (1 Timothy 2:13–14). In 1 Corinthians 11:8–9, he writes, "Man is not from woman, but woman from man. Nor was man created for the woman, but woman for the man."

Paul's presentation of the doctrine of original sin in Romans 5:12–20 depends on a historical Adam and a literal interpretation of the account in Genesis about how he fell. Furthermore, everything Paul has to say about the doctrine of justification by faith depends on that. "For as in Adam all die, even so in Christ all shall be made alive" (1 Corinthians 15:22). Clearly Paul regarded both the creation and fall of Adam as history, not allegory. Jesus Himself referred to the creation of Adam and Eve as a historical event (Mark 10:6). To question the historicity of these events is to undermine the very essence of Christian doctrine.

Moreover, if Scripture itself treats the creation and fall of Adam as historical events, there is no warrant for treating the rest of the creation account as allegory or literary device. Nowhere in all of Scripture are any of these events handled as merely symbolic.

In fact, when the New Testament refers to creation (Mark 13:19; John 1:3; Acts 4:24; 14:15; 2 Corinthians 4:6; Colossians 1:16; Hebrews 1:2, 10; Revelation 4:11; 10:6; 14:7), it always refers to a past, completed event—an immediate work of God, not a still-occurring process of evolution. The promised New Creation, a running theme in both Old and New Testaments, is portrayed as an immediate creation, too—not an eons-long process (Isaiah 65:17). In fact, the model for the New Creation is the original creation (cf. Romans 8:21; Revelation 21:1, 5).

Hebrews 11:3 even makes belief in creation by divine fiat the very essence of faith itself: "By faith we understand that the worlds were framed by the word of God, so that the things which are seen were not made of things which are visible." Creation *ex nihilo* (out of nothing) is the clear and consistent teaching of the Bible.

Evolution was introduced as an atheistic alternative to the biblical view of creation. According to evolution, man created God rather than vice versa. And as we have seen, the evolutionists' ultimate agenda is to eliminate faith in God altogether and thereby do away with moral accountability.

Intuition suggests a series of questions to the human mind when we contemplate our origin: Who is in control of the universe? Is there Someone who is sovereign—a Lawgiver? Is there a universal Judge? Is there a transcendent moral standard to live by? Is there Someone to whom we will be accountable? Will there be a final assessment of how we live our lives? Will there be any final judgment?

Those are the very questions evolution was invented to avoid.

Evolution was devised to explain away the God of the Bible—not because evolutionists really believed a Creator was unnecessary to explain how things began, but because they did not want the God of Scripture as their Judge. Marvin L. Lubenow writes:

> The real issue in the creation/evolution debate is not the existence of God. The real issue is the nature of God. To think of evolution as basically atheistic is to misunderstand the uniqueness of evolution. Evolution

was not designed as a general attack against theism. It was designed as a specific attack against the God of the Bible, and the God of the Bible is clearly revealed through the doctrine of creation. Obviously, if a person is an atheist, it would be normal for him to also be an evolutionist. But evolution is as comfortable with theism as it is with atheism. An evolutionist is perfectly free to choose any god he wishes, as long as it is not the God of the Bible. The gods allowed by evolution are private, subjective, and artificial. They bother no one and make no absolute ethical demands. However, the God of the Bible is the Creator, Sustainer, Savior, and Judge. All are responsible to him. He has an agenda that conflicts with that of sinful humans. For man to be created in the image of God is very awesome. For God to be created in the image of man is very comfortable.[8]

To put it simply, evolution was invented in order to eliminate the God of Genesis and thereby to oust the Lawgiver and obliterate the inviolability of His law. Evolution is simply the latest means our fallen race has devised in order to suppress our innate knowledge and the biblical testimony that there is a God and that we are accountable to Him (cf. Romans 1:28). By embracing evolution, modern society aims to do away with morality, responsibility, and guilt. Society has embraced evolution with such enthusiasm because people imagine that it eliminates the Judge and leaves them free to do whatever they want without guilt and without consequences.

The evolutionary lie is so pointedly antithetical to Christian truth that it would seem unthinkable for evangelical Christians to compromise with evolutionary science in any degree. But during the past century and a half of evolutionary propaganda, evolutionists have had remarkable success in getting evangelicals to meet them halfway. Remarkably, many modern evangelicals— perhaps it would even be fair to say most people who call themselves evangelicals today—have already been convinced that the Genesis account of creation is not a true historical record. Thus they have not only capitulated to evolutionary doctrine at its starting point, but they have also embraced a view that undermines the authority of Scripture at its starting point.

So-called theistic evolutionists who try to marry humanistic theories of modern science with biblical theism may claim they are doing so because they love God, but the truth is that they love God a little and their academic reputations a lot. By undermining the historicity of Genesis they are undermining faith itself. Give evolutionary doctrine the throne and make the Bible its servant, and you have laid the foundation for spiritual disaster.

Scripture, not science, is the ultimate test of all truth. And the further evangelicalism gets from that conviction, the less evangelical and more humanistic it becomes.

Scripture cautions against false "knowledge" (1 Timothy 6:20)—particularly so-called "scientific" knowledge that opposes the truth of Scripture. When what is being passed off as "science" turns out to be nothing more than a faith-based world-view that is hostile to the truth of Scripture, our duty to be on guard is magnified. And when naturalistic and atheistic presuppositions are being aggressively peddled as if they were established scientific facts, Christians ought to expose such lies for what they are and oppose them all the more vigorously. The abandonment of a biblical view of creation has already borne abundant evil fruit in modern society. Now is no time for the church to retreat or to compromise on these issues. To weaken our commitment to the biblical view of creation would start a chain of disastrous moral, spiritual, and theological ramifications in the church that will greatly exacerbate the terrible moral chaos that has already begun the unraveling of secular society.

With that in mind I undertook an earnest study of Genesis a couple of years ago. Although the bulk of my ministry has been devoted to a verse-by-verse exposition of the whole New Testament, I recently turned to the Old Testament and began preaching a series on Genesis in our church. This book is the fruit of my research and teaching in Genesis 1–3. We find there the foundation of every doctrine that is essential to the Christian faith. And the more carefully I have studied those opening chapters of Scripture, the more I have seen that they are the vital foundation for everything we believe as Christians.

Sadly, it is a foundation that is being systematically undermined by the very institutions that should be most vigorously defending it. More and more Christian educational institutions, apologists, and theologians are abandoning faith in the literal truth of Genesis 1–3. I recall reading a survey a few years ago that revealed that in one of America's leading evangelical accrediting associations, whose membership boasted scores of evangelical Bible colleges and universities, only five or six college-level schools remain solidly opposed to the old-earth view of creation. The rest are open to a reinterpretation of Genesis 1–3 that accommodates evolutionary theories. Scores of well-known Bible teachers and apologists see the whole question as moot, and some even aggressively argue that a literal approach to Genesis is detrimental to the credibility of Christianity. They have given up the battle—or worse, joined the attack against biblical creationism.

I'm thankful for those who are still faithfully resisting the trend-organizations like Answers in Genesis, the Creation Research Society, and the Institute for Creation Research. These organizations and others like them involve many expert scientists who challenge the presuppositions of evolutionists on technical and scientific grounds. They clearly demonstrate that scientific proficiency is not incompatible with faith in the literal truth of Scripture—and that the battle for the beginning is ultimately a battle between two mutually exclusive faiths—faith in Scripture versus faith in antitheistic hypotheses. It is not really a battle between science and the Bible.

My aim in this book is to examine what Scripture teaches about creation. Although I am convinced that the truth of Scripture has scientific integrity, for the most part I intend to leave the scientific defense of creationism to those who have the most expertise in science. My purpose is chiefly to examine what Scripture teaches about the origin of the universe and humanity's fall into sin and to show why it is incompatible with the naturalists' beliefs and the evolutionists' theories.

As Christians, we believe the Bible is truth revealed to us by God, who is the true Creator of the universe. That belief is the basic foundation of all genuine Christianity. It is utterly incompatible with the speculative presuppositions of the naturalists.

In Scripture the Creator Himself has revealed to us everything essential for life and godliness. And it starts with an account of creation. If the biblical creation account is in any degree unreliable, the rest of Scripture stands on a shaky foundation.

But the foundation is not shaky. The more I understand what God has revealed to us about our origin, the more I see clearly that the foundation stands firm. I agree with those who say it is time for the people of God to take a fresh look at the biblical account of creation. But I disagree with those who think that calls for any degree of capitulation to the transient theories of naturalism. Only an honest look at Scripture, with sound principles of hermeneutics, will yield the right understanding of the creation and fall of our race.

The Bible gives a clear and cogent account of the beginnings of the cosmos and humanity. There is absolutely no reason for an intelligent mind to balk at accepting it as a literal account of the origin of our universe. Although the biblical account clashes at many points with naturalistic and evolutionary hypotheses, it is not in conflict with a single scientific fact. Indeed, all the geological, astronomical, and scientific data can be easily reconciled with the biblical account. The conflict is not between science and Scripture, but between the biblicist's confident faith and the naturalist's willful skepticism.

To many, having been indoctrinated in schools where the line between hypothesis and fact is systematically and deliberately being blurred, that may sound naive or unsophisticated, but it is nonetheless a fact. Again, science has never disproved one word of Scripture, and it never will. On the other hand, evolutionary theory has always been in conflict with Scripture and always will be. But the notion that the universe evolved through a series of natural processes remains an unproven and untestable hypothesis, and therefore it is not "science." There is no proof whatsoever that the universe evolved naturally. Evolution is a mere theory—and a questionable, constantly changing one at that. Ultimately, if accepted at all, the theory of evolution must be taken by sheer faith.

How much better to base our faith on the sure foundation of God's Word! There is no ground of knowledge equal to or superior to Scripture. Unlike scientific theory, God's Word is eternally unchanging. Unlike the opinions of man, its truth is revealed by the Creator Himself! It is not, as many suppose, at odds with science. True science has always affirmed the teaching of Scripture. Archaeology, for instance, has demonstrated the truthfulness of the biblical record time and time again. Wherever Scripture's record of history may be examined and either proved or disproved by archaeological evidence or reliable, independent documentary evidence, the biblical record has always been verified. There is no valid reason whatsoever to doubt or distrust the biblical record of creation, and there is certainly no need to adjust the biblical account to try to make it fit the latest fads in evolutionary theory.

Therefore my approach in this book will be simply to examine what the biblical text teaches about creation. My goal is not to write a polemic against current evolutionary thinking. I don't intend to get into in-depth scientific arguments related to the origin of our universe. Where scientific fact intersects with the biblical record, I will highlight that. But my chief aim is to examine what the Bible teaches about the origin of the universe and then to look at the moral, spiritual, and eternal ramifications of biblical creationism to see how it relates to people in today's world.

I'm indebted to several authors who have treated this subject before and whose works were very helpful in framing my own thoughts on these matters. Chief among them are Douglas F. Kelly,[9] John Ankerberg and John Weldon,[10] Phillip E. Johnson,[11] Henry Morris,[12] and Ken Ham.[13]

Again, a biblical understanding of the creation and fall of humanity establishes the necessary foundation for the Christian world-view. Everything Scripture teaches about sin and redemption assumes the literal truth of the first three chapters of Genesis. If we wobble to any degree on the truth of this passage, we undermine the very foundations of our faith.

If Genesis 1–3 doesn't tell us the truth, why should we believe anything else in the Bible? Without a right understanding of our origin, we have no way to understand anything about our spiritual existence. We cannot know our purpose, and we cannot be certain of our destiny. After all, if God is not the Creator, then maybe He's not the Redeemer either. If we cannot believe the opening chapters of Scripture, how can we be certain of anything the Bible says?

Much depends, therefore, on a right understanding of these early chapters of Genesis. These chapters are too often mishandled by people whose real aim is not to understand what the text actually teaches, but to adjust it to fit a scientific theory. The approach is all wrong. Since creation cannot be observed or replicated in a laboratory, science is not a trustworthy place to seek answers about the origin and fall of humanity. Ultimately, the only reliable source of truth about our origin is what has been revealed by the Creator himself. That means the biblical text should be our starting place.

I am convinced the correct interpretation of Genesis 1–3 is the one that comes naturally from a straightforward reading of the text. It teaches us that the universe is relatively young, albeit with an appearance of age and maturity, and that all of creation was accomplished in the span of six literal days.

To those who will inevitably complain that such a view is credulous and unsophisticated, my reply is that it is certainly superior to the irrational notion that an ordered and incomprehensibly complex universe sprung by accident from nothingness and emerged by chance into the marvel that it is.

Scripture offers the only accurate explanations that can be found anywhere about how our race began, where our moral sense originated, why we cannot seem to do what our own consciences tell us is right, and how we can be redeemed from this hopeless situation.

Scripture is not merely the best of several possible explanations. It is the Word of God. And my prayer for you is that as we study the opening chapters of the Bible together you will believe what God has spoken.

1
CREATION: BELIEVE IT OR NOT

Genesis 1:1

I**T'S HARD TO IMAGINE** anything more absurd than the naturalist's formula
for the origin of the universe: *Nobody times nothing equals everything.* There
is no Creator; there is no design or purpose. Everything we see simply
emerged and evolved by pure chance from a total void.

Ask the typical naturalist what he believes about the beginning of all
things, and you are likely to hear about the big bang theory—the notion that
the universe is the product of an immense explosion. As if an utterly violent
and chaotic beginning could result in all the synergy and order we observe in
the cosmos around us. But what was the catalyst that touched off that big
bang in the first place? (And what, in turn, was the catalyst for *that*?)
Something incredibly large had to fuel the original explosion. Where did
that "something" originate? A big bang out of nowhere quite simply could
not have been the beginning of all things.

Is the material universe itself eternal, as some claim? And if it is, why hasn't
it wound down? For that matter, what set it in motion to begin with? What
is the source of the energy that keeps it going? Why hasn't entropy caused it
to devolve into a state of inertia and chaos, rather than (as the evolutionist
must hypothesize) apparently developing into a more orderly and increasingly
sophisticated system as the big bang expands?

The vast array of insurmountable problems for the naturalist begins at the
most basic level. What was the first cause that caused everything else? Where
did matter come from? Where did energy come from? What holds everything

together and what keeps everything going? How could life, self-consciousness, and rationality evolve from inanimate, inorganic matter? Who *designed* the many complex and interdependent organisms and sophisticated eco-systems we observe? Where did *intelligence* originate? Are we to think of the universe as a massive perpetual-motion apparatus with some sort of imper-sonal "intelligence" of its own? Or is there, after all, a personal, intelligent Designer who created everything and set it all in motion?

Those are vital metaphysical questions that *must* be answered if we are to understand the meaning and value of life itself. Philosophical naturalism, because of its materialistic and antisupernatural presuppositions, is utterly incapable of offering *any* answers to those questions. In fact, the most basic dogma of naturalism is that everything happens by natural processes; nothing is supernatural; and therefore there can be no personal Creator. That means there can be no design and no purpose for anything. Naturalism therefore can provide no philosophical basis for believing that human life is particularly valuable or in any way significant.

On the contrary, the naturalist, if he is true to his principles, must ulti-mately conclude that humanity is a freak accident without any purpose or real importance. Naturalism is therefore a formula for futility and meaningless-ness, erasing the image of God from our race's collective self-image, depreci-ating the value of human life, undermining human dignity, and subverting morality.

EVOLUTION IS DEGRADING TO HUMANITY

The drift of modern society proves the point. We are witnessing the aban-donment of moral standards and the loss of humanity's sense of destiny. Rampant crime, drug abuse, sexual perversion, rising suicide rates, and the abortion epidemic are all symptoms that human life is being systematically devalued and that an utter sense of futility is sweeping over society. These trends are directly traceable to the ascent of evolutionary theory.

And why not? If evolution is true, humans are just one of many species that evolved from common ancestors. We're no better than animals, and we ought not to think that we are. If we evolved from sheer matter, why should we esteem what is spiritual? In fact, if everything evolved from matter, nothing "spiritual" is real. We ourselves are ultimately no better than or different from any other living species. We are nothing more than protoplasm waiting to become manure.

As a matter of fact, that is precisely the rationale behind the modern animal-rights movement, a movement whose raison d'être is the utter degradation of the human race. Naturally, all radical animal-rights advocates are evolutionists. Their belief system is an inevitable byproduct of evolutionary theory.

People for the Ethical Treatment of Animals (PETA) is well known for its stance that animal rights are equal to (or more important than) human rights. They maintain that killing any animal for food is the moral equivalent of murder; eating meat is virtually cannibalism; and man is a tyrant species, detrimental to his environment.

PETA opposes the keeping of pets and "companion animals"—including guide dogs for the blind. A 1988 statement distributed by the organization includes this: "As John Bryant has written in his book *Fettered Kingdoms*, [companion animals] are like slaves, even if well-kept slaves."

Ingrid Newkirk, PETA's controversial founder, says, "There is no rational basis for saying that a human being has special rights. . . . A rat is a pig is a dog is a boy."[1] Newkirk told a *Washington Post* reporter that the atrocities of Nazi Germany pale by comparison to the killing animals for food: "Six million Jews died in concentration camps, but six *billion* broiler chickens will die this year in slaughterhouses."[2]

Clearly, Ms. Newkirk is *more* outraged by the killing of chickens for food than she is by the wholesale slaughter of human beings. One gets the impression she would not necessarily consider the extinction of humanity an undesirable thing. In fact, she and other animal-rights advocates often sound downright misanthropic. She told a reporter, "I don't have any reverence for life, only for the entities themselves. I would rather see a blank space where I am. This will sound like fruitcake stuff again but at least I wouldn't be harming anything."[3]

The summer issue of *Wild Earth* magazine, a journal promoting radical environmentalism, included a manifesto for the extinction of the human race, written under the pseudonym "Les U. Knight." The article said, "If you haven't given voluntary human extinction much thought before, the idea of a world with no people in it may seem strange. But, if you give it a chance, I think you might agree that the extinction of Homo sapiens would mean survival for millions, if not billions, of Earth-dwelling species. . . . Phasing out the human race will solve every problem on earth, social and environmental."[4]

That is worse than merely inane, irrational, immoral, or humiliating; it is *deadly*.

But there's even an organization called The Church of Euthanasia. Their Web page advocates suicide, abortion, cannibalism, and sodomy as the main ways to decrease the human population. Although the Web page contains elements of parody deliberately designed for shock value, the people behind it are deadly serious in their opposition to the continuance of the human race.[5] They include detailed instructions for committing suicide. The one commandment church members are required to obey is "Thou shalt not procreate." By deliberately making their views sound as outrageous as possible, they have received widespread coverage on talk shows and tabloid-style news programs. They take advantage of such publicity to recruit members for their cause. Despite their shocking message, they have evidently been able to persuade numerous people that the one species on earth that *ought* to be made extinct is humanity. Their Web site boasts that people in the thousands have paid the ten dollar membership fee to become church members.

That sort of lunacy is rooted in the belief that humanity is simply the product of evolution—a mere animal with no purpose, no destiny, and no likeness to the Creator. After all, if we got where we are by a natural evolutionary process, there can be no validity whatsoever to the notion that our race bears the image of God. We ultimately have no more dignity than an amoeba. And we *certainly* have no mandate from the Almighty to subdue the rest of creation.

And if a human being is nothing more than an animal in the process of evolving, who can argue against the animal-rights movement? Even the most radical animal-rights position is justified in a naturalistic and evolutionary world-view. If we really evolved from animals, we are in fact just animals ourselves. And if evolution is correct, it is a sheer accident that man evolved a superior intellect. If random mutations had occurred differently, apes might be running the planet and humans would be in the zoo. What right do we have to exercise dominion over other species that have not yet had the opportunity to evolve to a more advanced state?

Indeed, if man is merely a product of natural evolutionary processes, then he is ultimately nothing more than the accidental byproduct of thousands of haphazard genetic mutations. He is just one more animal that evolved from amoeba, and he is probably not even the highest life-form that will eventually evolve. So what is special about him? Where is his meaning? Where is his dignity? Where is his value? What is his purpose? Obviously he has none.[6]

It is only a matter of time before a society steeped in naturalistic belief fully embraces such thinking and casts off all moral and spiritual restraint. In fact, that process has begun already. If you doubt that, consider some of the televised debauchery aimed at the *MTV/Jerry Springer* generation.

EVOLUTION IS HOSTILE TO REASON

Evolution is as irrational as it is amoral. In place of God as Creator, the evolutionist has substituted chance—sheer fortune, accident, happenstance, serendipity, coincidence, random events, and blind luck. Chance is the engine most evolutionists believe drives the evolutionary process.

Naturalism essentially teaches that over time and out of sheer chaos, matter evolved into everything we see today by pure chance. And this all happened without any particular design. Given enough time and enough random events, the evolutionist says, *anything* is possible. And the evolution of our world with all its intricate ecosystems and complex organisms is therefore simply the inadvertent result of a very large number of indiscriminate but extremely fortuitous accidents of nature. Everything is the way it is simply by the luck of the draw. And thus chance itself has been elevated to the role of creator.

John Ankerberg and John Weldon point out that matter, time, and chance constitute the evolutionists' holy trinity. Indeed, these three things are all that is eternal and omnipotent in the evolutionary scheme: matter, time, and chance. Together they have formed the cosmos as we know it. And they have usurped God in the evolutionist's mind. Ankerberg and Weldon quote Jacques Monod, 1965 Nobel Prize-winner for his work in biochemistry. In his book *Chance and Necessity,* Monod wrote, "[Man] is alone in the universe's unfeeling immensity, out of which he emerged by chance. . . . Chance *alone* is at the source of every innovation, of all creation in the biosphere. Pure chance, absolutely free but blind, [is] at the very root of the stupendous edifice of evolution."[7]

Obviously, that is a far cry from being created in the image of God. It is also utterly irrational. The evolutionary idea not only strips man of his dignity and his value, but it also eliminates the ground of his rationality. If everything happens by chance, then in the ultimate sense, nothing can possibly have any real purpose or meaning. And it's hard to think of any philosophical starting point that is more irrational than that.

But a moment's reflection will reveal that chance simply *cannot* be the cause of anything (much less the cause of *everything*). Chance is not a force. The only legitimate sense of the word *chance* has to do with mathematical probability. If you flip a coin again and again, quotients of mathematical probability suggest that it will land tails up about fifty times out of a hundred. Thus we say that when you flip a coin, there's a fifty-fifty "chance" it will come up tails.

But "chance" is not a force that can actually flip the coin. Chance is not an intellect that designs the pattern of mathematical probabilities. Chance *determines* nothing. Mathematical probability is merely a way of measuring what actually *does* happen.

Yet in naturalistic and evolutionary parlance, "chance" becomes something that determines what happens in the absence of any other cause or design. Consider Jacques Monod's remark again: "Chance . . . is at the source of every innovation, of all creation." In effect, naturalists have imputed to *chance* the ability to cause and determine what occurs. And that is an irrational concept.

There are no uncaused events. Every effect is determined by some cause. Even the flip of a coin simply cannot occur without a definite cause. And common sense tells us that whether the coin comes up heads or tails is also determined by *something*. A number of factors (including the precise amount of force with which the coin is flipped and the distance it must fall before hitting the ground) determine the number of revolutions and bounces it makes before landing on one side or the other. Although the forces that determine the flip of a coin may be impossible for us to control precisely, those forces, not "chance," determine whether we get heads or tails. What may appear totally random and undetermined to us is nonetheless definitively determined by *something*.[8] It is not caused by mere chance, because chance simply does not exist as a force or a cause. Chance is nothing.

Fortune was a goddess in the Greek pantheon. Evolutionists have enshrined chance in a similar way. They have taken the myth of chance and made it responsible for all that happens. Chance has been transformed into a force of causal power, so that *nothing* is the cause of *everything*. What could be *more* irrational than that? It turns all of reality into sheer chaos. It therefore makes everything irrational and incoherent.

The entire concept is so fraught with problems from a rational and philosophical viewpoint that one hardly knows where to begin. But let's begin at the beginning. Where did matter come from in the first place? The naturalist would have to say either that all matter is eternal, or that everything appeared by chance out of nothing. The latter option is clearly irrational.

But suppose the naturalist opts to believe that matter is eternal. An obvious question arises: What caused the first event that originally set the evolutionary process in motion? The only answer available to the naturalist is that chance made it happen. It literally came out of nowhere. No one and nothing made it happen. That, too, is clearly irrational.

So in order to avoid *that* dilemma, some naturalists assume an eternal chain of random events that operate on the material universe. They end up with an eternal but constantly changing material universe governed by an endless chain of purely random events—all culminating in magnificent design without a designer, and everything happening without any ultimate cause. At the end of the day, it is still irrational. It eliminates purpose, destiny, and meaning from everything in the universe. And therefore it leaves no ground for anything rational.

In other words, *nihilism*—a belief that everything is entirely without meaning, without logic, and without reason—is the only philosophy that works with naturalism. The universe itself is incoherent and irrational. Reason has been deposed by pure chance.

And such a view of chance is the polar opposite of reason. Common-sense logic suggests that every watch has a watchmaker. Every building has a builder. Every structure has an architect. Every arrangement has a plan. Every plan has a designer. And every design has a purpose. We see the universe, infinitely more complex than any watch and infinitely greater than any man-made structure, and it is natural to conclude that Someone infinitely powerful and infinitely intelligent made it. "For since the creation of the world His invisible attributes, His eternal power and divine nature, have been clearly seen, being understood through what has been made" (Romans 1:20 NASB).

But naturalists look at the universe, and despite all the intricate marvels it holds, they conclude no one made it. Chance brought it about. It happened by accident. That is not logical. It is absurd.

Abandon logic and you are left with pure nonsense. In many ways the naturalists' deification of chance is worse than all the various myths of other false religions, because it obliterates all meaning and sense from everything. But it is, once again, pure religion of the most pagan variety, requiring a spiritually fatal leap of faith into an abyss of utter irrationality. It is the age-old religion of fools (Psalm 14:1)—but in modern "scientific" dress.

What could prompt anyone to embrace such a system? Why would someone opt for a world-view that eliminates all that is rational? It boils down to the sheer love of sin. People want to be comfortable in their sin, and there is no way to do that without eliminating God. Get rid of God and you erase all fear of the consequences of sin. So even though sheer irrationality is ultimately the only viable alternative to the God of Scripture, multitudes have opted for irrationality just so they could live guilt-free and shamelessly with their own sin. It is as simple as that.

Either there is a God who created the universe and sovereignly rules His creation, or everything was caused by blind chance. The two ideas are mutually exclusive. If God rules, there's no room for chance. Make chance the cause of the universe, and you have effectively done away with God.

As a matter of fact, if chance as a determinative force or a cause exists even in the frailest form, God has been dethroned. The sovereignty of God and chance are inherently incompatible. If chance causes or determines *anything*, God is not truly God.

But again, chance is not a force. Chance cannot make anything happen. Chance is nothing. It simply does not exist. And therefore it has no power to do anything. It cannot be the cause of any effect. It is an imaginary hocus-pocus. It is contrary to every law of science, every principle of logic, and every intuition of sheer common sense. Even the most basic principles of thermodynamics, physics, and biology suggest that chance simply cannot be the determinative force that has brought about the order and interdependence we see in our universe—much less the diversity of life we find on our own planet. Ultimately, chance simply cannot account for the origin of life and intelligence.

One of the oldest principles of rational philosophy is *ex nihilo nihil fit*. Out of nothing, nothing comes. And chance is nothing. Naturalism is rational suicide.

When scientists attribute instrumental power to chance they have left the realm of reason, they have left the domain of science. They have turned to pulling rabbits out of hats. They have turned to fantasy. Insert the idea of chance, and all scientific investigation ultimately becomes chaotic and absurd. That is precisely why evolution does not deserve to be deemed true science; it is nothing more than an irrational religion—the religion of those who want to sin without guilt.

Someone once estimated that the number of random genetic factors involved in the evolution of a tapeworm from an amoeba would be comparable to placing a monkey in a room with a typewriter and allowing him to strike the keys at random until he accidentally produced a perfectly spelled and perfectly punctuated typescript of Hamlet's soliloquy. And the odds of getting all the mutations necessary to evolve a starfish from a one-celled creature are comparable to asking a hundred blind people to make ten random moves each with five Rubik's Cubes, and finding all five cubes perfectly solved at the end of the process. The odds against *all* earth's life forms evolving from a single cell are, in a word, impossible.

Nonetheless, the absurdity of naturalism goes largely unchallenged today in universities and colleges. Turn on the Discovery Channel or pick up an issue of *National Geographic* and you are likely to be exposed to the assumption that chance exists as a force—as if mere chance spontaneously generated everything in the universe.

One Nobel laureate, Harvard professor George Wald, acknowledged the utter absurdity of this. Pondering the vast array of factors both real and hypothetical that would have to arise spontaneously all at once in order for inanimate matter to evolve into even the most primitive one-celled form of life, he wrote, "One has only to contemplate the magnitude of this task to concede that the spontaneous generation of a living organism is impossible." Then he added, "Yet here we are—as a result, I believe, of spontaneous generation."[9] How did Wald believe this impossibility came about? He answered:

"Time is in fact the hero of the plot. The time with which we have to deal is of the order of two billion years. What we regard as impossible on the basis of human experience is meaningless here. Given so much time, the 'impossible' becomes possible, the possible probable, and the probable virtually certain. One has only to wait: time itself performs the miracles."[10] Given enough time, that which is impossible becomes "virtually certain." That is sheer double-talk. And it perfectly illustrates the blind faith that underlies naturalistic religion.

There is no viable explanation of the universe without God. So many immense and intricate wonders could not exist without a Designer. There's only one possible explanation for it all, and that is the creative power of an all-wise God. He created and sustains the universe, and He gives meaning to it. And without Him, there is ultimately no meaning in anything. Without Him, we are left with only the notion that everything emerged from nothing without a cause and without any reason. Without Him, we are stuck with that absurd formula of the evolutionist: Nothing times nobody equals everything.

EVOLUTION IS ANTITHETICAL
TO THE TRUTH GOD HAS REVEALED

By contrast, the actual record of creation is found in Genesis 1:1: "In the beginning God created the heavens and the earth." It would be hard to state an answer to the great cosmic question any more simply or directly than that.

The words of Genesis 1:1 are precise and concise beyond mere human composition. They account for everything evolution *cannot* explain. Evolutionary philosopher Herbert Spencer, one of Darwin's earliest and most enthusiastic advocates, outlined five "ultimate scientific ideas": time, force, action, space, and matter.[11] These are categories that (according to Spencer) comprise everything that is susceptible to scientific examination. That simple taxonomy, Spencer believed, encompasses all that truly exists in the universe. *Everything* that can be known or observed by science fits into one of those categories, Spencer claimed, and nothing can be truly said to "exist" outside of them.

Spencer's materialistic world-view is immediately evident in the fact that his categories leave room for nothing spiritual. But set aside for a moment the rather obvious fact that something as obvious as human intellect and emotion do not quite fit into any of Spencer's categories.[12] A moment's reflection will reveal that evolutionary principles *still* cannot account for the actual origin of *any* of Spencer's categories. The evolutionist must practically assume the eternality of time, force, action, space, and matter (or at least one of these[13]—and then he or she proceeds from there to hypothesize about) how things have developed out of an originally chaotic state.

But Genesis 1:1 accounts for all of Spencer's categories. "In the beginning"—that's *time*. "God"—that's *force*.[14] "Created"—that's *action*. "The heavens"—that's *space*. "And the earth"—that's *matter*. In the first verse of the Bible God laid out plainly what no scientist or philosopher cataloged until the nineteenth century. Moreover, what evolution still cannot possibly explain—the actual origin of everything that science can observe—the Bible explains in a few succinct words in the very first verse of Genesis.

About the uniqueness of the Bible's approach to creation, Henry Morris writes:

> Genesis 1:1 is unique in all literature, science, and philosophy. Every other system of cosmogony, whether in ancient religious myths or modern scientific models, starts with eternal matter or energy in some form, from which other entities were supposedly gradually derived by some process. Only the Book of Genesis even attempts to account for the ultimate origin of matter, space, and time; and it does so uniquely in terms of special creation.[15]

And thus in that very first verse of Scripture, each reader is faced with a simple choice: Either you believe God *did* create the heavens and the earth, or you believe He *did not*. If He did not, He does not exist at all, nothing has any purpose and nothing makes any sense. If on the other hand there is a creative intelligence—if there is a God—then creation is understandable. It is possible. It is plausible. It is rational.

Ultimately, those are the options every reader of Genesis is faced with. Either the vast array of complex organisms and intelligence we observe reflect the wisdom and power of a personal Creator (and specifically, the God who has revealed Himself in Scripture), or all these marvels somehow evolved spontaneously from inanimate matter, and no real sense can be made of anything.

Even among the best scientists who have left their mark on the scientific world, those who think honestly and make honest confessions about origins will admit that there must be a creative intelligence. (Einstein himself firmly believed that a cosmic intelligence *must* have designed the universe, though like many others today who accept the notion of intelligent design, he avoided the obvious conclusion that if there's a "Cosmic Intelligence" powerful enough to design and create the universe, that "Intelligence" is by definition Lord and God over all.) And although the scientific and academic communities often mercilessly attempt to silence such opinions, there are nonetheless many men of integrity in the scientific community who embrace the God of Scripture and the biblical creation account.[16]

God *did* create the heavens and the earth. And there is only one document that credibly claims to be a divinely revealed record of that creation: the Book of Genesis. Unless we have a creator who left us with no information about where we came from or what our purpose is, the text of Genesis 1–2 stands for all practical purposes unchallenged as the only divinely revealed description of creation. In other words, if there is a God who created the heavens and the earth, and if He revealed to humanity any record of that creation, Genesis is that record. If the God of Scripture did not create the heavens and the earth, then we have no real answers to anything that is truly important. Everything boils down to those two simple options.

So whether we believe the Genesis record or not makes all the difference in the world. Douglas F. Kelly, professor of systematic theology at Reformed Theological Seminary, has written on this subject with great insight. He says, "Essentially, mankind has only two choices. Either we have evolved out of the slime and can be explained only in a materialistic sense, meaning that we are made of nothing but the material, or we have been made on a heavenly pattern."[17]

He's right. Those are ultimately the only two options. We can either believe what Genesis says, or not. If Genesis 1:1 is true, then the universe and everything in it was created by a loving and personal God and His purposes are clearly revealed to us in Scripture. Further, if the Genesis account is true, then we bear the stamp of God and are loved by Him—and *because* we are made in

His image, human beings have a dignity, value, and obligation that transcends that of all other creatures. Moreover, if Genesis is true, then we not only have God's own answers to the questions of what we are here for and how we got where we are, but we also have the promise of salvation from our sin.

If Genesis is *not* true, however, we have no reliable answer to anything. Throw out Genesis and the authority of *all* Scripture is fatally compromised. That would ultimately mean that the God of the Bible simply doesn't exist. And if some other kind of creator-god does exist, he evidently doesn't care enough about his creation to provide any revelation about himself, his plan for creation, or his will for his creatures.

There are, of course, several extrabiblical accounts of creation from pagan sacred writings. But they are all mythical, fanciful, and frivolous, featuring hideously ungodly gods. Those who imagine such deities exist would have to conclude that they have left us without any reason for hope, without any clear principles by which to live, without any accountability, without any answers to our most basic questions, and (most troubling of all) without any explanation or solution for the dilemma of evil.

Therefore if Genesis is untrue, we might as well assume that no God exists at all. That is precisely the assumption behind modern evolutionary theory. If true, it means that impersonal matter is the ultimate reality. Human personality and human intelligence are simply meaningless accidents produced at random by the natural processes of evolution. We have no moral accountability to any higher Being. All morality—indeed, all truth itself—is ultimately relative. In fact, truth, falsehood, goodness, and evil are all merely theoretical notions with no real meaning or significance. Nothing really matters in the vast immensity of an infinite, impersonal universe.

So if Genesis is false, nihilism is the next best option. Utter irrationality becomes the only "rational" choice.

Obviously, the ramifications of our views on these things are immense. Our view of creation is the necessary starting point for our entire world-view. In fact, so vital is the issue that Francis Schaeffer once remarked that if he had only an hour to spend with an unbeliever, he would spend the first fifty-five minutes talking about creation and what it means for humanity to bear the image of God—and then he would use the last five minutes to explain the way of salvation.[18]

The starting point for Christianity is not Matthew 1:1, but Genesis 1:1. Tamper with the Book of Genesis and you undermine the very foundation of Christianity. You cannot treat Genesis 1 as a fable or a mere poetic saga without severe implications to the rest of Scripture. The creation account is where God starts His account of history. It is impossible to alter the beginning without impacting the rest of the story—not to mention the ending. If Genesis 1 is not accurate, then there's no way to be certain that the rest of Scripture tells the truth. If the starting point is wrong, then the Bible itself is built on a foundation of falsehood.

In other words, if you reject the creation account in Genesis, you have no basis for believing the Bible at all. If you doubt or explain away the Bible's account of the six days of creation, where do you put the reins on your skepticism? Do you start with Genesis 3, which explains the origin of sin, and believe everything from chapter 3 on? Or maybe you don't sign on until sometime after chapter 6, because the Flood is invariably questioned by scientists, too. Or perhaps you find the Tower of Babel too hard to reconcile with the linguists' theories about how languages originated and evolved. So maybe you start taking the Bible as literal history beginning with the life of Abraham. But when you get to Moses' plagues against Egypt, will you deny those, too? What about the miracles of the New Testament? Is there any reason to regard *any* of the supernatural elements of biblical history as anything other than poetic symbolism?

After all, the notion that the universe is billions of years old is based on naturalistic presuppositions that (if held consistently) would rule out all miracles. If we're worried about appearing "unscientific" in the eyes of naturalists, we're going to have to reject a lot more than Genesis 1–3.

Once rationalism sets in and you start adapting the Word of God to fit scientific theories based on naturalistic beliefs, there is no end to the process. If you have qualms about the historicity of the creation account, you are on the road to utter Sadduceeism—skepticism and outright unbelief about *all* the supernatural elements of Scripture. Why should we doubt the literal sense of Genesis 1–3 unless we are also prepared to deny that Elisha made an ax-head float or that Peter walked on water or that Jesus raised Lazarus from the dead? And what about the greatest miracle of all—the resurrection of Christ? If we're going to shape Scripture to fit the beliefs of naturalistic scientists, why stop at all? Why is one miracle any more difficult to accept than another?

And what are we going to believe about the end of history as it is foretold in Scripture? All of redemptive history ends, according to 2 Peter 3:10–12, when the Lord uncreates the universe. The elements melt with fervent heat, and everything that exists in the material realm will be dissolved at the atomic level, in some sort of unprecedented and unimaginable nuclear meltdown. Moreover, according to Revelation 21:1–5, God will immediately create a new heaven and a new earth (cf. Isaiah 65:17). Do we really believe He can do that, or will it take another umpteen billion years of evolutionary processes to get the new heaven and the new earth in working order? If we really believe He can destroy *this* universe in a split second and immediately create a whole new one, what's the problem with believing the Genesis account of a six-day creation in the first place? If He can do it at the end of the age, why is it so hard to believe the biblical account of what happened in the beginning?

So the question of whether we interpret the Creation account as fact or fiction has huge implications for every aspect of our faith. These implications will become even more clear as we work our way through the text to the biblical account of Adam's fall. But the place to hold the line firmly is here at Genesis 1:1.

And that is no oversimplification. Frankly, believing in a supernatural, creative God who made everything is the only possible rational explanation for the universe and for life itself. It is also the only basis for believing we have any purpose or destiny.

In the beginning God created the heavens and the earth.

—Genesis 1:1

2
HOW DID CREATION HAPPEN?

SCRIPTURE CLEARLY TEACHES that God created the universe out of *nothing*. He spoke it into existence by His Word. In fact, one of the unique features of the creation account in Genesis is a repeated stress on divine creation by *fiat*[1]—meaning that a simple decree from God brought the created thing into being. It's one of the fundamental tenets of true faith: "By faith we understand that the worlds were framed by the word of God, so that the things which are seen were *not made of things which are visible*" (Hebrews 11:3, emphasis added).

Evolution teaches the exact opposite. Evolution turns the creation event into a process that spanned billions of years and is still not complete. Evolutionists further insist that neither life itself nor any of the various species of living creatures came into being by immediate creation from nothing, but that they all emerged first from inanimate matter and then from pre-existing life-forms through a series of slow changes and genetic mutations that took some twenty billion years (or longer)—and that everything is still evolving. The modern scientific community has demanded and received almost universal acceptance of these basic principles of evolutionary theory.

Of course, as we noted in the previous chapter, time is the hero of all the evolutionists' theories. If the universe is not billions and billions of years old, we can discard evolutionary theory from the outset. On the other hand, if we accept the evolutionists' theory that the universe has existed for countless epochs, we must adjust our interpretation of Scripture to accommodate an old earth and thereby capitulate to one of evolution's most essential dogmas. Unfortunately, many Christian leaders today are advocating the latter approach.

WAS THE EARTH SHAPED BY CONSTANCY OR BY CATASTROPHE?

The hypothesis that the earth is billions of years old is rooted in the unbiblical premise that what is happening now is just what has always happened. This idea is known as uniformitarianism. It is the theory that natural and geological phenomena are for the most part the results of forces that have operated continuously, with uniformity, and without interruption, over billions and billions of years. Uniformitarians assume that the forces at work in nature are essentially fixed and constant. Scientists who hold this view explain nearly all geological phenomena in terms of processes that are still occurring. The uniformitarian sees sedimentary rock strata, for example, and assumes that the sediments that formed them resulted from the natural, slow settling of particles in water over several million years. A uniformitarian observes the Grand Canyon and assumes the natural flow of the Colorado River carved that immense chasm over many ages with a steady (though constantly decreasing) stream.

Uniformitarianism was first proposed around the beginning of the nineteenth century by two British geologists, James Hutton and his best-known disciple, Charles Lyell. Lyell's work *Principles of Geology* was an explicit rejection of creation- and flood-based explanations for geological formulations. Lyell insisted that all the features of earth's geology must be explainable by natural, rather than supernatural, processes. He regarded all biblical or supernatural explanations as inherently unscientific and therefore false. In other words, he began with the presupposition that Scripture itself is untrue. And his work essentially canonized atheistic naturalism as the basis for "scientific" research.

As we have noted previously, naturalism itself is a religious belief. The conviction that nothing happens supernaturally is a tenet of faith, not a fact that can be verified by any scientific means. Indeed, an a priori rejection of everything supernatural involves a giant, irrational leap of faith. So the presuppositions of atheistic naturalism are actually no more "scientific" than the beliefs of biblical Christianity. That obvious fact seems to have escaped Lyell and many who have followed him.

Nonetheless, Lyell's uniformitarian theory was enormously influential on other scientists of his age. (Darwin even took a copy of Lyell's work with him when he sailed on the *Beagle* in 1831.) And from the first publication of Lyell's work until today, the hypothesis that the earth is ages old has dominated secular science. The theory of evolution itself was the predictable and nearly immediate result of Lyell's uniformitarian hypothesis.

Of course, modern scientists have expanded their estimates of the age of the earth beyond anything Lyell himself ever imagined. But the basic theory of uniformitarianism first emerged from Lyell's antibiblical belief system.

The opposite of uniformitarianism is catastrophism, the view that dramatic geological changes have occurred in sudden, violent, or unusual events. A catastrophist observing sedimentary rock formations or large canyons is more likely (and more accurately) to interpret them as the result of massive flooding. Of course, this yields a much younger time frame for the development of earth's geological features. (A sudden flood, for example, can produce a thick layer of sediment in a few hours. That means a large stratum of sedimentary rock, which a uniformitarian might assume took millions of years to form, could actually be the result of a single flash flood.) Catastrophism therefore poses a major challenge to the evolutionary timetable, eliminating the multiple billions of years demanded to make the evolutionary hypothesis work. And for that reason it is rejected out of hand by most evolutionists.

But a moment's reflection will reveal that the fossil record is impossible to explain by any uniformitarian scheme. For a living creature to become fossilized (rather than to decay and turn to dust—Job 34:15), it must be buried immediately under a great weight of sediment. Apart from a catastrophic deluge on a scale unlike any observed in recent history, how can we explain the existence of massive fossil beds (such as the Karoo formation fossil field in Africa, which is thought to hold eight hundred billion vertebrate fossils)? Natural sedimentation over several ages cannot explain how so many fossils came to be concentrated in one place. And every inhabited continent contains large fossil beds where millions of fossilized species are found together in large concentrations, as if all these creatures were destroyed and buried together by massive flooding. Fossils of sea creatures are even found on many of the world's highest mountain tops. How do uniformitarians explain such phenomena? The only way they can: They constantly increase their estimate of the age of the earth.

Scripture expressly condemns uniformitarianism in 2 Peter 3:4. Peter prophesied that this erroneous view would be adopted in the last days by scoffers—men walking after their own lusts—who imagine that "all things continue as they were from the beginning of creation." The apostle Peter goes on to write, "For this they willfully forget: that by the word of God the heavens were of old, and the earth standing out of water and in the water, by which the world that then existed perished, being flooded with water" (vv. 5–6).

In other words, the plain teaching of Scripture is that this world's history has *not* been one of uniform natural and geological processes from the beginning. But according to the Bible, there have been at least two global cataclysmic events: creation itself and a catastrophic worldwide flood in Noah's time. These would sufficiently explain virtually all the geological and hydrological features of the earth as we know it.[2]

In fact, large-scale catastrophic forces are the only really plausible explanation for some geological features. Not far from where I live is an area known as Vasquez Rocks. It has the appearance of a rugged moonscape (and is a familiar site in science-fiction films, where it is often employed as a setting for scenes depicting exotic planets). Its main features are massive shards of jagged rock strata, broken sharply and thrusting out of the ground to great heights. Whatever force stood those rocks on end was obviously sudden and violent, not slow and gradual. The entire region is filled with similar evidences of catastrophe. Not far away is the notorious San Andreas fault. There, where the roadway has been cut into the hillside, travelers may observe violently twisted rock strata. These features are mute evidence to extraordinary forces that have shaped the topography of Southern California—far exceeding the power of any known earthquake. Such phenomena are what we might expect, given the historicity of the biblical record. Scripture says, for example, that when the Flood began, "all the fountains of the great deep were broken up" (Genesis 7:11). No doubt the Flood was accompanied by volcanic activity, massive geological movements, and the shifting of the earth's tectonic plates. Such a catastrophe would not only explain twisted and upthrust rock strata, but it would also easily explain why so many of the earth's mountain ranges give evidence of having once been under the sea. Uniformitarians cannot agree on any feasible explanation for features like these.

A massive flood would also explain the formation of the Grand Canyon. In fact, it would be a better explanation of how the canyon came to be than any uniformitarian hypothesis. The features of the canyon itself (extremely deep gorges with level plateaus at the rims) suggest that it was formed by rapid erosion. A strikingly similar formation is Providence Canyon, near Lumpkin, Georgia—a spectacular canyon that covers more than eleven hundred acres. In the early 1800s the entire area was flat farmland. By the mid 1800s, farmers had completely cleared the area of trees and their root systems, leaving the area susceptible to erosion. In 1846, heavy rainfall began forming small gullies and crevices. These expanded with every successive rainfall. By the 1940s, nearby buildings and towns had to be moved to accommodate the growing canyon. Today the canyon comprises sixteen fingers, some more than one mile in length. At places the distance from the canyon floor to the rim is as high as a fifteen-story building. Today it is a scenic area, lush with trees and wildlife, often called "Georgia's Little Grand Canyon." Its features are indistinguishable from canyons geologists claim took billions of years to form.[3]

Douglas F. Kelly writes:

> The uniformitarian assumption that millions of years of geological work (extrapolating from present, slow, natural processes) would be required to explain structures such as the American Grand Canyon for instance, is called into serious question by the explosion of Mount St. Helens in the state of Washington on the 18 of May 1980. Massive energy equivalent to 20 million tons of TNT destroyed 400 square kilometers of forest in six minutes, changing the face of the mountain and digging out depths of earth and rock, leaving formations not unlike parts of the larger Grand Canyon. Recent studies of the Mount St. Helens phenomenon indicate that if attempts were made to date these structures (which were formed in 1980) on the basis of uniformitarian theory, millions of years of formation time would be necessarily postulated.[4]

Christians who reinterpret the biblical text to try to accommodate the uniformitarians' old-earth hypotheses do so unnecessarily. To imagine that the earth was formed by natural processes over billions and billions of years through slow and steady evolution is to deny the very essence of what Scripture teaches about the earth's creation. It is to reject the clear account of God Himself that He created the earth and all its life in six days.

WHICH CAME FIRST— THE CHICKEN OR THE EGG?

One rather obvious fact ignored by many is that the universe was mature when it was created. God created it with the *appearance* of age. When He created trees and animals, for example, He created them as mature, fully developed organisms. According to the biblical account, He did not create just seeds and cells. He certainly did not plant a single cell programmed to evolve itself into a variety of creatures. He made trees with already-mature fruit (Genesis 1:11). He didn't merely create an egg; He made chickens already full grown. (Thus Genesis 1:21 plainly answers the familiar conundrum.) He created Adam full grown and fully capable of marriage and procreation.

Did Adam have a navel? It's worth noting that some modern creationists, including Ken Ham (whose work I have the utmost respect for), believe the answer is no, because the navel is a scar left from the umbilical cord, and a created being would have no use for such a scar.[5]

The question of whether Adam had a navel may sound frivolous, but in medieval and renaissance times it was often the subject of intense debate. Artists who depicted Adam and Eve in the garden were faced with a theological dilemma: Should our first parents be portrayed with navels, or not? Not a few artists solved the problem by painting fig leaves large enough to extend above where the navel would be. But in his famous painting that is the centerpiece of the Sistine Chapel's ceiling, Michelangelo gave Adam an impressive bellybutton. And he was fiercely criticized for it by some of the sterner theologians of his day.

But is it really so far-fetched to think that God would have created Adam with a navel? After all, the navel is an integral part of normal human anatomy. The structure of our abdominal muscles and vascular system is designed to accommodate the navel. I know of no necessary theological or biblical reason to *insist* that Adam and Eve could not have had them. Our first parents surely appeared like normal adults in every respect. They were probably given calluses to protect the soles of their feet like any normal adult, and the edges of their teeth were no doubt smooth, as if from normal use, rather than sharp, as if they had never been used.

Of course, the whole question of whether Adam and Eve had bellybuttons (or calluses or smooth-edged teeth) is purely speculative. Scripture simply does not address the issue. So while the question itself is intriguing, there's no need to revive a trivial debate with medieval intensity.

The fact remains, however, that Adam certainly had many features associated with maturity. He wasn't created as an embryo or an infant. He was a fully grown man. There is no reason to doubt that he had normal adult features; he certainly would have had fully developed muscles; and we know he was created with enough knowledge to tend the garden, name the animals, and talk with God. Without any growth, history, or experience, he was still a mature adult man.

Suppose a modern scientist could travel back in time and arrive in the garden moments after Adam's creation. If he examined Adam, he would see adult features. If he could converse with Adam, he would find a man with adult knowledge and fully formed language skills. But if he interpreted those things as conclusive proof that Adam was more than one hour old, he would simply be wrong. When we're dealing with things created *ex nihilo*, evidences of maturity or signs of age do not constitute proof of antiquity.

And what if that same time-traveling scientist did a botanical study of a newly created oak tree? He would observe the size of the tree, note the tree's fruit (acorns), and probably conclude that the tree itself was many years old. What if he cut down one of the trees to examine its growth rings? Would he find growth rings inside, indicating that the tree had been there for many seasons? Why not? Those rings of xylem and phloem are not only signs of the tree's age, but they also compose the tree's vascular system. They are essential to the strength of a large tree as well. But if our imaginary scientist concluded on the basis of tree rings that the tree was ninety years old, he would be wrong again. The garden itself was created mature, fully functional, and therefore with the appearance of age.

The garden was no doubt filled with creatures that had every appearance of age. On day seven, when the Lord rested from His labor, everything was fully mature and fully functional. The eagles soaring overhead might appear to be thirty years old, but they were less than a week old. Elephants roaming around might have had full tusks and appeared to be fifty years old, but they were merely one day old. Any mountains, rivers, or other geological features probably also appeared to have been there for some time. There were no doubt beautiful waterfalls and canyons, and other features that the typical geologist would surmise had been formed by several ages of wind and water or volcanic eruptions and earthquakes. But the fact is that they were all made in one day. And when Adam looked up into the heavens and saw that incredible expanse with millions of bright stars, he was seeing light from millions of light-years away— even though those stars had all had been there less than four days. The light he saw was itself part of God's creation (Genesis 1:3. See chapter 5 for a discussion of how light from distant stars might be instantly visible on earth).

All those marks of age and maturity are part of every creative miracle. When Jesus turned water to wine, for example, He utterly bypassed the fermentation and aging process. He made wine instantly from water, and those who tasted it testified that it was the best wine of all (John 2:10)—meaning it was mature and well seasoned already, even though it was an instantaneous creation. When He multiplied the loaves and fishes, He created bread and fish that were already cooked and ready to eat.

We certainly expect people who reject Scripture and despise God to accept the notion that the universe has existed for eons and eons. For obvious reasons, they want to eliminate every supernatural explanation for the origin of humanity. They don't want any binding moral law or omnipotent Judge to whom they must be accountable. So of course they embrace the naturalistic theories of evolution and an ancient earth with great enthusiasm.

But it is shocking and disturbing to see how the idea that the earth is billions of years old has begun to dominate even the evangelical Christian community. In recent years a number of leading evangelical theologians, Bible commentators, and apologists have begun arguing that it is now necessary to go beyond the plain meaning of the creation account in Genesis and try to adapt our understanding of creation as closely as possible to the theories currently in vogue in secular science. If we insist on a literal six-day creation and a young age for the universe, they claim, we will sacrifice our academic credibility and weaken our testimony to those educated in the theory of evolution.

SHOULD WE APPRAISE SCRIPTURE BY SCIENCE, OR VICE VERSA?

Perhaps the leading evangelical figure in the effort to harmonize Genesis with current scientific theories is Hugh Ross, a former astrophysicist who is now a full-time apologist and advocate for old-earth creationism. (Dr. Ross employs the term "progressive creationism" to describe his views.)

Ross, to his credit, says he affirms without reservation the absolute authority and inerrancy of Scripture. He accepts the biblical testimony that God created each species of living creature individually. He does not believe that lower life-forms evolved into higher ones, or that humans evolved from animal species. In fact, he regards Adam and Eve as historical figures, the literal parents of the entire human race. In all these ways, the views advocated by Hugh Ross are far superior to those of theistic evolutionists or other professing Christians who imbibe evolutionary theory and conclude that the early chapters of Genesis are merely myth or error. Unlike them, Hugh Ross is an evangelical. The doctrinal statement his ministry publishes is a straightforward statement of basic evangelical convictions. His books are endorsed by a Who's Who of evangelical leaders.

So what's the problem? Simply this: Hugh Ross has embraced selected theories of big bang cosmology, which he regards as undisputed fact—including the notion that the universe and the earth are billions of years old—and he employs those theories as lenses through which to interpret Scripture. In effect, he makes Scripture subservient to science—and he does so without carefully separating scientific fact from scientific theory.

Hugh Ross is convinced modern scientific theories can give us a superior understanding of the basic facts related to the origin of the universe. All Ross's books therefore argue, in effect, that the findings of modern science are necessary to interpret the Bible's true meaning. According to Ross, our generation—thanks to the evolutionists' big bang theory—is now able to understand the true meaning of the biblical creation narratives in a way no previous generation ever could. In effect, he believes the modern scientific opinion about the age and origin of the universe is *essential* to explain what Scripture really meant all along. He is therefore convinced that Scripture aims to teach us that creation was a process that took billions of years, not just one week, to complete. And that means all past generations from Moses through the late twentieth century have been clueless as to the true meaning of Genesis.

Obviously, Ross himself does not accept *all* the claims of evolutionists. But if his views are correct, we should be able to separate what is factual from what is theoretical in modern science, and use the *facts* of science as a guideline for interpreting the biblical creation account. This approach, he insists, yields an understanding of Genesis that perfectly harmonizes with modern cosmology's belief that the universe is some twenty billion years old.

Unfortunately, Ross himself seems to use a completely arbitrary method to determine which doctrines of modern science should be regarded as fact and which are mere theory.

For example, the big bang theory itself is still highly controversial, even among Ross's fellow astronomers. It is only the latest in a long line of "scientific" explanations of how the universe came to be. Big bang cosmology itself is in constant flux. (For example, scientists once believed that the entire universe emerged when an unimaginably enormous mass of matter exploded, but the theory currently in vogue is that all the matter of the universe emerged from a particle that was infinitesimally small.) Yet despite all the uncertainty surrounding the big bang, Hugh Ross regards it as an "unshakably established" fact,[6] and he insists that it sheds necessary light on the true meaning of Scripture.

Ross also advocates a scheme of long paleontological eras that he claims harmonizes perfectly with the six days of Scripture. In order to maintain his view, he is forced to ignore or dismiss in a facile way some rather obvious difficulties. For example, plant life appears on day three in the biblical account, but the sun, essential to sustaining those plants, doesn't appear until day four. And insects aren't created until day six, which would be millions of years after the appearance of plant life, if Ross's view of the "days" is correct. Of course, the paleontological sequence Ross proposes is by no means universally accepted by scientists; it is merely one of several popular theories.[7] But Ross treats it as authoritative fact and lets it dictate his whole understanding of the Bible's six days of creation.

Ross treats many similarly questionable theories as indisputable facts. He believes, for example, that science has proven irrefutably that the Flood of Noah's era could not really have been the sort of worldwide deluge a literal reading of Genesis 7:19–24 would clearly indicate. He apparently believes science has established with absolute certainty the existence of pre-Adamic hominids—subhuman creatures who were perfectly manlike in appearance. He states as a matter of fact that "bipedal, tool-using, large-brained hominids roamed the earth at least as long ago as one million years"[8]—long ages before he believes Adam appeared on the scene. And in order to explain how species like that arose and disappeared before Adam's creation Ross also insists that the world was filled with bloodshed, death, violence, and decay for countless millennia—even prior to the Fall of Adam and the curse of Genesis 3:14–19.

Reading through Ross's books, one is at a complete loss to discover *how* he determines which modern scientific ideas are facts and which ones are mere theories. He constantly cites "the latest research findings," "recent studies," "current estimates," "newer data"—while acting as if he were citing matters of well-established, universally accepted fact. Dr. Ross's tendency to treat questionable theories as if they were irrefutable fact is well documented.[9] The conclusion is inescapable that his own arbitrary judgment is the main standard by which he determines which scientific ideas are established facts and which are mere theory.

But the question of whether a scientific doctrine is truly fact or merely theory is not one that can be brushed aside if one accepts Dr. Ross's views, because his entire system is built on the idea that Scripture and the facts of science are equal in authority.

According to Ross, *general revelation* (the display of divine glory that is evident in creation) is every bit as essential and as authoritative as *special revelation* (the truth God has revealed in Scripture). Indeed, Ross would be perfectly happy to give science a place in the canon. "God's revelation is not limited exclusively to the Bible's words," he says. *"The facts of nature may be likened to a sixty-seventh book of the Bible."*[10]

Ross seems to try to back away from the implications of that statement, but he cannot:

> Some readers might fear I am implying that God's revelation through nature is somehow on an equal footing with His revelation through the words of the Bible. Let me simply state that truth, by definition, is information that is perfectly free of contradiction and error. Just as it is absurd

to speak of some entity as more perfect than another, so also one revelation of God's truth cannot be held as inferior or superior to another.[11]

In other words, Ross clearly *does* believe "that God's revelation through nature is . . . on an equal footing with His revelation through the words of the Bible." No other sensible conclusion may be drawn from his words. If the facts of nature might as well be written down and stitched into the Bible as a "sixty-seventh book," then there is no reason to subjugate science to Scripture, rather than vice versa.

After all, if the voice of nature really *does* speak with the same clarity and authority as the inspired words of Scripture, who could argue with Ross's approach?

IS GENERAL REVELATION EQUAL TO SPECIAL REVELATION?

But how much and what kind of truth does God reveal through nature? Hugh Ross seems to believe that general revelation alone is sufficient to tell us all we need to know about God and creation. "God reveals himself faithfully through the 'voice' of nature as well as through the inspired words of Scripture," Ross writes.[12] What about the truth of the gospel? Is it discernable to someone who observes only nature and the cosmos apart from Scripture? Ross seems to suggest that it is, and in support he cites Colossians 1:23, where we are told that the gospel "has been proclaimed to every creature under heaven" (NIV).[13] Thus Ross implies that nature, like Scripture, is a *sufficient* revelation, able to make people wise unto salvation and thoroughly equip them for every good work (cf. 2 Timothy 3:15–17).

Ross claims the classic evangelical view of a literal six-day creation and a young earth is rooted in a faulty "single revelational theology," which he defines as "the belief that the Bible is the only authoritative source of truth."[14] He refers to his own view as "dual revelation theology"—and in support of his view he supplies a list of Scripture references that establish the doctrine of general revelation, chiefly Psalm 19:1–4 and Romans 1:19–20.

Reading Ross's treatment of the subject, one might get the impression that young-earth creationists deny general revelation altogether. But the reality is that *all* evangelical theologians recognize the legitimate place of general revelation. In the passages Ross cites, Scripture plainly states that "The heavens declare the glory of God" (Psalm 19:1). The revelation of God and His glory through nature is obvious enough so that anyone who rejects the God of the Bible is "without excuse" (Romans 1:19–20). The Romans 1 passage even says the evidence of creation reveals to everyone certain "invisible attributes" of God, namely "His eternal power and Godhead" (i.e., His divinity).

But those passages do not teach what Dr. Ross claims they teach. They certainly do not put nature on an equal footing with Scripture. In fact, Jesus Himself expressly debunked the notion that nature and Scripture are equivalent forms of revelation when He said, "Heaven and earth will pass away, but My words will by no means pass away" (Matthew 24:35; cf. Mark 13:31).

Furthermore, nothing in Scripture suggests that *everything* we need to know about God is revealed to us in nature. On the contrary, the whole point of Psalm 19 is to underscore the necessity, the absolute sufficiency, and the preeminence of *special* revelation—Scripture. Nature simply puts God's glory on display in a mute testimony that declares His majesty, power, divinity, and existence to all—and leaves them without excuse if they ignore or reject the God of the Bible. In other words, natural revelation is sufficient to condemn sinners, but not to save them. Scripture, on the other hand, is perfect, sure, right, pure, clean, and altogether true (vv. 7–9). Unlike the general revelation available to us in nature, the truth of Scripture converts the soul, makes wise the simple, enlightens the eyes, and endures forever (vv. 7–9). So the psalm plainly underscores the *superiority* of Scripture. Its whole point is that the revelation of God in nature is not as powerful, as enduring, as reliable, as clear, or as authoritative as Scripture. Scripture is a *sufficient* revelation; nature is not. Scripture is clear and complete; nature is not. Scripture therefore speaks with more authority than nature and should be used to assess scientific opinion, not vice versa.

Unlike nature, Scripture is *perspicuous*; its meaning is clear and easy to understand. Not all Scripture is *equally* perspicuous, of course. Some portions are notoriously hard to understand (2 Peter 3:16), and even the simplest passage of Scripture must be correctly interpreted in order to yield its true meaning. But the perspicuity and the comprehensiveness of Scripture are vastly superior to that of nature. And therefore Scripture should be the rule by which we measure science, rather than the reverse approach.

Hugh Ross places too much stress on the value of general revelation. He errs in making general revelation and special revelation exact parallels—as if everything Scripture says about its own authority and sufficiency were true of nature as well. Worse, his view of "the facts of nature" is framed by current scientific hypotheses about the age and origin of the universe. So Ross is actually suggesting that evolutionists' theories (or at least some of them) ought to be esteemed as highly as biblical revelation. In practice, however, he and other progressive creationists have made scientific theories a *superior* authority, because they employ those theories as a rule by which they interpret the statements of the Bible. Current scientific theory has thus become an interpretive grid through which progressive creationists read and explain Scripture. They have made science the interpreter of Scripture in a manner that is completely unwarranted. In effect, they have simply borrowed ideas from modern scientific theory and imported those thoughts *into* the text of Scripture. The actual language of the text is thus obscured or overturned in favor of an unbiblical idea that has been imposed on it. Such a method naturally yields an interpretation that is utterly disconnected from and often flatly contrary to the actual words of Scripture. And frankly, that is the only way anyone could ever read the testimony of Scripture and conclude that the universe is billions of years old.

IS THE UNIVERSE YOUNG OR OLD?

In fact, it is virtually impossible to begin with a straightforward reading of Genesis and arrive at the opinion that the universe is older than a few thousand years.

Take the age of the human race, for example. Hugh Ross believes, on the basis of the fossil record, that the creation of Adam may have occurred as much as fifty thousand years ago.[15] But Genesis contains a detailed genealogy that traces the development of the human race from Adam to Abraham and beyond. The genealogy includes a chronology with the exact ages of individuals when their offspring were born. Archbishop James Ussher did a careful analysis of the genealogies in the seventeenth century and concluded that the date for Adam's creation was 4004 B.C. Some scholars have suggested that there may be gaps in the genealogy, in which a generation or two is skipped and the name of a grandson or great-grandson is substituted for the name of a son. Such gaps can be demonstrated in some biblical genealogies. (In Matthew 1:8, for instance, Matthew skips three generations from Joram to Uzziah, apparently to maintain a symmetry in the genealogy.) No such gaps can be proven in the detailed genealogies of Genesis 5 and 11. But even allowing for some possible gaps, it's inconceivable that the date for Adam's creation could be much more than ten thousand years ago. As Henry Morris has written, "At the outside, it would seem impossible to insert gaps totaling more than about five thousand years in these chapters without rendering the record irrelevant and absurd. Consequently, the Bible will not support a date for the creation of man earlier than about 10,000 B.C."[16]

What about the notion that the "days" of creation were long epochs? We'll examine this question more closely in the chapters to come, but for now it is sufficient to point out that nothing in the immediate context suggests that these early chapters of Genesis are to be interpreted figuratively. Jesus treated the biblical creation account as history (Matthew 19:4), as did the apostles Paul (2 Corinthians 4:6) and Peter (2 Peter 3:5). It is presented as straightforward history. Indeed, the only reason for interpreting the six days of Genesis as long epochs is for the sake of harmonizing Genesis with recent scientific theories. As Edward J. Young observed:

> What strikes one immediately [about such an approach] is the low esti-
> mate of the Bible which it entails. Whenever "science" and the Bible are
> in conflict, it is always the Bible that, in one manner or another, must
> give way. We are not told that "science" should correct its answers in the
> light of Scripture. Always it is the other way round. Yet this is really sur-
> prising, for the answers which scientists have provided have frequently
> changed with the passing of time. The "authoritative" answers of pre-
> Copernican scientists are no longer acceptable; nor, for that matter, are
> many of the views of twenty-five years ago.[17]

But the order of creation itself rules out the possibility that the "days" of Genesis 1 were really long ages. For example, plant life was created on day three, including flowering plants and seed-producing trees (1:12). But birds didn't appear until the fifth day (v. 21), and earth-bound animal creatures—

including insects ("creeping thing[s]," v. 24)—were not created until the sixth day. As every gardener knows, there is a necessary symbiosis between most flowering plants and the insect kingdom that utterly rules out the existence of one apart from the other. All these different, interdependent life-forms could not have evolved together simultaneously; neither could the flowering plants have been created thousands of years before the insects and birds.

Scripture says *all* these creatures were made in a week's time. Life did not appear slowly and gradually on the earth, in increasing degrees of complexity, and over many ages of time. That is what evolution teaches. The Bible stresses the sudden and immediate *ex nihilo* creation of everything in the universe. It was all created in a very short time, despite its incredible vastness and complexity.

Obviously, the mind steeped in modern science and its antisupernatural bias struggles to fathom how so much could occur in so short a time. But there's no reason a Christian should doubt that God could have created everything fully mature in a nanosecond if He chose to do so. There's *certainly* no reason a Christian should balk at believing that God created everything in six days. After all, that is what a straightforward reading of Scripture plainly teaches.

Nonetheless, Hugh Ross evidently thinks the intricacy and perfection of creation is an argument against a young earth. After listing several scientific "proofs" that the universe is billions of years old, he writes:

> One further consideration from an altogether different perspective concerns the nature of creativity itself. Observe any skilled sculptor, painter, or poet, a craftsman of any kind. Observe the painstaking yet joyful labor poured into each object of his design. Examine the creation on any scale, from a massive galaxy to the interior of an atom, from a whale to an amoeba. The splendor of each item, its beauty of form as well as of function, speaks not of instantaneous mass production, but rather of time and attention to detail, of infinite care and delight.[18]

The argument seems to suggest that God could not possibly have created such an intricate universe in only six days' time. Yet the whole point of Genesis 1–2 is that God's creative power, like the universe itself, is unfathomable to the human mind. With His infinite power and wisdom, He had no need of eons to design and perfect His creation. He simply spoke the word and brought forth out of nothing everything we see. And Scripture says He did it in six days.

Absolutely nothing in the text of Genesis 1:1–2:3 speaks of evolution or long geological ages in the creation process. The text itself is in fact a straightforward refutation of all evolutionary principles. Theistic evolution, billion-year-old-earth theories, and "progressive creationism" are all refuted if we simply take the statements of Genesis at face value. Only by denying key expressions or interpreting them in a nonliteral sense can the Christian read any degree of evolution or "progressive creation" into the Genesis account.

Consequently, it's a very difficult task for any commentator or exegete to impose old-earth theories on the biblical creation account. In order to attempt it at all, they must begin by obscuring the obvious historical sense of the passage, and turning instead to literary devices such as allegory, myth, legend, or poetic expressions.

And in doing so, they are attempting to make the Word of God bow the knee to godless naturalism and its everchanging theories. We ought rather to allow the unchanging, authoritative Word of God to inform our understanding, and let science bow the knee to Scripture.

Dr. Ross remains an evangelical who believes in the historicity of Adam and Eve precisely because at some juncture he decided to accept the revealed truth of Scripture *instead of* the theories of modern science. It would be much better to recognize the superiority of Scripture up-front and make Scripture the authority whereby *all* scientific theory is evaluated. That is the historic principle of *sola Scriptura*. Christians who hold to the authority of Scripture over scientific theory will not be ashamed when all the true facts come in. Remember, Christ Himself said, "Heaven and earth will pass away, but My words will by no means pass away" (Matthew 24:35). The Word of God still stands unchanged after thousands of years, while the theories of secular science change dramatically with every new generation.

Heaven and earth *will* pass away. As mentioned in the previous chapter, the universe will one day dissolve as quickly as it came into being (2 Peter 3:10–12), only to be replaced immediately by a new heaven and new earth (Revelation 21:1–5). And the biblical account of the first creation will be fully vindicated.

The earth was without form, and void; and darkness was on the face of the deep. And the Spirit of God was hovering over the face of the waters. Then God said, "Let there be light"; and there was light. And God saw the light, that it was good; and God divided the light from the darkness. God called the light Day, and the darkness He called Night. So the evening and the morning were the first day.

—*Genesis 1:2–5*

3
LIGHT ON DAY ONE

Genesis 1:2–5

THE FIRST DAY OF CREATION defines and delimits what the Bible means by the word *day* throughout the context of the first chapter of Genesis. Those who believe the days of creation were long ages invariably make much of the fact that the sun was not created until the fourth day, and on this basis they argue that the days could not have been solar, twenty-four-hour days. The word *day*, they point out, is used elsewhere in Scripture to speak of long or indeterminate periods of time. For example, "the day of the Lord" is an expression used throughout Scripture to signify an eschatalogical era in which God pours out His wrath upon the earth. Moreover, 2 Peter 3:8 says, "With the Lord one day is as a thousand years, and a thousand years as one day." Thus old-earth creationists argue that the days of creation might well have been long eras that roughly correspond to modern geological theories about the so-called Precambrian, Paleozoic, Mesozoic, Tertiary, and Quaternary eras.

The problem with this view is that nothing in the passage itself suggests that the days were long epochs. The days are defined in Genesis 1:5: "God called the light Day, and the darkness He called Night. So the evening and the morning were the first day." Night and day, evening and morning are demarcated by rhythmic phases of light and darkness from the very beginning. The very same expression, "the evening and the morning were the [nth] day" is employed for each of the six days of creation (vv. 5, 8, 13, 19, 23, 31), underscoring the fact that the days were the same and that they had clearly defined boundaries.

The only cadence of light and darkness defined anywhere in this context is the day-night cycle that (after day four) is governed by the sun and moon (v. 18). There is no reason to believe the rhythm was greatly altered on day four. That means the duration of "the evening and the morning" on the first day of creation was the same as the evening and morning of any solar day.

Indeed, the word *day* is sometimes used figuratively in Scripture to speak of an indeterminate period of time ("the day of your gladness"—Numbers 10:10). But throughout Scripture, wherever the word is modified by a number ("He rose again the third day"—1 Corinthians 15:4), the clear reference is to a normal solar day.

Nothing in Scripture itself permits the view that the days of creation were anything other than literal twenty-four-hour days. Only extrabiblical influences—such as the theories of modern science, the views of higher criticism, or other attacks against the historicity of Scripture—would lead anyone to interpret the days of Genesis 1 as long epochs. In effect, old-earth creationists have subjugated Scripture to certain theories currently popular in big bang cosmology. Cosmological theories have been imposed on Scripture as an interpretive grid and allowed to redefine the length of the creation days. Such an approach is *not* evangelical, and because it compromises the authority of Scripture at the start, it will inevitably move people away from an evangelical understanding of Scripture, no matter how tenaciously the proponents of the view attempt to hold to evangelical doctrine. To accommodate our understanding of Scripture to secular and scientific theory is to undermine biblical authority.

Hugh Ross and other old-earth creationists respond to this argument by pointing out that Augustine and certain other church fathers interpreted the days of creation nonliterally. "Their scriptural views cannot be said to have been shaped to accommodate secular opinion," Ross claims.[1]

Indeed, Augustine did take a nonliteral view of the six days of creation. He wrote, "What kind of days these were it is extremely difficult, or perhaps impossible for us to conceive, and how much more to say!"[2]

But what Ross *doesn't* tell his readers is that Augustine and those who shared his views were arguing that God created the entire universe instantly, in a less than a nanosecond—indeed, outside the realm of time completely. Far from agreeing with Ross and modern science that creation was spread over billions of years, Augustine and others who shared his view went the opposite direction and foreshortened the time of creation to a single instant. They did this because they had been influenced by Greek philosophy to believe that a God who transcends time and space could not create in the realm of time. So they collapsed the six days to a single instant. Augustine wrote, "Assuredly the world was made, not in time, but simultaneously with time."[3] That was precisely what Augustine's study of the works of secular philosophers had taught him. In other words, his views on this question *were*, after all, an accommodation to secular opinion. (And such opinions *did* eventually erode the early church's commitment to the authority of Scripture.)

However, Augustine opposed the notion of an ancient earth as vigorously as any modern evangelical critic of old-earthism. He included an entire chapter in *The City of God* titled, "Of the Falseness of the History Which Allots Many Thousand Years to the World's Past." His criticism of those who believed the earth is ancient was straightforward: "They say what they think, not what they know. They are deceived, too, by those highly mendacious documents which profess to give the history of many thousand years, though, reckoning by the sacred writings, we find that not 6,000 years have yet passed."[4]

Indeed, nothing in Scripture itself would ever lead anyone to think that the world is billions of years old or that the days of creation were long eras. Instead, by defining the days of creation according to the light cycle that separates day from night, Scripture states as explicitly as possible that the days of creation were equal in length to normal solar days. And part of the wonder of creation is the ease and speed with which God formed something so unimaginably vast, complex, intricate, and beautiful. The emphasis is not, as Hugh Ross suggests, on "time and attention to detail."[5] Rather, what the biblical account aims to stress is the infinite majesty and power of the Almighty One who accomplished so much, so perfectly, in so short a time, with nothing more than His Word.

Old-earth creationism diminishes the biblical emphasis on creation by divine fiat, setting up a scenario where God tinkers with creation over long epochs until the world is finally ready to be inhabited by humans made in His image. This is quite contrary to what Genesis teaches.

That is not to suggest, as Augustine did, that everything was created in an instant. According to Scripture, there is a progression to God's creative work. He did it over six days' time and rested on the seventh day. This is not because He needed that much time to create, and certainly not because He needed the rest. But He thereby gave a pattern for the cycle of work and rest He deemed right for humanity to live by. This established the measure of a week, which to this day is reflected in the calendar by which the entire world measures time. We'll examine this more closely when we deal with the seventh day.

And He sovereignly chose to devote each day to a specific aspect of creation. Day one saw the creation of time, matter, and light.

The creation of time is implied by the words "In the beginning." The beginning of what? Time itself. Before this, there was no measurement of time and no passage of time. God Himself existed in all His perfection, outside of time, in a realm we cannot even imagine. Our thoughts about timelessness are limited, because everything we know is subject to the passage of time.

Much has been written about the timelessness of God. It is a profound and difficult concept, and I do not propose to deal with it in any great depth, except to affirm that Scripture teaches it. It is the very thing Peter spoke of in 2 Peter 3:8 when he wrote, "With the Lord one day is as a thousand years, and a thousand years as one day." (That verse, by the way, has nothing to do with the length of the creation days. Peter was affirming God's timelessness; Genesis clearly indicates that creation took place in time.) God is not limited by the ticking of a clock. He can accomplish in a nanosecond as much as He can accomplish in a quadrillion years. And both are alike to Him. He knows the details of the future with as much certainty as He knows the past. Scripture underscores God's timelessness by referring to Him as "Lord God Almighty, Who was and is and is to come!" (Revelation 4:8). God Himself says, "I am the Alpha and the Omega, the Beginning and the End . . . who is and who was and who is to come, the Almighty" (1:8). Even the eternality, and hence the timelessness, of Christ is suggested by Hebrews 13:8: "Jesus Christ is the same yesterday, today, and forever."

But along with the universe, God created time. That, I believe, is the very thing the words "In the beginning" in Genesis 1:1 mean to teach. With God's first creative activity, time emerged from eternity.

And matter emerged from that which is immaterial. Out of nothing, in an instant, the universe—with all its space and matter—was made by God's decree. It is impossible to tell what form the matter took, but notice that the stars and planets were not created until day four. The universe—at least its energy and mass—began to exist in some form, though the light-giving stars and planets had not yet taken shape. What shape everything was in is not spelled out in explicit detail. But I like the paraphrase of Genesis 1:1 that was proposed by Henry Morris: "The transcendent, omnipotent Godhead called into existence the space-mass-time universe."[6] We know from verse 2 that the earth existed in a formless, barren state, shrouded in darkness and water or mist of some sort. A similar barrenness no doubt characterized the whole universe. But in that first instant of creation, the "space-mass-time universe" began to exist.

Other than that, day one is notable for one thing: light. Of all God's creation, the thing that most clearly reveals and most closely approximates His glory is light. That's why He Himself is called "the Father of lights, with whom there is no variation or shadow of turning" (James 1:17). In other words, all true spiritual light emanates from Him. No matter how He turns, He casts no shadow, nor is He ever in the shadows, because He is pure light, "and in Him is no darkness at all" (1 John 1:5). Like the sun, but more perfectly than the sun, He broadcasts light with no taint of any shadow. "Light dwells with Him" (Daniel 2:22), and He "[dwells] in unapproachable light, whom no man has seen or can see" (1 Timothy 6:16). Created light represents His glory more nearly than any other aspect of creation. Like Him, it illuminates and makes known all else. Without light, all creation would remain cold and dark. So it is fitting that light was created on day one.

Here is the biblical account of God's activity on that first day of creation:

> In the beginning God created the heavens and the earth. The earth was without form, and void; and darkness was on the face of the deep. And the Spirit of God was hovering over the face of the waters. Then God said, 'Let there be light'; and there was light. And God saw the light, that it was good; and God divided the light from the darkness. God called the light Day, and the darkness He called Night. So the evening and the morning were the first day. (Genesis 1:1–5)

Verse 1 is a general statement. The rest of Genesis 1 unfolds the sequence of God's creative work.

THE BATTLE FOR THE BEGINNING

THE BARREN PLANET

As day one emerges from eternity, we find the earth in a dark and barren condition. Three phrases are used in verse 2 to describe the original state of the earth. It was "without form, and void", "darkness was on the face of the deep", and "the Spirit of God was hovering over the face of the waters." Those three expressions describe the condition of the earth at the dawning of day one.

The construction of the Hebrew phrase that opens verse 2 is significant. The subject comes before the verb, as if to emphasize something remarkable about it. It might be translated, "As to the earth, it was formless and void." Here is a new planet, the very focus of God's creative purpose, and it was formless and void. The Hebrew expression is *tohu wa bohu*. *Tohu* signifies a wasteland, a desolate place. *Bohu* means "empty." The earth was an empty place of utter desolation.

The same expression is used in Jeremiah 4:23. There, Jeremiah is lamenting the doom of Israel. He says in verse 19, "O my soul, my soul! I am pained in my very heart! My heart makes a noise in me; I cannot hold my peace." Why? Because the trumpet signaling God's judgment of Israel had sounded. "Destruction upon destruction is cried, For the whole land is plundered" (v. 20). And he borrows the very words from Genesis 1:2: "I beheld the earth, and indeed it was without form [*tohu*], and void [*bohu*]; And the heavens, they had no light" (v. 23). That is how he describes the condition of Judah under the devastating destruction that was brought upon it by the judgment of God. What was once a fruitful land had become a wilderness (v. 26). It was a wasted, devastated place without any inhabitants. It had lost its former beauty. It didn't have any form. It didn't have any beauty. It had reverted to a state of barrenness that reminded Jeremiah of the state of the earth in the beginning, before God's creative work had formed it into something beautiful.

Isaiah borrows the same expression. Prophesying the destruction that would come in the day of the Lord's vengeance against the Gentiles, he says their land will be turned into desolation. "He shall stretch out over it the line of confusion [*tohu*] and the stones of emptiness [*bohu*]" (Isaiah 34:11). That pictures God as the architect of judgment, using a plumb line of *tohu*, which is kept taut by weights made of *bohu*.

So these words speak of waste and desolation. They describe the earth as a place devoid of form or inhabitants—a lifeless, barren place. It suggests that the very shape of the earth was unfinished and empty. The raw material was all there, but it had not yet been given form. The features of earth as we know it were undifferentiated, unseparated, unorganized, and uninhabited.

Some have suggested that an indeterminate interval of many billions of years is hidden between verses 1 and 2. This theory, known as the "gap theory," was once quite popular, and is featured prominently in the *Scofield Reference Bible*. According to the gap theory, God created a fully-functional earth in verse 1. That ancient earth ostensibly featured a full spectrum of animal and plant life, including fish and mammals, various species of now-extinct dinosaurs, and other creatures that we know only from the fossil record.

Proponents of the gap theory suggest that verse 2 ought to be translated, "The earth became without form, and void." They speculate that as a result of Satan's fall, or for some other reason, the prehistoric earth was laid waste by an untold calamity. (This presupposes, of course, that Satan's fall or some other evil occurred sometime in the gap between Genesis 1:1 and 1:2.) Then, according to this view, God created all the life-forms that we now see and thus remade earth into a paradise in six days of *re*creation.

Like other old-earth theories, the gap theory is supposed to explain the fossil record and harmonize the biblical account with modern scientific theories about a multiple-billion-year-old earth.

Most who hold to the gap theory suggest that the sun was not *created* on day four; it was merely made visible on that day by the clarifying of earth's atmosphere or the receding of a vapor cloud that had encircled the earth. Other than that, the gap theory has one advantage over most other old-earth views: It allows for a straightforward literal interpretation of the creation days of Genesis 1.

But the theory is accepted by relatively few today, because the biblical and theological problems it poses are enormous. For example, in Genesis 1:31, *after* God had completed all His creation, He declared it "very good"—which would not be a fitting description if evil had already entered the universe. Furthermore, if the fossil record is to be explained by an interval in the white space between Genesis 1:1 and 1:2, that means death, disease, suffering, and calamity were common many ages before Adam fell. Yet Scripture says Adam's sin was the event that introduced death and calamity into God's creation: "By man came death" (2 Corinthians 15:21); "Through one man sin entered the world, and death through sin" (Romans 5:12). The gap theory also flatly contradicts Exodus 20:11: "For in six days the Lord made the heavens and the earth, the sea, and all that is in them, and rested the seventh day."

The plain meaning of the text seems to be that the barrenness described in verse 2 is simply the original state of the universe in the twenty-four hours immediately following its initial creation. It is not a state of desolation into which the earth *fell*; it is how the universe appeared *in situ*, before God finished His creative work. The picture it conjures up is reminiscent of a potter wishing to fashion a beautiful vessel and then fill it to be used. He first takes a lump of unformed clay and places it on the wheel to mold and fit it to his purpose. In a similar way, God began with raw material. He first created a basic mass of elements that contained everything necessary to make a habitat for the life He would later create. And then using that mass of elements, He carefully shaped it and formed it into the perfect finished work He had planned from the beginning. So aside from the life-forms He created, His work throughout those first six days is comparable to the potter's finishing work. It was mostly a process of perfecting what He had already created in the beginning.

According to Scripture, it all began in total darkness. Not only was the universe barren and utterly uninhabited; it was also engulfed in total, absolute darkness. God had not yet created light. Verse 2 says, "darkness was on the face of the deep."

The word *deep* in Scripture is an expression used for the sea (cf. Isaiah 51:10). And the phrase in Genesis 1:2 is followed by a parallelism: "The Spirit of God was hovering over the face of the waters." This suggests the earth's surface *was* water. It was a vast ocean—the deep—a global, primordial ocean that covered the entire planet. And it was all engulfed in the blackness of a universal darkness.

Water, so vital to the nourishment of the life that was to come, was already earth's most prominent feature. This original watery state of the earth is referred to in Psalm 104:5–6: "You who laid the foundations of the earth, so that it should not be moved forever, You covered it with the deep as with a garment; the waters stood above the mountains."

Who can fathom what a formless, empty, watery earth, utterly devoid of light, might have been like? It did not remain in such a dark and barren condition very long. God instantly set to work fashioning the material He had created.

THE BROODING SPIRIT

Look again at that closing sentence of verse 2: "And the Spirit of God was hovering over the face of the waters." Remember, the earth was an undeveloped, unformed, lifeless mass of matter hung in space, covered by water, and engulfed in darkness. And the Spirit of God was hovering over the surface of it. The Spirit of God enveloped it, surrounded it, and guarded over it. He was the creative Agent who would oversee formation out of the formlessness and the filling of the void.

The Hebrew word for "hovering" is an interesting word that evokes the image of a hen brooding over her chicks. The word indicates superintending, divine care, and supervision. The same Hebrew word appears twice more in the Old Testament—once in Deuteronomy 32:11, where the imagery is that of an eagle hovering over its nest (the King James Version translates it as "fluttereth" in that verse); and once in Jeremiah 23:9, where it is translated "shake"—describing the prophet's bones quaking with shock at the Word of the Lord. The word implies movement, and Henry Morris has therefore suggested that the final phrase in Genesis 1:2 could be translated, "the Spirit of God *vibrated* over the face of the waters"—signifying the transmission of energy from Creator to creation, and identifying the Holy Spirit as the "Prime Mover" who sets all of creation in motion.[7]

In his book, *Creation and Change*, Douglas F. Kelly writes:

> This "brooding" of the Spirit of God over the waters is a major detail in the creation account, not a minor one. It demonstrates vividly the biblical worldview of a God whose hand and direct presence are never lifted from the elements and working of the material order. This . . . is the direct antithesis of any sort of philosophical Deism or theological Dualism, both of which assume a vast gap between the living God and the space, time cosmos. Deism pictures a remote deity unable or unwilling to intervene immediately in the natural realm. That assumption explains much of the

traditional and contemporary resistance to the biblical teaching of creation, as well as to the reality of miracles, Christ's incarnation and intercessory prayer. It must be remembered that the deistic gap between God and the world is merely a philosophical assumption; an axiom of naturalistic religion, as it were, not a scientific fact.[8]

In other words, this underscores God's direct activity in all aspects of creation. He didn't create a mechanism for evolution and leave the universe to develop to maturity on its own. He was directly and personally involved in every aspect of creation. Every bit of it—from the tiniest subatomic particle to the grandest galaxy—shows His handiwork. It is the work of His fingers (Psalm 8:3).

And yet notice also that as the Genesis account unfolds, virtually every aspect of creation is the immediate effect of God's Word. He merely says, "Let there be light"—and there was light (1:3). He says, "'Let the earth bring forth the living creature according to its kind . . . '; and it was so" (v. 24). He accomplishes it all instantly by His sovereign decree. So powerful is His Word that He speaks, and at once it is done. Only in the case of Adam is a creative *process* described: God "formed man of the dust of the ground, and breathed into his nostrils the breath of life" (2:7).

All of this speaks of an immediate, instantaneous creation by divine decree. There is no need for epochal time periods to allow nature to shape and mold the face of the earth. Scripture says all the work of giving form to the formless and filling the void is the immediate work of God Himself. He does it merely by issuing a command. Thus His absolute sovereignty is stressed in the very act of creation.

Yet at the same time, the intimacy of His involvement with the formation of the world is pictured by the imagery of the Holy Spirit, who hovers over the face of the waters, incubating the fledgling creation and then superintending its maturing process with the attentive care of a mother hen guarding a nest of hatchlings.

That imagery also denotes a particular focus on this planet. From this point on, the entire creation account is told from the perspective of an observer on earth. It is the Holy Spirit's own perspective. This planet is the nucleus of God's creative purpose. It is the paradise He created as a habitat for creatures whom He would make in His own image—the very pinnacle of His creative work.

And the fact that earth alone, of all known planets, seethes with life, is directly owing to the Holy Spirit's activity described in Genesis 1:2. The entire Bible testifies that the Spirit of God is the source of all life and creation. "By His Spirit He adorned the heavens" (Job 26:13). Job testified, "The Spirit of God has made me, and the breath of the Almighty gives me life" (Job 33:4). "By the word of the Lord the heavens were made, and all the host of them by the breath of His mouth" (Psalm 33:6). The word translated "breath" is the same as the Hebrew word for "spirit." David the psalmist noted the Holy Spirit's role in the formation of all creatures: "You send forth Your Spirit, they are created" (Psalm 104:30).

Scripture also teaches that the Spirit of God is essential for the sustaining of life. He still blankets and nurtures His creation. "For in Him we live and move and have our being" (Acts 17:28). "In [His] hand is the life of every living thing, and the breath of all mankind" (Job 12:10).

THE CLARIFYING LIGHT

After the creation of the original material universe, the most significant feature of day one is the creation of light. "Then God said, 'Let there be light'; and there was light" (v. 3). Science cannot understand light, much less explain how it came about. This verse simply says it was created by an order from God. The One who is uncreated light brought created light into existence. The One who dwells in unapproachable light illuminated His creation with a brilliant object lesson about His glory.

What form this light took is not clear. Whether it was merely an ethereal glow or a light that emanated from a specific place is nowhere stated. Actual lights, such as the sun, moon, and stars, were not created until the fourth day. These were permanent light bearers. But light itself, the *reality* of light, was created on day one. And instantly it separated day from night.

Douglas F. Kelly writes:

> The speaking into existence of the created light is the first of a series of
> three separations accomplished by the Creator which were essential to

make the chaos into a cosmos. On Day One light separates day and night; on Day Two the "firmament" separates the upper waters from the earth, constituting an atmosphere or "breathing space"; on Day Three, the waters below the heavens are collected into seas, and thus separated from the dry land. These three separations show the mighty hand of God shaping and organizing the dark, watery mass in the direction of a beautiful garden; a fit and lovely dwelling place for plants, animals and humankind.[9]

The picture this suggests is that of someone who comes to arrange items in a dark room, and before he does anything else, he turns on the light.

But this involved more than a separation between light and darkness. The creation of light also inaugurated the measurement of earth's time by periods of day and night. Regular intervals of light began to be interspersed with intervals of darkness. And in verse 5 we are told, "God called the light Day, and the darkness He called Night. So the evening and the morning were the first day." Thus the rhythm of days and nights began. Perhaps the earth was already rotating on its axis, with light illuminating one side and darkness veiling the other.

Various suggestions have been made about what this light might have been. Could it have been a mass of glowing matter that was later shaped into the sun? Or (as seems more likely) could it have been a disembodied light, an ethereal temporary brilliance decreed by God to illuminate His creation until permanent lights were set in place? The nature of this light is not described. We are simply told that light existed because God told it to exist. And it should not be difficult for us to believe that One whose glory is described as pure light could command light to appear even before there were any stars or sun to embody that light.

What is light? Even the best physicists struggle to explain it. It has characteristics of both particles and waves. Light photons behave like particles, like tiny specks of dust, except that they have no volume. The energy of a photon is concentrated in a finite space, existing at any given moment in a specific location, yet moving at a definable, measurable velocity. And that is why we speak of the "speed" of light. Yet light also exhibits the characteristics of a wave, which is not a finite entity. A wave, unlike a particle, exists in no finite space; it has a variable frequency; and it may be illustrated mathematically as a sine curve that has no beginning or end. Wave motion, unlike particle motion, involves the transfer of energy from point to point without the transfer of matter. A light wave is essentially a deformation of electric and magnetic fields. To complicate matters further, light waves can behave like particles, and the particle-like photons can behave like waves.

Light is a form of energy. It is essentially electromagnetic radiation, including every frequency from long-wave radiation, radio waves, microwaves, and infrared waves at the high end, to ultraviolet, x-rays, and gamma radiation at the low end. In the middle is visible light, including the entire rainbow of colors. The different colors are simply varying wavelengths of light in the spectrum. White light—what we normally think of when we hear the word *light*—is not a pure color itself; it is a combination of all the colors in the visible spectrum.

The appearance of everything we see is a result of how light waves reflect off objects. But the range of different light waves is infinite and includes far more than is visible to our eyes. When you listen to the radio, for example, you are hearing a signal that is broadcast using technology that takes advantage of the properties of light. Multiple frequencies enable us to tune our radios to multiple stations, ranging from shortwave frequencies that travel vast distances, to long-wave (FM) frequencies that are more localized.

Even some of the spectra of light that are invisible to the human eye have properties that make other types of vision possible. Infrared rays, for example, are not visible to normal human eyesight, but they provide enough illumination to enable detailed photographs to be taken in the dark. Modern science has made night-vision instruments possible by using light that is normally invisible to the human eye.

To describe all the marvels of light would provide ample material for an entire set of books. You have probably experimented with light reflection and light refraction using mirrors and prisms. Prisms separate the colors of light because as the light passes through the prism its direction is bent. Different color waves, moving at different speeds, come out of the prism separated into a visible spectrum. Eyeglass lenses refract light in a precise enough fashion to correct the deficiencies of our failing eyesight. Concave lenses spread light rays apart; convex ones bring light rays closer together. This ability of lenses to manipulate light enables optometrists to prescribe eyeglasses that correct our vision with a high degree of accuracy.

Fine strands of fiberoptic material use the reflective properties of light to carry tiny pulses of light across vast distances at literally the speed of light with pinpoint precision. Those pulses—basically rapidly flashing on–off signals—enable modern undersea cables to carry digitized telephone calls, video images, and other forms of data from continent to continent literally at light speed. All of this is possible because of the marvelous properties of light.

Light waves, unlike sound waves or shock waves, can travel through a vacuum. That is why we can see the stars at night. If you were to take a bell and enclose it in a plexiglass container, then pump all the air out of the container to create a near vacuum, you could still see the bell, of course, but you would not be able to hear it ring—because sound waves cannot travel across a vacuum.

Yet, amazingly, light cannot be seen by the human eye except when it interacts with matter. A beam of light shining up into the sky at night would be invisible if there were not tiny particles in the air that reflect it. A flashlight turned on in outer space will send out a beam that is completely invisible, except where it strikes an object.

Nothing known to us in the universe moves faster than the speed of light. Light in a vacuum travels 186,282 miles per second. But no matter how fast you are moving, the speed of light appears to be the same speed as if you were not moving at all. (In other words, moving toward a light source, even at a very high rate of speed, will not accelerate the speed at which the light appears to travel toward you, and moving away from light will not slow down its apparent motion. Nothing else in the universe has this property.)

According to currently accepted theories of physics, if an object or person were able to travel into space at a velocity approaching light speed, time and distance would be foreshortened for them compared to what a stationary observer on earth would experience. So a traveler making a round-trip journey to a distant star at near light speed would return to find more time had passed on earth than in his spaceship. His watch and even his appearance would reflect this difference. If he had a twin brother, the traveler would be younger than his earthbound twin. The farther and faster he travels, the more pronounced this effect would be. If he traveled the distance of one light-year, the "year" required for him to travel so far is only a year from the perspective of a stationary observer. To the traveler himself, it would be as if far less than a year had passed. So travel approaching the speed of light would play havoc with our perception of time.

Perhaps nothing in all of physics is more fascinating or more mysterious than light. Light is the single most important source of energy and heat on earth. Without light, life on earth would be impossible. Virtually all the earthly mechanisms we depend upon for the transfer of energy are derived, ultimately, from light. Wind, the water cycle, and ocean waves would all cease if the earth were to remain in utter darkness for very long. The earth would quickly turn cold and all life would cease. That's why light was the vital starting point in the process of creation.

Scripture says, "God saw the light, that it was good" (Genesis 1:4). "It was good" becomes the refrain that runs through the biblical creation account. This statement stresses the divine origin and perfection of all that was created. Creation was good because God is good. All that He created was good. He declared light good because it was a reflection of Himself. He is the standard and definition of all that is good. Douglas F. Kelly sums this point up beautifully with a quotation from Novatian, a third-century theologian:

> What could you possibly say then that would be worthy of Him? He is more sublime than all sublimity, higher than all heights, deeper than all depth, clearer than all light, brighter than all brilliance, more splendid than all splendour, stronger than all strength, mightier than all might, more beautiful than all beauty, truer than all truth, more enduring than all endurance, greater than all majesty, more powerful than all power, richer than all riches, wiser than all wisdom, kinder than all kindness, better than all goodness, juster than all justice, more merciful than all mercy. Every kind of virtue must of necessity be less than He who is the God and source of everything.[10]

And creation itself, in its pristine state, was a reflection of the goodness of God. No aspect of creation sums this up more clearly than the creation of light. It is sheer brilliance, unfathomable energy, the very thing that was most needed for the formless void to begin to take shape as a paradise of pure goodness.

Energy permeates the cosmos. If you took a canister of completely empty space—a total vacuum, with no molecules of matter in it—then froze it to absolute zero so that even the radiation were taken out of it, there would still be something in that space: energy in massive proportions.

This is known as zero-point energy. It fills even the "emptiness" of space. Most scientists now believe that a volume of empty space no larger than a coffee cup contains enough energy to evaporate all the oceans of the world. Where does this energy come from? Science has no explanation for it. Clearly, it is part of God's creation. Either it was inherent in the original creation of matter and space, or it is an aspect of what occurred the moment God said, "Let there be light."

But it was never God's plan as Creator that there be perpetual visible light with no darkness. So He "divided the light from the darkness" (v. 4). Both light and darkness suited His creative plan. He "called the light Day, and the darkness He called Night" (v. 5). So it was, and so it has always been. The same constant cycle of light and darkness, day and night, has defined the character of this earth since day one.

Verse 5 concludes the biblical description of the first day: "So the evening and the morning were the first day."

It was a spectacular first day. Just in case someone might think this was a long evolutionary process, verse 5 says emphatically, "And there was evening and there was morning, one day." That's a literal translation of the Hebrew word order. It doesn't describe a billion-year-long process; it describes one day—one cycle of light and dark—evening and morning.

And thus the work of creation is underway.

Then God said, "Let there be a firmament in the midst of the waters, and let it divide the waters from the waters." Thus God made the firmament, and divided the waters which were under the firmament from the waters which were above the firmament; and it was so. And God called the firmament Heaven. So the evening and the morning were the second day. Then God said, "Let the waters under the heavens be gathered together into one place, and let the dry land appear"; and it was so. And God called the dry land Earth, and the gathering together of the waters He called Seas. And God saw that it was good. Then God said, "Let the earth bring forth grass, the herb that yields seed, and the fruit tree that yields fruit according to its kind, whose seed is in itself, on the earth"; and it was so. And the earth brought forth grass, the herb that yields seed according to its kind, and the tree that yields fruit, whose seed is in itself according to its kind. And God saw that it was good. So the evening and the morning were the third day.

—Genesis 1:6–13

4

WHEN HE MARKED OUT
THE FOUNDATIONS OF THE EARTH

Genesis 1:6–13

IN PROVERBS 8, the voice of wisdom speaks. This personification of wisdom is regarded by most commentators as one of the classic Old Testament references to God the Son, the Second Person of the Trinity. He declares His own eternality:

> The Lord possessed me at the beginning of His way,
> Before His works of old.
> I have been established from everlasting,
> From the beginning, before there was ever an earth.
> When there were no depths I was brought forth,
> When there were no fountains abounding with water.
> Before the mountains were settled,
> Before the hills, I was brought forth;
> While as yet He had not made the earth or the fields,
> Or the primeval dust of the world.
> When He prepared the heavens, I was there,
> When He drew a circle on the face of the deep,
> When He established the clouds above,
> When He strengthened the fountains of the deep,
> When He assigned to the sea its limit,
> So that the waters would not transgress His command,
> When He marked out the foundations of the earth,

Then I was beside Him as a master craftsman;
And I was daily His delight,
Rejoicing always before Him. (Proverbs 8:22–30)

Verses 22–26 describe Christ's existence with the Father in eternity past. But beginning in verse 27, He describes creation with words that perfectly parallel the Genesis account: "When He prepared the heavens, I was there, when He drew a circle on the face of the deep."

The "circle on the face of the deep" in verse 27 seems to refer to the firmament that was created on day two of creation, establishing the celestial waters above and the sea beneath, with a breathable atmosphere separating them. Verse 28 then describes how the Creator assigned the limits of the sea, as dry land emerged from the waters that originally covered the whole earth. That occurred on day three. According to this passage from Proverbs, Wisdom, which is none other than the divine Logos, was "beside [God the Father] as a master craftsman" (v. 30). That harmonizes perfectly with the testimony of John 1:1–3, which states that the Logos was with God, and is Himself God, and "without Him nothing was made that was made."

Those first three days of creation were foundational. Each day is marked by a significant division that occurs. On day one, as we saw in the previous chapter, light was divided from darkness. On day two, a firmament divided the waters above the earth from the waters below. And on day three, the dry land was separated from the sea.

All of this was necessary to make the earth habitable. Those were the first and foundational steps toward making a cosmos out of the chaos described in verse 2.

Days two and three of creation saw monumental changes as the formless void took on its finished look.

DAY TWO: THE FIRMAMENT

As the second day dawned, the earth was still covered with water. It probably had the appearance of a seething cauldron of mud, with no dry land and no breathable atmosphere. Its entire surface was a liquid soup of elements, predominantly water, situated in a spherical shape and hung on nothing in space (cf. Job 26:7).

"Then God said, 'Let there be a firmament in the midst of the waters, and let it divide the waters from the waters.' Thus God made the firmament, and divided the waters which were under the firmament from the waters which were above the firmament; and it was so" (Genesis 1:6–7).

Notice once again that God accomplished His work simply by speaking the word. He commanded the water to separate, and He placed an expanse, or a "firmament" between the water that remained on the earth and the water that rose above the expanse.

The word "firmament" is the Hebrew word *raqiya*. It speaks of something that is spread out. It is derived from a verb that means "to spread an overlay." A verb form of the same word is used, for example, in Exodus 39:3 to speak of the hammering of gold into thin sheets. Gold when hammered easily flattens and spreads out into a plate, and that is how gold plates were made to overlay the ark and other fixtures in the temple.

So the imagery of Genesis 1:6 is that of a vast expanse, a protective layer that overlays the earth and divides the waters below (the sea of water that covered the earth) from the waters above (which could refer to atmospheric water, clouds, and water vapor; or it might describe some kind of ice-crystal or water-vapor canopy that encircled the antediluvian world). In other words, the expanse in-between—the firmament—includes the earth's breathable atmosphere.

God called this expanse heaven (v. 8). It seems to refer primarily to the sky immediately above us—the atmospheric heavens. But the word *firmament* is also sometimes used to signify the stellar heavens beyond earth's atmosphere, as in verse 14. In 2 Corinthians 12, when Paul speaks of being "caught up to the third heaven," he is referring to the earth's atmosphere as the first heaven, the space beyond earth's atmosphere as the second heaven, and the heaven where God dwells as the third heaven. The firmament described here—the overlay that divided the waters below from the waters above—is the first heaven. According to Genesis 1:1, the heavens of outer space had already been created. So the firmament described in verses 7–8 is the earth's atmosphere.

Apparently there was no atmosphere on the earth in the beginning, but on the second day, God spoke it into existence. He released some of earth's water and sent it up, and He made a firmament of breathable gases between that water above and the water below. And as that firmament formed, the upper waters, in the form of a layer of mist or vapor, rose into the sky, giving the appearance of a transparent vault, or an invisible dome, rising up from earth's surface. A similar effect can be seen at times when the weather changes. And as recently as Victorian times, a popular way of signifying fair weather was to say, "The glass is rising high today." The formation of the firmament also had the appearance of a glass dome rising above earth's surface.

Moses' account is notable for the absence of any mythological features. All other ancient literature about the origin of the earth included fantastic legends about gods and sea monsters and cosmic battles that supposedly explained the emergence of earth's atmosphere and the formation of the land out of the sea. The Babylonians, for example, said that earth and heaven were separated when the god Marduk defeated Tiamat, the ocean-goddess, and cut her body in two. Half of her body became the earth, and the other half became the heavens.

The biblical account is of an entirely different character. What the Bible says is entirely reasonable. God divided the waters, and some rose into the upper atmosphere. The remaining waters still engulfed the earth. And in-between was an expanse, the firmament, which He called heaven. Again, this firmament was simply the earth's breathable atmosphere.

Verse 6 records the decree that made it happen: "Then God said, 'Let there be a firmament in the midst of the waters, and let it divide the waters from the waters.'" Verse 7 reiterates the process in order to show that precisely what He ordered is what happened: "Thus God made the firmament, and divided the waters which were under the firmament from the waters which were above the firmament; *and it was so*" (emphasis added).

Notice that this is expressly described as a creative act, accomplished by decree from God. It was not a natural process that occurred spontaneously through long natural processes. To imagine it that way is to miss the very point this passage is teaching. On day two God was still employing creative power in proportions that are beyond our capacity to understand. There is no need for any scientific or naturalistic explanation of how this might have occurred. God *made* the firmament (v. 7).

The Hebrew verb translated "made" in that verse is *asah*. It is different from *bara*, the verb used for "created" in verse 1. And because of that word difference, some have argued that verse 7 doesn't describe an act of creation, but rather a providential act that employed natural processes to bring the firmament into place. But the Hebrew words are synonyms. They are even used in a parallel sense in Genesis 2:3, which says, "God blessed the seventh day and sanctified it, because in it He rested from all His work which God had created [*bara*] and made [*asah*]."

The context makes clear that *asah* in verse 7 describes an act of *fiat* creation, because verse 6 describes the decree by which God ordered the firmament to come into being. It also clearly involves the creation of something that never before existed.

One of the most difficult issues raised by this passage is the question of what "the waters which were above the firmament" refers to. Some creationists, including Henry Morris, believe that this was a protective canopy that remained in place until the Flood of Noah's time. Those who hold this view suggest that the waters above the firmament were a transparent vapor or a layer of water molecules at the outer edge of the atmosphere that kept the earth in a kind of a hothouse environment. This might explain why prior to the Flood it was common for humans to live more than nine hundred years. According to the hypothesis, the water canopy shielded people from the sun's more harmful rays, regulated the climate at a perfect temperature, and provided other benefits that increased the longevity of life on earth. But at the Flood, according to this theory, that canopy fell and contributed to the deluge that drowned the earth.

Other scientists, however, including some who hold biblical views of creation, believe the canopy theory poses more problems than it solves. It is a question for scientists, not exegetes, to argue over, because Scripture does not explicitly teach that such a canopy existed. "The waters which were above the firmament" needn't refer to a canopy of water; it might merely refer to the water vapor that continually floats above the earth's surface. All Genesis 1:6–7 says is that there was a division so that some of the water rose above the firmament and the rest stayed on the surface of the earth. That, frankly, could either describe a canopy of water surrounding the earth that is no longer there, or it could be a reference to water vapor like that which hovers above the firmament even today. I'm inclined to think it describes a unique atmospheric condition that existed prior to the Flood, because Scripture says that before the Flood there was no rain (Genesis 2:5), and at the Flood, the windows of heaven opened and the waters above contributed to the deluge that wiped out all life on earth except for the creatures Noah had taken on the ark (Genesis 7:11–12).

But the firmament itself was the breathable atmosphere, or the sky. The word *firmament* is used throughout Scripture to signify this (Genesis 1:20; Daniel 12:3).

"And God called the firmament Heaven" (v. 8). Because the firmament constitutes the visible heavens, Scripture speaks of the stars as being "in the firmament" (Genesis 1:14–15; 17), just as we say the stars are "in the sky" even today.

Psalm 104:2 celebrates the work of day two in picturesque terms: "[You] stretch out the heavens like a curtain." The psalm goes on to employ the symbolic imagery of a master builder to describe how God held the waters above in their place: "He lays the beams of His upper chambers in the waters, who makes the clouds His chariot, who walks on the wings of the wind." Thus the psalmist praises the wisdom of God that is revealed in the work of day two.

Notice that day two is the only day in which God does not expressly say of His work, "It was good" (cf. Genesis 1:4, 10, 12, 18, 21, 25). Surely this is a significant omission. It cannot mean that the second day's work was *not* good. But it does seem to imply that the work of day two was an incomplete step toward making the earth habitable. The stage of creation that began on day two wasn't complete until day three, when dry land emerged from the water and the earth was made fit for living things. At that point, the world was finally shaped into a habitable condition, and then God pronounced His verdict: "It was good" (v. 10).

But verse 8 signals the end of day two before that verdict is expressly pronounced: "So the evening and the morning were the second day."

DAY THREE: THE SEA AND DRY LAND

As day three dawns, the earth is still uninhabited, uninhabitable, and not in its final form. Its entire surface is still covered with water. But by the end of the day there will be not only dry land, but also vegetation.

Many who deny a literal six-day creation claim that such rapid changes are not possible. Obviously, land submerged under the sea in the morning would not normally be dry enough to support the planting of vegetation by evening. And the massive global tectonic changes that would be necessary to cause whole continents to appear from the sea would hardly seem feasible in the *same* twenty-four-hour period that plant life emerges.

That might seem to be a powerful and persuasive argument if we were talking about natural processes. But Scripture is describing the creative work of God, with whom all things are possible (Matthew 19:26). One might as well argue that the instantaneous multiplying of loaves and fishes was impossible because, after all, it takes time for fish to be hatched, grow to maturity, and be caught, cooked, and prepared for eating. If the laws of nature set limits on the creative power of God, we might as well rule out miracles altogether. But the laws of nature place no limit on what God can do (Genesis 18:14; Jeremiah 32:27). And for that reason, our understanding of science should never govern whether we take God's Word literally or not.

It is nonetheless interesting and ironic that secular physicists trying to explain the origin of the earth on purely scientific principles face a similar dilemma. Scientists who hold to the big bang theory must explain how a universe full of matter appeared out of nowhere in an instant. According to an article in the *Los Angeles Times*:

> The Big Bang is looking more supernatural all the time. About 20 years ago, the late Carl Sagan famously said that Big Bang science would eventually show that the universe was created without any creator. Since then, the picture has changed quite a bit, one reason why, in the years before his 1996 death, Sagan himself began to advocate science-and-religion studies.
>
> The leading contemporary development in Big Bang thinking is a

93

theory called "cosmic inflation," which holds that the entire universe popped out of a point with no content and no dimensions, essentially expanding instantaneously to cosmological size. Now being taught at Stanford, the Massachusetts Institute of Technology and other top schools, this explanation of the beginning of the universe bears haunting similarity to the traditional theological notion of creation *ex nihilo*, "out of nothing."[1]

The article goes on to quote "one of the world's foremost astronomers, Allan Sandage of the Observatories of the Carnegie Institution in Pasadena, Calif., [who] recently proposed that the Big Bang could only be understood as 'a miracle,' in which some higher force must have played a role."

Ultimately, *no* theory about the origin of the universe is tenable without an all-wise and all-powerful Creator. Adding multiple billions of years to the time frame doesn't even solve the problem; it only pushes it further back in time. In the end, only a miracle can account for the existence of the universe.

As Christians, we believe in the limitless miracle-working ability of our Almighty Creator. Therefore it should not tax our faith when we read that dry land and plant life rose up out of the sea in a day's time at the behest of our sovereign God. Why should we read that and think it unreasonable? Why should we reinterpret the clear statements of Scripture and try to turn this into an ages-long evolutionary process? Why cannot we simply take God at His Word?

Scripture describes day three in these terms:

> Then God said, "Let the waters under the heavens be gathered together into one place, and let the dry land appear"; and it was so. And God called the dry land Earth, and the gathering together of the waters He called Seas. And God saw that it was good. Then God said, "Let the earth bring forth grass, the herb that yields seed, and the fruit tree that yields fruit according to its kind, whose seed is in itself, on the earth"; and it was so. And the earth brought forth grass, the herb that yields seed according to its kind, and the tree that yields fruit, whose seed is in itself according to its kind. And God saw that it was good. So the evening and the morning were the third day. (Genesis 1:9–13)

The description of this day begins with the exact same words we find at the beginning of each day's chronicle: "Then God said. . . ." (vv. 3, 6, 11, 14, 20, 24). The repeated phrase emphasizes the fact that everything comes into being from nothing. God simply speaks it into existence.

And here is the third foundational division. Remember, on the first day God divided light from darkness. On the second day He divided the water below from the water above. Now, on the third day, He divides the land from the sea.

After the firmament was created, the earth was still completely engulfed in water. No doubt beneath the water was solid matter, but it was still hidden under "the face of the deep" (v. 2)—under the surface of a global ocean.

Notice God's creative decree: "Let the waters under the heavens be gathered together into one place, and let the dry land appear" (v. 9). The Septuagint (an ancient Greek translation of the Old Testament) uses the word *sunagogen*, the same word from which we get *synagogue*, meaning "a gathering place." So the waters surrounding the earth were gathered into one place, and at the same time land began to appear. The land was instantly dry, too, because that is what God decreed. "And it was so" (v. 9).

This might describe the formation of one massive continent, because the waters were gathered "into one place." In fact, most geologists think today's continents show evidence of having drifted apart from a single mass. That continental separation may have occurred during the Flood, when "all the fountains of the great deep were broken up" (Genesis 7:11). Or this initial creation might have involved multiple continents, because in verse 10, God calls the gathering together of the waters "seas"—a plural term, suggesting that although the waters were gathered into "one place," they were contained in several distinct but interconnected basins, just as we see today.

In any case, land emerged for the first time out of the water. The cataclysm that brought this about at the command of God is almost inconceivable. All of a sudden rock and earth, still in its unformed condition and buried under the depths of a global sea, started to move to the surface of the water. As the land pushed up from the depths, the water was displaced, gathering itself into one place—a massive ocean containing numerous "seas" but now distinct from the landmass. Perhaps chemical reactions occurred along with the massive tectonic movements, so that minerals, rock, and fertile soil were instantly formed out of the primordial ocean. But notice that what emerged was neither mud nor slime, but "dry land" (vv. 9–10), instantly ready to sustain plant life. It was a staggering act of creation.

It is the clear testimony of Scripture that God made this happen instantaneously. Job 38 confirms the fact. Here the Lord is talking to Job—and it is clear that the Lord is not an evolutionist. He reminds Job that the creature is in no position to question the Creator:

> Now prepare yourself like a man;
> I will question you, and you shall answer Me.
> Where were you when I laid the foundations of the earth?
> Tell Me, if you have understanding.
> Who determined its measurements? Surely you know!
> Or who stretched the line upon it?
> To what were its foundations fastened?
> Or who laid its cornerstone,
> When the morning stars sang together,
> And all the sons of God shouted for joy? (vv. 3–7).

Then the Lord describes what He did on day three of creation:

> Or who shut in the sea with doors,
> When it burst forth and issued from the womb;
> When I made the clouds its garment,
> And thick darkness its swaddling band;
> When I fixed My limit for it,
> And set bars and doors;
> When I said, "This far you may come, but no farther,
> And here your proud waves must stop!" (vv. 8–11)

The psalmist describes the same thing in Psalm 104:5–9:

> You who laid the foundations of the earth,
> So that it should not be moved forever,
> You covered it with the deep as with a garment;

The waters stood above the mountains.
At Your rebuke they fled;
At the voice of Your thunder they hastened away.
They went up over the mountains;
They went down into the valleys,
To the place which You founded for them.
You have set a boundary that they may not pass over,
That they may not return to cover the earth.

All of this, together with the quotation from Proverbs 8 cited at the beginning of the chapter, affirms that water covered the entire earth at the very beginning, and in a direct act of sovereign creation, God separated the land from the sea. Scripture gives a consistent account of how the land arose from the sea and its boundaries were set. The action is always attributed directly to God. He did it just as it is described in Genesis 1:9–10. There is no reason to try to explain it in natural terms. It was a creative miracle wrought by divine fiat.

As He did on days one and two, God named what He had made. "And God called the dry land Earth, and the gathering together of the waters He called Seas" (v. 10). There is now earth, sea, and heaven—a tripartite eco-system, now ready for life. Thus Scripture says what it omitted to say in the account of day two: "And God saw that it was good" (v. 10). It was earth, essentially as we know it, except that it was utterly devoid of life. Everything necessary for the sustenance of life was there, but life itself had not yet been created.

THE END OF DAY THREE: PLANT LIFE

"Then God said, 'Let the earth bring forth grass, the herb that yields seed, and the fruit tree that yields fruit according to its kind, whose seed is in itself, on the earth'; and it was so" (v. 11).

Notice again that plant life appeared because God decreed it. He spoke it into existence. It was not an accidental byproduct of some chemical reaction. It was not the result of long, evolving, natural processes. It was the immediate result of His sovereign command.

This, by the way, represents one of the inexplicable steps of creation that evolution simply cannot explain by any reasonable theory: the generation of life from that which is inanimate. As author and biochemist Michael Behe has pointed out, evolution can deal only with "systems that are already working." By definition, that which does not function simply cannot "evolve." It is therefore impossible for inanimate matter to produce biological systems by "evolution." Before any evolution can occur, some type of living organism would first have to be produced directly and immediately. In Behe's words, even in an evolutionary framework, the original biological system could not have been produced gradually. "It would have to arise as an integrated unit, in one fell swoop, for natural selection to have anything to work on."[2] So evolution utterly fails as an explanation for how life came about.

But here we see precisely how it happened. God spoke. "'Let the earth bring forth grass, the herb that yields seed, and the fruit tree that yields fruit according to its kind, whose seed is in itself, on the earth'; *and it was so*" (v. 11, emphasis added). Vegetation of every kind appeared instantly at His Word. Three Hebrew nouns are used. The first, *deshe*, is translated "grass," but it is a general term for vegetation. The other two nouns, *ʿeseb* and *ʿets*, speak of herbaceous plants and trees, respectively.

Both herb and tree yield seed, each "according to its kind." God made them not only capable of reproduction, but also ready for it. He created fully mature vegetation with seed already in it, ready to be dispersed.

Incidentally, one of the great wonders of creation is the way seed dispersal works. God designed an astonishing variety of ways for seeds to be carried from place to place. Some seeds are feathery and light or aerodynamically shaped and can be carried by wind. Others are carried by birds and animals—by adhering to animal fur or by being eaten and later deposited in the creature's droppings. There are hundreds of creative ways for seeds to be dispersed. This one aspect of creation alone reveals that a marvelous creative mind planned and shaped everything we see.

Notice that God created plants, not merely seeds. He made them mature, already fully rooted and developed, already bearing fruit and seed, already multiplying. As we see consistently throughout the Genesis account, from the moment He creates something, it appears as if it has been there for some time.

The seed contained in the vegetation was preprogrammed with DNA and genetic information to assure that each would reproduce "according to its kind" (vv. 11–12). That same phrase is repeated ten times in the first chapter of Genesis. The Hebrew word for "kind" is *min*, and it is roughly equivalent to the English word *species*. (Though man-made classification systems employing terms like *genus* and *species* can be misleading and are not necessarily in harmony with the biblical measure of what constitutes a "kind.")³ This is not a technical term, however. It simply designates a category of related organisms capable of breeding with one another.

The fact that creatures reproduce according to their own kind is a fundamental rule of genetics. Each organism has a unique DNA structure, with genes and chromosomes that determine all its characteristics. Careful breeding can emphasize or minimize certain characteristics within genotypes, but no amount of cross-pollination can cause a whole new life-form to arise from the species that exist. And boundaries are set on which species may be cross-pollinated. Attempting to crossbreed an oak tree with a fungus would not produce any offspring whatsoever, much less a whole new species.

Absolutely nothing in this section of Scripture—and for that matter nothing anywhere in the Bible—suggests that any living species evolved from another species. The plain language of the text means that each "kind" was directly created *ex nihilo*.

In fact, it is fair to say that this crucial phrase, "according to its kind," clearly refutes the very heart of the evolutionary idea. It debunks the notion that all life descended from a common source, and it sets a limitation on the degree of difference between any creature and its offspring. Plants cannot bring forth anything but more plants with characteristics inherited from their parents. Trees can produce only similar trees. Likewise, animals can reproduce only more animals of their own kind. The offspring may have slightly different characteristics from either of their parents, but those characteristics will nonetheless be inherited from the parents' genetic makeup. Crossbreeding cannot produce new species. Above all, plant life cannot produce animal life. There is no known process by which a plant, or any combination of plants, lacking the higher faculties of intelligent life, could ever produce animal offspring. Plants reproduce according to their own kind. Those are fundamental genetic principles, and they contradict the whole basis of the evolutionary theory. (We'll have more to say about this in chapter 6 when we examine day five of creation.)

The seed is the part of the organism that makes reproduction possible. A pollinated seed contains a complete genetic map for the offspring of the plant. Its characteristics as an adult plant are already programmed into the seed's genetic code from the moment the seed is pollinated, and that is what determines that each organism will produce "according to its kind."

Henry Morris writes:

> It should also be mentioned that the formation of plants, even in such complex forms as fruit trees, occurred before the creation of any form of animal life. This, of course, is quite logical, but it does flatly contradict the accepted evolutionary system, which has marine animals, both invertebrates and vertebrates, evolving hundreds of millions of years before the evolution of fruit trees and other higher plants. Furthermore, many plants require pollination by insects, but insects were not made until the sixth day of creation, which argues against the possibility that the days of creation could have been long ages. The idea of theistic evolution is counter to the biblical record of creation in practically every passage.[4]

Clearly and in plain language, what Genesis 1:11–12 describes is the origin of all vegetable life. It accounts for the creation of all plant species. It also sets forth the means God designed to ensure the continuity and stability of what He had made. There is nothing here that permits the belief that any new species arose through any evolutionary process. There is nothing here that demands a long era instead of a twenty-four-hour day. All of it is perfectly understandable if we simply take it at face value.

It also reveals to us the all-wise hand of an intelligent Creator. It solves the great conundrum evolution cannot explain: how so much intricate design and functionality can be built into the universe. All of that wonderful complexity—from the carefully balanced gases in our atmosphere to the incredible means by which plants reproduce—is clear evidence of intelligent design. It reflects the goodness and the wisdom of God. It ought to direct us to seek Him where He has most clearly revealed Himself—in the text of Scripture. Anyone who looks at creation without recognizing the infinite intelligence behind it is willfully blind.

God Himself looked at it and saw that it was good (v. 12). And then day three signs off with the standard formula: "So the evening and the morning were the third day" (v. 13). Again, a literal translation of the Hebrew is "Evening, morning—the third day." Nothing about the language suggests that it is figurative. Morris writes:

> The terms "evening" (Hebrew *ereb*) and "morning" (Hebrew *boqer*) each occur more than one hundred times in the Old Testament and always have the literal meaning—that is, the termination of the daily period of light and the daily period of darkness, respectively. Similarly, the occurrence of "day" modified by a numeral (e.g., "third day") is a construction occurring more than one hundred times in the Pentateuch alone, always with a literal meaning. Even though it may challenge our minds to visualize the lands and seas, and all plants, being formed in one literal day, that is exactly what the Bible says! We are not justified at all in questioning either God's power to do this or His veracity in telling us that He did.[5]

Of all the days of Genesis 1, this third day brought about the most dramatic changes in the way the earth looked. At the beginning of the day the face of the earth was covered with water and probably had the appearance of a seething cauldron of mud. By the end of the day it was a paradise of green-covered earth, decorated with all the hues of various flowers and trees, set in the midst of a spectacular blue ocean. No wonder God saw that it was good. It was good—a perfect environment for life, and a paradise for the creature God planned to make in His own image.

Then God said, "Let there be lights in the firmament of the heavens to divide the day from the night; and let them be for signs and seasons, and for days and years; and let them be for lights in the firmament of the heavens to give light on the earth"; and it was so. Then God made two great lights: the greater light to rule the day, and the lesser light to rule the night. He made the stars also. God set them in the firmament of the heavens to give light on the earth, and to rule over the day and over the night, and to divide the light from the darkness. And God saw that it was good. So the evening and the morning were the fourth day.

—Genesis 1:14–19

5
LIGHTS IN THE HEAVENS

Genesis 1:14–19

NATURALISTIC SCIENCE has always struggled to explain all the stars and planets that exist in the universe. How could so much have evolved out of nothing? How did the stars get scattered across such a vast expanse of space? Why is there such diversity among them? What set the stars ablaze, and where did the planets come from?

Genesis 1 gives a simple answer: God made them all. He spoke them into existence. Their vastness, their complexity, their beauty, and their sheer number all reveal the glory and the wisdom of an all-powerful Creator. And they remind us how amazing it is that such a great Creator would lavish His grace and favor on the human race. After all, from the perspective of size, our whole world constitutes only an infinitesimal speck in the vastness of all He created.

David celebrated this fact in Psalm 8:3–4:

> When I consider Your heavens, the work of Your fingers,
> The moon and the stars, which You have ordained,
> What is man that You are mindful of him,
> And the son of man that You visit him?

As David gazed into an unfathomably large universe, he realized it was just finger work for God. As great as the universe is, God is infinitely greater. And the human race is nothing by comparison.

Yet God's creative purpose has always had the human race at its center. We alone of all His creatures are made in His image. The entire creation account in Genesis 1 is told from an earthly perspective, underscoring the centrality of this tiny planet in the creative purpose of God.

Even the creation of the stars is recounted from an earthly perspective, so that the sun and moon appear as two great lights, while vast galaxies of stars appear as lesser luminaries, being mentioned almost as a footnote in verse 16: "the stars also."

Here is the complete biblical account of day four:

> Then God said, "Let there be lights in the firmament of the heavens to divide the day from the night; and let them be for signs and seasons, and for days and years; and let them be for lights in the firmament of the heavens to give light on the earth"; and it was so. Then God made two great lights: the greater light to rule the day, and the lesser light to rule the night. He made the stars also. God set them in the firmament of the heavens to give light on the earth, and to rule over the day and over the night, and to divide the light from the darkness. And God saw that it was good. So the evening and the morning were the fourth day. (Genesis 1:14–19)

As we arrive on day four, we enter a second phase of God's creative work. Notice the correlation between days one through three and days four through six. Days one and four, two and five, and three and six contain unmistakable parallels. A comparison of the two phases looks like this:

Phase 1	Phase 2
Day 1: light	Day 4: luminaries
Day 2: the firmament and the waters below	Day 5: birds and fish
Day 3: dry land	Day 6: land creatures

Everything from day four on is finishing work, as God fills and populates that which was once formless and void. And the first thing to be filled is the vast expanse of heaven.

As we have seen from the beginning and will see throughout the entire week of creation, God accomplishes His creative work by *fiat*. "Then God said, 'Let there be lights in the firmament'" (v. 14). There is no process and no passage of time; that which He creates comes into being instantly by His Word alone. That is why theories that add multiple billions of years to the age of the earth do nothing to advance biblical understanding. Creation is not a process God initiated; it is something God *completed*. He literally spoke it into existence. In the words of the psalmist:

> By the *word* of the Lord the heavens were made,
> And all the host of them by the breath of His *mouth*.
> He gathers the waters of the sea together as a heap;
> He lays up the deep in storehouses.
> Let all the earth fear the Lord;
> Let all the inhabitants of the world stand in awe of Him.
> For He *spoke*, and it was done;
> He *commanded*, and it stood fast.
> (Psalm 33:6–9, emphasis added)

In other words, what God made did not evolve. He gave the order, and it came into existence complete and fully functioning.

The entire panoply of heaven—including the moon, the sun, the stars, and countless galaxies—was complete and fully functioning on the day God made it. It still functions as He designed it, with a complexity that is staggering.

From our perspective, it appears that the stars are fixed in place. They are not. They move vast distances at incredible speeds. But because the distances are so great, from the viewpoint of earth the stars appear to be in the same place all the time. Mariners for thousands of years have been able to chart their course by the stars because they don't *appear* to be moving.

But they *are* moving. Even the sun has a circuit (cf. Psalm 19:6), and the entire solar system moves with it, in constant orbit around the center of our galaxy, the Milky Way. Astronomers using radio telescopes recently calculated that it would take the earth about 226 million years to complete a full orbit of the galactic center. That is exactly the path God designed the earth to travel, and it all began in a moment, when He created all the stars and set them in motion with a single word.

As we saw on day one, God had already created light and separated the light from the darkness. Where did that original light come from and what form was it in? We do not know because Scripture does not say. But from an earthly perspective it seems to have been an exact parallel to sunlight, separating day from night with a rhythm that continued after day four and was then measured from an earthly perspective by the rising and setting of the sun.

The original light was most likely a disembodied and diffused light of some kind. It might have been a pure display of divine glory, much like the light that will shine in New Jerusalem, described in Revelation 21:23: "The city had no need of the sun or of the moon to shine in it, for the glory of God illuminated it." In any case, its source was very clearly God, the Father of lights and the giver of every good and perfect gift (James 1:17).

But on day four, God created the sun and moon to be permanent heavenly luminaries. The source and creator of the light was still God, but from now on there would be light-bearing bodies that would perpetually shine their light on the earth at the proper intervals and seasons. God gave the decree: "Let there be lights in the firmament of the heavens to divide the day from the night; and let them be for signs and seasons, and for days and years; and let them be for lights in the firmament of the heavens to give light on the earth" (Genesis 1:14–15). And, as always happens when God commands decretively, "it was so."

The stars and heavenly bodies are an incredibly complex and wonderful aspect of creation. Consider some of the reasons why God created them.

SEPARATION

First of all, the stars and heavenly bodies were given to separate day from night. God Himself had already separated light from darkness on day one, and He had already named the light day and the darkness night (v. 5). The introduction of the sun and stars on day four doesn't alter the definition, nor is there any suggestion that it changes the rhythm or the duration of the days. Rather, sun and moon are set in place as permanent markers "to divide the day from the night" (v. 14).

What had been a disembodied blanket of diffused supernatural light was superseded by a universe full of light-bearing bodies. The alternation between day and night continued, but now heavenly bodies provided the varying degrees of light.

There were two "great lights"—a greater light (the sun) to rule the day, and a lesser light (the moon) to rule the night. These two great heavenly luminaries were positioned above the earth to provide light and to govern the passing of day and night.

The language is picturesque: "to rule the day . . . to rule the night." We're not to think this signifies anything similar to the pagan idea that the heavenly bodies themselves were deities. We stress again that there are no such mythological or allegorical features anywhere in the Genesis account. Although it speaks of the sun "ruling" the day and the moon "ruling" the night, the imagery is not at all like that of the ancient Babylonian or Sumerian accounts of creation, where the sun and moon were personified and made into gods or godlike beings—deities that supposedly governed the details of life on earth. The biblical account has nothing in common with such fanciful pagan notions.

In fact, all such myths are expressly excluded by the Old Testament (cf. Deuteronomy 4:19). Instead, this speaks of how the heavenly bodies govern our days, nights, months, and years—and thus they control our life patterns. The heavenly bodies are presented to us as created objects, absent any personality traits and devoid of any of the trappings of deity. They "rule" only in a figurative sense. In other words, their light oversees the earth and governs its passage from day to night.

The sun, of course, *radiates* light, while the moon merely *reflects* light. But from an earthly perspective, both are light sources. The Genesis account does not aim at a scientific explanation of how the moon gives light. It simply reveals that the divine purpose for the moon was to provide illumination by night, and that purpose is perfectly fulfilled through the reflective light cast by the moon.

The sun and the moon are fascinating heavenly bodies. The sun is an immense ball of flame. Its diameter measures 865,000 miles, which is about 109 times the diameter of the earth. Its volume is 1.3 million times greater than that of the earth, meaning that if the sun were hollow, it would take more than a million earth-sized objects to fill it. If the sun were the size of a bowling ball, the earth by comparison would look like a poppy seed. Most scientists believe the sun is composed of 70 percent hydrogen, 28 percent helium, 1.5 percent carbon, nitrogen, and oxygen, and less than .5 percent other elements. The surface temperature of the sun is estimated at about 10 thousand degrees Fahrenheit, and scientists believe the temperature at its core is 27 million degrees Fahrenheit.

By the way, it is worth pausing to note that many scientists believe the earth and planets of our solar system were once part of the sun and were somehow spun off and sent into their orbits by some explosion on the sun, or else they were formed in a collision of the sun with another heavenly body. If that were true, we might expect Earth, Mars, Venus, and Mercury to have similar compositions of elements, all similar to and derived from the sun. They don't. Ninety-eight percent of the sun is hydrogen and helium. But less than 1 percent of the elements on the planets are hydrogen and helium. Furthermore, the planets themselves are all different, unique in their composition. The appearance of the planets themselves confirms this. Each is distinctive, with its own peculiar look and singular design.

In addition, Venus, Uranus, and Pluto spin the opposite direction from the rest of the planets. The moons of the various planets orbit in different directions and on different routes compared to the planets' polar bearings. All that diversity is the fingerprint of a Creator.

As stars go, the sun is only small- to medium-sized. Astronomers classify it as a yellow dwarf. By comparison, many stars, known as supergiants, are as much as one thousand times larger than our sun. One such supergiant star that we can observe is Betelgeuse. Its size varies, because it seems to pulsate. And at times it is at least six hundred times larger than our sun.

The distance from the earth to the sun is about ninety-three million miles. At that distance, it takes about eight and a half minutes for light to travel from the sun to the earth. So the light you see at the first glimpse of a 6:00 A.M. sunrise is light that left the sun when it was about 5:51 A.M. at your location on the earth.

The sun's brightness remains fairly constant, but occasionally eruptions flare up on its surface. Dark spots, known as sunspots, also appear at times and seem to rotate with the sun's surface. These variations are not visible to the naked eye, but they can cause dramatic weather changes and electrical storms on earth, as well as stormlike conditions in space. Solar flares are the largest known explosions in the solar system. A single flare of typical size is equivalent to several million 100-megaton hydrogen bombs. The energy sent out from such explosions can play havoc with power systems on earth. In 1989 a Canadian power plant was knocked out by energy from a solar flare, leaving millions of customers without power for several hours.[1]

Yet the sun maintains an amazing balance of light and energy that is perfect to sustain life on earth. If the brightness or temperature of the sun were increased or decreased by only a few percentage points either way, life as we know it would soon end on earth.

The moon is also an immense body. Its diameter is more than one-fourth that of the earth's, and it is larger than the planet Pluto. Its surface temperature varies enormously compared to that of the earth. Depending on whether it is in sunlight or darkness, the moon's surface can be as hot as 215 degrees Fahrenheit or as cold as -243 degrees Fahrenheit.

The moon circles the earth like a far-off satellite in a slightly elliptical orbit that varies from 221,000 miles at its closest point (the perigee) to 252,000 miles at its furthest point (the apogee). The moon completes a full orbit around the earth every 27.3 days, traveling a distance of almost a million and a half miles each month.

The same side of the moon always faces the earth, and therefore if you stand on the moon, the earth is always at the same place in the sky. The lunar phases we see from the earth are caused by the position of the sun relative to the moon. The moon appears full when the side of the moon that faces the earth is also facing the sun. As the sun's position moves out of alignment with the earth, the amount of the moon that appears in shadow increases.

The moon has virtually no atmosphere, so there is no diffusion of the reflected light at the moon's surface. Standing on the moon, the sky appears black, even in bright daylight. And viewing the moon through a telescope, its features may be seen from earth with amazing clarity.

The moon, like the sun, helps keep the perfect balance of earth's life-sustaining environment. Ocean tides are caused by the moon's gravitational pull. High tides align with the moon on both sides of the earth. The earth bulges slightly both toward and away from the moon, and this affects the water level of the oceans. As the earth rotates on its axis, those bulges move across the face of the earth. That is why there are two high and low tides each day. The size of the tides varies depending on how close the moon is to earth and where it lines up with the sun. (The sun's gravity also has an effect on earth's tidal ebb and flow.) These tides are vital to the balance of earth's ecosystems.

Scientists have proposed a number of theories about how the moon might have been formed by natural processes. Some have suggested it split off from the earth or was violently torn from the earth by a collision with a massive body the size of Mars. Some believe it was formed elsewhere in the solar system and captured by the earth's gravitational pull. Others believe it formed along with the earth as a kind of double planet. Each of these explanations poses major problems. For example, three minerals have been discovered on the moon that are unknown on earth, undermining the theory that moon and earth were once a single body. The dynamics of how the moon might have broken off and escaped earth's gravitational pull are also impossible to explain by any known model. For this reason there is no real consensus among scientists and evolutionists on the question of how the moon was formed—even though some twenty billion dollars has been spent by modern scientists trying to answer the question of how the moon "evolved."

The Bible's explanation avoids all such difficulties: God simply created the moon and placed it in orbit around the earth. He did this on day four of creation week.

REGULATION

Scripture gives a second reason why God created the sun, moon, and stars. These heavenly bodies would not only mark the passing of days and nights, but they would also be permanent signposts: "Let them be for signs and seasons, and for days and years" (Genesis 1:14).

The Hebrew word for "signs" is *oth*, meaning "beacons" or "signals." It suggests that the heavenly bodies were set in place to serve as signs for the inhabitants of the earth. What were they signs of? Some have suggested that this could refer to navigation signs. Indeed, as noted earlier, the stars have been used as navigation beacons from time immemorial. Sailors using nothing but the stars have plotted their courses on the open seas for thousands of years.

Others might imagine that this means the stars were given for astrological signs or omens of important events to come. It was by a star, for example, that God led the Magi to the Christ child in Matthew 2. But astrology is an occult and pagan practice, and all such forms of fortunetelling are strictly forbidden in Scripture (Deuteronomy 18:10–12; Isaiah 7:12–14).

One surprisingly popular view is that the gospel is revealed through the signs of the zodiac. The zodiac *could* be interpreted in a myriad of ways (as a comparison of any two random horoscopes will show). Some have suggested that it gives an account of the gospel in pictorial fashion. Virgo supposedly speaks of the virgin mother, the serpent is ostensibly Satan, and some of the other constellations are said to picture Christ in various stages of humility and triumph. E. W. Bullinger wrote an entire book titled *The Witness of the Stars* in 1893 outlining the gospel through the signs of the zodiac. The view has been revived recently and promoted by D. James Kennedy and Chuck Missler. Some have even suggested that the zodiac is an extrabiblical witness to the gospel through which multitudes who have never had the Scriptures preached to them might find Christ. The problem with this view is that it is based on nothing but sheer imagination. One thing is certain: The zodiac has never communicated the gospel in any sensible way to those who are most obsessed with it. And there is no credible record of anyone who ever discovered the gospel message in the stars that way.

But the context of Genesis 1 makes clear what kind of "signs" the stars were to be. They were markers to indicate times and seasons: "for signs and seasons, and for days and years" (v. 14). And in that way they regulate our lives. They set our calendars. They determine the length of a year. They divide the year into seasons. And they mark the passage of our days and nights.

In that sense, the whole pulse of human life is governed and regulated by the heavenly bodies. The sun determines our days. The moon determines the months. And the stars, sun, and moon all determine our seasons and years. Our whole calendar is thus determined by the stars, and even seasonal weather patterns are determined by the sun and moon. Because the earth is tilted on its axis, the sun's rays strike different parts of the earth at different angles throughout the year. That produces the seasons that are so critical for the rejuvenation of life, the growing of crops, and the flourishing of the earth. It is all in perfect balance and works to bless humanity with a variety of climates and weather patterns. The perfection with which these all operate is one of the great proofs that they were designed by a wise and gracious Creator.

The length of our days and even our sleep patterns are set in perfect harmony with the amount of time it takes the earth to complete one full rotation. Even the precise tilt of the earth's axis is vital in maintaining earth's seasons. Imagine how different life would be if the earth suddenly began rotating at one-third its current speed. Days would be three times longer. We would be forced to stagger our sleep so that sometimes we would sleep during sunlight hours and remain awake during long hours of darkness. The variation in daytime and nighttime temperatures would be dramatically altered. Every rhythm of our lives would be overthrown.

But all life on earth is perfectly suited to a twenty-four-hour day, and according to Scripture, that is because the same Creator who made all living things also determined and fixed the length of our days.

The story is told of Charles Boyle, the fourth Earl of Orrery, a devoted Christian and brilliant thinker who was fascinated with Kepler's and Newton's discoveries about planetary motion and the intricate design of the universe. Boyle hired a watchmaker to design a working mechanical model of the solar system that demonstrated the motion of the planets around the sun. (Such a model is called an *orrery*, after its designer.) Boyle was showing the model to an atheistic scientist, who was very impressed with the clockwork model. The atheist said, "That's a very impressive model. Who made it for you?"

"No one made it," Boyle wryly replied. "It just happened."

The point was clear. No one really believes such intricate design is the product of happenstance. It reflects the work of an intelligent mind, a Master Designer, who set things in their proper place and started them in motion. In fact, there is a principle in philosophy known as the Orrery theorem, which says that if the model of any system in nature requires intelligent design, the natural system itself must have required at least as much intelligence in the original design.

Since the actual stars and planets and their functions are so much more infinitely grand and intricate than any clockwork model, they must have been designed by an infinitely greater mind. Scripture plainly says they are the product of the mind of God. It frankly requires a stubborn skepticism to conclude otherwise.

God created the sun, moon, and stars to precise specifications, and as we have seen, they regulate our lives in the sense that they determine the length of our days, months, and years; they determine the seasons in a year, and they mark every facet of our clocks and calendars. The stellar bodies thus determine when we eat, when we work, and when we sleep. And all of this was set in motion perfectly on day four of creation.

Think of it: The rotation of the earth on its axis is what determines a twenty-four-hour day. The moon's orbits around the earth determine our months. And the earth's revolutions around the sun determine our years. Interestingly, there is nothing in the celestial bodies that determines a week. And yet humanity universally numbers the calendar by weeks. Where did that come from? The creation week of Genesis 1. It was the period of time in which God created the universe, and ever since, it has governed how humanity marks time.

Days and years are respectively the shortest and the longest measures of time definitely fixed by the movement of the heavenly bodies. And, as Genesis 1:14 plainly states, even the framework of the seasons is fixed by the moon, sun, and stars God created on day four.

ILLUMINATION

The third and perhaps most obvious reason for the heavenly bodies is to provide permanent light fixtures that illuminate the earth. Genesis 1:15 notes this purpose: "And let them be for lights in the firmament of the heavens to give light on the earth."

God said it, "and it was so." That same familiar phrase appears again in connection with God's creative activity on day four. That is a technical phrase that means it was made permanent. It became a fixed, established condition. Again, this militates against the idea of progressive creationism. The condition of the stars and planets was not something that occurred by any evolutionary process. God spoke it into existence. He fixed it. It was firm. It was established. In the words of Psalm 33:9, "He spoke, and it was done; He commanded, and it stood fast."

By whatever means God had previously illuminated the earth—whether it was a supernatural light source, a disembodied and diffused light, or latent energy from the initial creation—it was no longer necessary. The sun henceforth would permanently give light to the earth by day, and the moon and stars would illuminate the night.

From day four on, sunlight became the chief source of light and energy on earth. Some stars supply energy to earth in the form of x-rays and radio signals, but because of its proximity to earth, and because of the nature of the light that it radiates, the sun outshines them all. It emits its radiation energy in a large spectrum of wavelengths, and the shorter the wavelength, the higher the frequency and the greater the energy. But most of the sun's energy comes to us in the form of visible light. (You will recall our discussion of the marvels of light in chapter 3.)

Within the visible light spectrum, violet light is at the high-energy end and red light is at the low-energy end. Even these invisible light rays supply energy. Photons of ultraviolet light, for example, are what cause our skin to burn if we are exposed to the sun too long. And at the opposite end of the spectrum, infrared rays can be felt as heat, even though infrared light radiates less energy than the photons in the visible region.

Almost every segment of the light spectrum is essential for sustaining life on earth. Ultraviolet rays are vital for photosynthesis—the process by which plants, and even some bacteria, use energy to produce sugar, carbohydrates, and other nutrients from carbon dioxide. In the process they release oxygen. That means earth's vegetation works like "lungs" for the planet, taking the carbon dioxide emitted by other living creatures and converting it back to nutrients and oxygen. Again, an incredibly intelligent design is revealed in the way the environment works. All of this is made possible by the light emitted from the sun.

How does the sun generate its light without quickly burning out? Until recently, the almost universally accepted scientific theory was that the sun's energy is produced when hydrogen is converted to helium by nuclear fusion at the sun's core. But that is no longer clear. Nuclear fusion produces subatomic particles called neutrinos that travel at the speed of light, even through solid objects. (Neutrinos can even travel through solid iron at the speed of light the same way light travels through empty space.) If hydrogen were being converted to helium by the sun, it would produce neutrinos at a predictable rate, and those neutrinos would be measurable on earth. Beginning in the 1960s a scientist named Raymond Davis began conducting an experiment designed to measure the neutrinos being emitted by the sun. He collected the neutrinos in a massive tank filled with 100,000 gallons of cleaning fluid (perchloroethylene, which is mostly chlorine), located at the Homestake Gold Mine in South Dakota. When neutrinos pass through chlorine, they produce a radioactive isotope of argon. By measuring the argon produced in the cleaning fluid, Davis was able to measure the neutrinos given off by the sun. But measurements revealed only a third the number of neutrinos that were expected according to the models scientists were then using. Now the question of how the sun generates light is again being debated by scientists. It is yet another example of how scientific theories are in constant flux—in contrast to Scripture, which never changes.

Look again at Genesis 1:16: "God made two great lights: the greater light to rule the day, and the lesser light to rule the night. He made the stars also." Again, we are given an unmistakable affirmation of divine creation. This was not a prolonged process. God *made* the lights. According to the psalmist in Psalm 8:3, they are "the work of [God's] fingers." And while that is admittedly an anthropomorphic expression, it underscores the fact that this was a direct, creative act of God. It does not speak of slow formation through natural and evolutionary processes. It is an instant creation.

Notice the closing phrase of Genesis 1:16: "He made the stars also." The economy of words is staggering. So much could have been said about the vast star systems that fill the immense universe. Scientists know relatively little about the stars, but it would be enough to fill several volumes. There are countless stars in the universe, each one unique, and each surrounded with wonder. Some are binary stars—two-star systems in which the stars actually orbit one another. Other lights in the heavens that appear as stars to us are actually nebulae—hazy, cloudlike clusters of stars. Many are unfathomably large. Consider the fact that our own sun is more than one million times larger than the earth by volume. Yet some of the vast nebulae astronomers have observed are more than one million times larger and brighter than our sun. Each star in the heavens is different from all others. Like fingerprints and snowflakes, they reveal the vast diversity reflected in God's creative wisdom.

The closest star to our solar system is Alpha Centauri. It is actually a triple-star system, with one star similar to our sun and two smaller red stars nearby. The center of this star system is 4.35 light-years away, and the smallest of the three stars, Alpha Centauri C (also known as Proxima Centauri) defines the outside edge of the system, only 4.22 light years from us. That means when observers from earth look at Alpha Centauri in the night sky, they are seeing light that left that star system nearly four and a half years earlier. And that is the *closest* star visible in the night sky. Most stars are immeasurably farther away than that.

That raises a fair question: If the universe is no more than ten thousand years old, as most young-earth creationists believe, and as I believe Scripture plainly teaches, how can we see light that theoretically should have taken millions of years to reach us? That's a reasonable question, and I believe there is a reasonable answer. It seems clear that when God created the stars, because He created them to illuminate the earth and be signs of our seasons, He also supernaturally enabled the light to traverse those vast expanses of space immediately. If He is capable of designing such an immense and intricate universe in the first place, He is certainly capable of getting the light across the vast reaches of space in accordance with His purpose. Don't imagine that the light from the stars is merely an illusion or a deception. Scripture indicates those are real stars out there, and what we are seeing is actually light from the stars, not an illusion. So it appears that at the moment of the stars' creation, God accelerated the light so that it would reach the earth in an instant.

Remember that according to Einstein's theory of general relativity, time is not a constant. Some creationists who are trained in physics believe it is theoretically possible for a dilation in time to enable light to travel those vast distances instantly.[2] After all, as we noted in the previous chapter, even many scientists who subscribe to big bang cosmology now believe that the universe itself exploded out of nothing to its immense proportions in an instantaneous "miracle."[3]

Again, science can only attempt to explain these mysteries by means of ever-changing theories. But the testimony of Scripture stands sure and unchanging: On the fourth day, "He made the stars also."

Genesis 1:18 repeats the now-familiar verdict of God. "God saw that it was good." Everything worked precisely the way He planned it. It was good.

There was no defect. There was no deficiency. There is no room for evolution, because everything that was created was already good, just as God made it to be.

"So the evening and the morning were the fourth day" (v. 19). On this day, for the first time, evening and morning were marked by light from the moon and light from the sun respectively. The rhythm of morning and evening continued as it had from the beginning, but now it was governed, as it has been ever since, by the setting and rising of the sun. Creation week has now passed the halfway point. And God's glory and splendor were already being revealed in all that He had made. As the psalmist wrote, "O Lord, our Lord, how excellent is Your name in all the earth, who have set Your glory above the heavens!" (Psalm 8:1).

That was, after all, the supreme purpose of God in creation: to display His glory. That glory is marvelously revealed in the expanse of the heavens. It is perfectly reflected in the vast array of stars and planets God created on day four. When we gaze into the heavens and consider those stars, our hearts ought to be moved like the psalmist's to praise God for the glory of His creation. And we ought to recoil from any suggestion that these things came into being by accidental causes or natural processes.

C. S. Lewis wrote:

> If the solar system was brought about by an accidental collision, then the appearance of organic life on this planet was also an accident, and the whole evolution of Man was an accident too. If so, then all our present thoughts are accidents—the accidental by-product of the movement of atoms. And this holds for the thoughts of the materialists and astronomers as well as for anyone else's. But if their thoughts are merely accidental by-products, why should we believe them to be true? I see no reason for believing that one accident should be able to give me a correct account of all the other accidents.[4]

Elsewhere, Lewis wrote:

> Each particular thought is valueless if it is the result of irrational causes. Obviously, then, the whole process of human thought, what we call

Reason, is equally valueless if it is the result of irrational causes. Hence every theory of the universe which makes the human mind a result of irrational causes is inadmissible, for it would be a proof that there are no such things as proofs. Which is nonsense. But Naturalism, as commonly held, is precisely a theory of this sort.[5]

The only reasonable explanation for the stars and our solar system is what we read in Scripture: "God set them in the firmament of the heavens" (Genesis 1:17). Scripture says an understanding of this is actually inborn in every human heart: "because what may be known of God is manifest in them, for God has shown it to them" (Romans 1:19).

"For since the creation of the world His invisible attributes are clearly seen, being understood by the things that are made, even His eternal power and Godhead" (v. 20). And that is why it ought to be the most natural thing in the world for us to gaze at the expanse of the heavens and echo what the psalmist wrote, "The heavens declare the glory of God; and the firmament showeth his handiwork" (Psalm 19:1 KJV).

Then God said, "Let the waters abound with an abundance of living creatures, and let birds fly above the earth across the face of the firmament of the heavens." So God created great sea creatures and every living thing that moves, with which the waters abounded, according to their kind, and every winged bird according to its kind. And God saw that it was good. And God blessed them, saying, "Be fruitful and multiply, and fill the waters in the seas, and let birds multiply on the earth." So the evening and the morning were the fifth day.

—Genesis 1:20–23

6
AN ABUNDANCE OF LIVING CREATURES
Genesis 1:20–23

BY DAY FIVE of creation, earth's environment and the heavenly realm were complete, and from here on the creative work of God consisted primarily in filling the earth with living creatures.

Scripture makes a clear distinction between plant and animal life. Trees and plants are nowhere in Scripture referred to as "living creatures" or "living souls." Those designations are reserved for animals, insects, birds, fish, and humans—in short, things that move and have central nervous systems. Plants, of course, are biological organisms—living things in that sense. They have genetic structures, biological systems, and the ability to reproduce after their own kind. But they do not have conscious life, and that is why plants and trees are never referred to as "living creatures" or "living souls" in the sense Scripture uses those expressions.

Day five therefore marks the appearance of the first *living creatures* on earth:

> Then God said, "Let the waters abound with an abundance of living creatures, and let birds fly above the earth across the face of the firmament of the heavens." So God created great sea creatures and every living thing that moves, with which the waters abounded, according to their kind, and every winged bird according to its kind. And God saw that it was good. And God blessed them, saying, "Be fruitful and multiply, and fill the waters in the seas, and let birds multiply on the earth." So the evening and the morning were the fifth day. (Genesis 1:20–23)

Here God populates the seas and the skies. Remember that this day is a kind of counterpart to day two, where the seas and the skies—the hydrosphere and the atmosphere—were divided by the creation of the firmament. Now the hydrosphere and the atmosphere are populated with "an abundance of living creatures" (v. 20).

Once again, as always, the means of creation is a decree from God. "Then God said" (v. 20). When God creates Adam on day six, He does so by forming him from the dust of the earth. If evolution were correct, we might expect to find God creating sea creatures from some preexisting life form—some plants or algae. But what Scripture says is that He spoke the full array of sea creatures into existence immediately, out of nothing. "Great sea creatures," including whales, massive sting rays, great white sharks, and giant squid, are all included, as is "every living thing that moves, with which the waters abounded" (v. 21).

There's a deliberate redundancy in the Hebrew expression, a literary device called *paranomasia,* in which different forms of the same word are repeated for emphasis. A literal rendering would be, "let the waters swarm with swarming things." A similar expression is used in verse 11, which could be literally rendered, "let the earth vegetate with vegetation."[1] The two expressions ("vegetate" and "swarm") make a contrast, and the emphasis here is on movement—specifically the animation of living creatures that can move and migrate at will, in contrast to plant life, which is essentially stationary.

And instantly the seas began to swarm with living creatures everywhere. I believe this includes even freshwater bodies, which also would have begun to teem with life at the Lord's command.

In verse 21, the Hebrew noun in the expression "every living *thing*" is *nephesh,* the same word translated "soul," in the King James Version of Genesis 2:7: "the LORD God formed man of the dust of the ground, and breathed into his nostrils the breath of life; and man became a living *soul.*" *Nephesh* literally means "that which breathes." It speaks of soulish life, creaturely life, as opposed to the merely organic life of plants. And it is used in Genesis 1:21 for the very first time. So again, these are the first "living creatures" in the biblical sense of that expression.

This is a remarkable step in the creative process, as profound as the creation of a whole universe of heavenly bodies on day four. The vastness and complexity of the forms of life God created probably rivals that of the stars. It includes everything from the smallest amoebas and microscopic animals to the "great whales" mentioned in the King James Version.

CREATION

Notice that verse 21 explicitly says "God *created*" them. The Hebrew verb is *bara,* which always speaks of direct creation. It explicitly rules out the possibility that these creatures evolved through some ages-long process. Together with the description of how God decreed their existence by speaking the command, it demands that we understand the origin of these creatures as an act of fiat creation, not an evolutionary process.

There is a clear and very specific emphasis on the vast array of creatures God created. "Great sea creatures" were created as well as "every living thing that moves" (v. 21). What is described here is antithetical to the notion that God made simple organisms that developed through natural processes into more complex ones. The description explicitly includes plankton as well as fish, eels as well as whales, and probably sea otters as well as sea-going dinosaurs. He spoke them into existence at once, all on the same day—in fact, all at the same moment. All were created in massive swarms that filled the seas. There is no other reasonable way to interpret the words without seriously undermining the truthfulness of the Genesis account.

Verse 20 says the same thing about bird life: "Let birds fly above the earth across the face of the firmament of the heavens." And verse 21 describes how it was so: "So God created . . . every winged bird according to its kind." He didn't merely seed the process with a few simple life forms that later mutated and developed into more complex ones. He created innumerable species, each "according to its kind."

And notice that the birds were created with the ability to fly. This wasn't a skill acquired through any evolutionary process. It is what they were created to do.

Thus God populated the sea and He populated the sky.

I recently listened to a taped lecture from a science professor at one of the most prestigious universities in Southern California. He was describing how he believed the evolutionary process occurred. He was convinced that the ability to swim, the ability to fly, and the ability to travel on land were acquired characteristics. He assured his students that all these abilities were the result of every life-form's natural instinct for self-preservation. (Where that instinct came from he did not speculate, but he was dogmatic in stating that it was the engine that made evolution work.)

He imagined that the earliest complex life-forms came into existence when single-celled creatures morphed by sheer accident into more complex life-forms. They found they could sustain themselves by consuming the simpler life-forms, and they developed means of moving so that they could feed.

They soon began consuming one another too. Through a process of accidental mutations that took billions of years, some of these primitive microorganisms developed into more complex and larger creatures that eventually learned to breathe air and moved onto the land to escape their predators.

He pictured the earth at this point as being populated with a variety of primitive, slithering reptiles and simple, smaller creeping things, which he referred to as "snakes" and "bugs." The snakes started eating the bugs, and the bugs, knowing that they faced the threat of extinction, sought inventive ways to get away from the snakes. Some of the bugs grew wings and developed the ability to fly. Others burrowed into the ground. Then the snakes began to die out for lack of food, and in order to preserve their species, some of them grew legs and devised other ways to climb trees and dig in the earth in order to have access to the bugs.

Eventually, he said, the snakes developed hollow bones and feet and bodies. Some of them developed wings and the ability to fly so that they could get more bugs. And through similar processes, he assured his students, great families of birds and mammals and other forms of animal life developed. It's all very simple, he said. The creatures that did *not* develop means of survival died out. It was all accomplished by the survival of the fittest.

That, of course, is the fundamental evolutionary idea. In comparison to the biblical account it is fanciful, preposterous, and genetically impossible. But it is the view that dominates modern scientific theories about origins. You can hear similar lectures at virtually every major university in the world.

Why would anyone deem such an absurd scheme more believable than the biblical account of creation? There is only one reason ultimately: Fallen humanity hates the God of the Bible, and the complexity and wisdom seen in creation is the single greatest rational obstacle to an atheistic world-view.

Consider the variety of wonders in the creation of sea life. Take the archerfish, for example. Archerfish live in fresh water and ocean estuaries, mostly in Southeast Asia. They have the unique ability to spit jets of water at insects resting on leaves and branches that overhang the water. Their upper palate is grooved, so that when the tongue is pressed against the roof of the mouth, it forms a tube. By forcing their gills shut, they can shoot a powerful jet of water with pinpoint accuracy. By doing this, they knock insects to the surface of the water, where they are easy prey for the archerfish. Their aim is accurate up to five feet, and they have a very keen binocular vision that enables them to judge distances with uncanny precision. They even have an instinctive ability to compensate for the refraction caused by the water's surface. Archerfish are also shaped and colored with a natural camouflage that makes them nearly invisible from above.

How could the archerfish have evolved such skills? Was it a survival instinct that caused them to evolve? Certainly not. Archerfish can and often do feed the same way other fish feed. They could survive perfectly well without their amazing feats of archery. They seem to prey on insects just for sport.

Another interesting creature is the sea horse. Sea horses are a kind of fish, but they are unlike any other. Their horselike heads are perpendicular to their bodies, giving them the appearance from which they derive their name. Despite their appearance they have no neck and cannot turn their heads. Their scales are fused into a bony armor plate that makes them unappetizing to predators. Their jaws are fixed and they are toothless, so they eat by sucking in tiny shrimp from the sea water. They swim vertically in the water and can grip with their tails to hang onto kelp in order to avoid being carried away by currents. Most amazingly, they reproduce by means of an unusual role-reversal. The female actually deposits her eggs in a womblike pouch in the male-and gestation therefore takes place in the male's body. When the eggs hatch, he goes through labor and gives birth to live seahorses. The male then nurtures the young the way females do in most species. What can account for these amazing features? There are no evidences of any transitional species between seahorses and other fish. That's because they did not evolve from other species; they were a unique part of God's original creation.

Then there are hermit crabs. Unlike other crabs, hermit crabs have no outer shell of their own. Their abdomen is soft, and they would be easy prey for predators if they did not have a means of protection. So they borrow used shells from various gastropods. They always use empty shells, never killing live occupants. And they will migrate from shell to shell as they outgrow their homes. The crab's body is naturally twisted to fit perfectly into the host shell. The crab's legs are perfectly designed for its habitat. It uses only the two legs immediately behind its claws for walking. The other legs grip the borrowed shell. The crab's enlarged right claw serves as a door to cover the shell's opening when the crab retreats inside. These crabs have a symbiotic relationship with sea anemones. Sea anemones have stinging cells that repel most other creatures, but hermit crabs often form partnerships with the anemones and carry them around on their shells, with the same anemone making the switch to a new host shell when the crab migrates. The anemone feeds off the leftovers from the crab's meals, and the crab is protected from predators by the anemone.

Could the crabs have evolved these features? Certainly not. The loss of its own protective shell would be contrary to evolution's principle of the survival of the fittest. And the evolution of a body so perfectly suited to the borrowed shell of another creature is impossible to explain by evolutionary principles. The hermit crab is simply more evidence of an intelligent Creator.[2]

Sea cucumbers are another amazing species. These are spineless, sluglike sea creatures with five rows of tube feet that run lengthwise, like the seams of a football. They have a mouth at one end that is surrounded by tentacles. The sea cucumber feeds by stationing itself where an ocean current brings it a steady supply of plankton, tiny shrimp, and other organic particles. It spreads the tentacles to collect the food and then sticks the tentacles in its mouth, one at a time, sucking the food off. A peculiar variety of fish known as the pearlfish takes shelter during the day inside the sea cucumber, where it feeds on the internal organs of the sea cucumber. The sea cucumber is not harmed by this, because it can regenerate its own organs. At night, the pearlfish travels through the sea cucumber's alimentary canal and emerges to supplement its diet with small crustaceans.

The sea cucumber has an amazing defense mechanism. When attacked, it will expel its own internal organs. The predator is usually satisfied with this feast, and the sea cucumber simply regenerates a new set of organs. Another defense mechanism is a gluelike substance the creature secretes. If this substance happens to get in your hair, you will not be able to get it off without shaving the hair. The secretion is so sticky that it can even be used to bind wounds.

Could all this be the product of evolutionary chance? Certainly not. It is more proof that an all-wise Creator designed each of these creatures.

One could choose virtually any creature from the sea and recite a similar list of creative marvels. Think of the amazing instinctive intelligence of whales and dolphins. The oceans are filled with an enormous variety of creatures, including starfish, jellyfish, electric eels, great white sharks, squid, octopus, shellfish, and crustaceans of all kinds. There are innumerable microorganisms, plankton, shrimp, and other tiny creatures. There are even some amazing fish that live at depths where life was once thought impossible. All of that was created instantly when God gave the word on day five.

And Genesis 1:21 contains an astonishing phrase: "great sea creatures." The New American Standard Bible renders it "great sea monsters." The Hebrew word is *tannin*, which can refer to any large creature, or it can mean "dragon" or "sea-serpent." The reference to one specific kind of creature seems significant. Why are the *tannin* singled out? Perhaps the answer is found in the fact that ancient Egyptian and Mesopotamian mythology was filled with fantastic tales about sea monsters. These were supposed to be gods, and the ancient pagans feared these sea-creature deities, as if they were the embodiment of evil. Such myths were common at the time Moses wrote this account. So here the biblical text simply states that God created even the largest, most monstrous creatures of the deep. They are not gods to be feared; they are created beings like every other form of life God created. And the biblical text underscores that fact, debunking all the pagan myths about them.

He also created "every winged bird according to its kind" (v. 21). Again, this speaks of the immediate creation of every variety of flying creature. As clearly as possible, the biblical text states that all of them were created together by the Lord's command; not one species evolved from another.

The variety of bird life is as remarkable and awe-inspiring as every other facet of creation. The fabulous assortment of colors and contrasts among birds is well known to even the most casual bird watcher. It reveals as clearly as any aspect of our world the Creator's love of beauty and diversity.

Stunning bright-pink flamingos, radiantly colored parrots, thick-plumed peacocks, long-legged cranes, spectacular long-tailed pheasants, and fancy-plumed cockatoos are familiar to us all. Everything from eagles and hawks to hummingbirds and doves reveals an amazingly rich creative originality. The life that fills our skies is as full of marvels as the life that fills our seas.

Consider pelicans, for example. The wingspan of some pelicans can reach up to six and a half feet. They have a long bill with an expandable pouch underneath that can hold up to three times more food than the pelican's stomach. They swallow their food whole, and it can be amusing to watch a pelican swallow a large pouch full of food with such a narrow neck. Incredibly, these massive birds dive for their food from heights of nearly sixty feet. With their awkward shape and long neck, such a dive appears impossibly dangerous, and yet pelicans are prodigious fishers. Their pouch is designed to scoop through the water like a net, trapping food while letting sea water escape. Are these magnificent birds the product of happenstance, or do they reflect the wisdom of a Creator? The answer is obvious.

The albatross is another amazing bird. With a wingspan of nearly twelve feet, it is the largest of all nonextinct flying birds. An adult albatross can fly one thousand miles in a single day. They stay aloft most of the time, landing only on the water or on boats to rest. They manage these great feats of flight by gliding long distances with their massive wings fully extended. They use air currents to gain altitude, not flapping their wings for long periods of time. A young albatross might circle the world up to seven times before ever touching solid earth. The only time an albatross will come onto land is when it breeds in the Antarctic region, and it may not breed for as long as three years, laying only one egg in a breeding season. An albatross can drink sea water, and it excretes the excess salt through its nasal passages. Some of them live up to eighty years. Could such amazing features evolve by any known natural process? Hardly. Evolution has no way to account for such remarkable characteristics—especially in a species that is so inefficient at breeding. The albatross is a unique creature that could only have been designed by an all-wise Creator.

The red-cockaded woodpecker has four strong toes that enable it to cling firmly to the sides of trees. It uses its long, sharp beak to chisel holes in long-leaf pine trees and builds its nests in holes it has chiseled out of living trees. A single bird might spend three years excavating a home. The woodpecker's primary predator is the rat snake. Rat snakes can climb trees, so as a protective measure, the woodpecker drills small holes above and below its nest-hole. Resin seeps from the small holes and oozes down the side of the tree. When the rat snake comes in contact with the resin, its scales get gummy and the snake is unable to climb the tree. In order to keep the sap flowing, the woodpecker must maintain the resin holes on a daily basis. The bird's presence is helpful, not hurtful, to the tree, because it feeds on insects and carpenter ants, which destroy trees.

A woodpecker can peck up to five hundred times per minute, striking the wood with a tremendous force at a rate of eight times per second. The bird's beak hits the wood at a speed of about thirteen miles per hour, which means the head impacts the tree with more force than you would feel if you ran headlong into a tree while running as fast as you could. Imagine doing that five hundred times in a minute! But the woodpecker's head is constructed with a built-in shock-absorbing system that cushions the brain. Such a wonderful creature could only be the product of intelligent design.

In mammals and virtually all other animals, the male carries XY chromosomes, and females have XX chromosomes. Thus in most species, it is the male who determines the sex of the offspring. But in birds (as in moths and butterflies) the situation is reversed, so that female birds carry the XY chromosome and males have the XX configuration.

Bird migration is another amazing example of the Creator's infinite wisdom. Many birds migrate long distances each year with uncanny precision. Arctic terns hold the record for the longest migration. They travel from the North Pole to the South Pole and back again each year. Most birds that migrate long distances fly mostly at night. They do this because one of the main ways they navigate is by the stars. Studies have shown that even birds raised entirely indoors can orient themselves properly the first time they see the stars. Tests done in planetariums show that birds know which direction to fly even in an artificial sky if the stars are properly placed. But when the star alignment in the planetarium is confused, the birds are confused as well.

How did birds acquire such abilities? They didn't acquire them at all.

They are inborn abilities designed into the birds by an intelligent Creator. Other bird instincts, such as the knowledge of how to construct so many different kinds of well-designed nests, also reveal the wisdom of the Creator.

Every aspect of creation is filled with equally amazing wonders. How could this be if it all happened merely by chance? The clear answer is that it couldn't. Creation occurred just as Scripture says it did.

"And God saw that it was good" (v. 21). His own goodness is reflected in what He made. Even in our fallen state, we can see His goodness when we observe how carefully and flawlessly He designed what He made. All the wonderful sea creatures, from sea cucumbers to giant whales—and all the birds that fill our skies, from the common starling to the most magnificent eagle—demonstrate His infinite goodness in their unique ways. He made all these marvelous creatures for His own good pleasure, and He continually oversees every detail of His creation by a loving, sovereign providence. Jesus said not even one sparrow falls to the ground apart from His Father's will (Matthew 10:29).

PROCREATION

All living organisms have three amazing properties. First, they are *self-sustaining*, meaning that they have means by which they sustain their own life—getting nourishment, breathing their atmosphere (even fish in the water), and defending themselves from predators or other threats in their habitat. All of them have unique ways of doing this that are perfectly suited to their environment. Second, they are *self-repairing*. If injured, they have means to heal. If fatigued, they can recoup strength by rest. Third, they are *self-reproducing*. They have built into them some means by which they can propagate and thereby produce more organisms of their own species. All three of those capabilities are inherent features of life itself.

And that fact argues powerfully for an intelligent Designer. Consider the difficulty in creating a machine that is self-sustaining, self-repairing, and self-reproducing. Such machines currently exist only in theory. They are called "Von Neumann machines" after a Hungarian scientist and mathematician named John Von Neumann, who lived in the first half of the twentieth century. Von Neumann hypothesized that it should be possible to create a machine that would sustain itself, repair itself, and reproduce itself. Modern research into artificial intelligence still draws heavily on Von Neumann's work, and modern computers are based on his groundbreaking ideas. But science has not yet been able to develop a truly self-sustaining, self-repairing, and self-replicating machine. The difficulty and complexity of creating something with all those capabilities is still out of reach for modern science.

Yet remarkably, every single living cell has all those capabilities. If this isn't convincing proof of an intelligent Designer, what is?

God built into His creation means by which every species He created could procreate. Not only at the level of individual cells, but on a much broader scale, every living species has the ability to reproduce; and the means by which various species procreate are nearly as diverse as the forms of life themselves.

Genesis 1:22 says, "And God blessed them, saying, 'Be fruitful and multiply, and fill the waters in the seas, and let birds multiply on the earth.'" The mention of procreation in this context demolishes the notion that the Biblical language is merely a symbolic account of how things evolved. Scripture is expressly teaching that God completed His creation of all the sea creatures and birds *before* He gave the order to reproduce. If evolution were true, it would mean that animal reproduction must have already been going on for billions of years before so many species of sea creatures and birds could emerge. If Genesis 1 were merely symbolic language describing how life evolved on earth, this verse would be wholly superfluous.

The inescapable message of this passage is that God created all the various birds and sea creatures with all their unique features in place, with all the diversity of species already established, and with the ability to reproduce "according to their kind" (v. 21). Those who imagine that all these different species emerged by evolution from a common source have simply rejected the clear meaning of this text.

Notice that expression, "according to its kind," which appears twice in verse 21, twice in verse 24, three times in verse 25, and once each in verses 11 and 12. It is used every time procreation is mentioned in the Genesis account. It underscores the very truth evolution denies: that when living creatures reproduce, they can produce only creatures similar to themselves. Apes do not give birth to humans.

Multitudes in the political and academic world today decry that fact as mere religious dogma. They fight to silence it from being taught in schools. Yet it is not merely religious dogma; it is what we learn from every scientific principle of genetics. Science has never observed, and never will observe, the evolution of one species into a new life form. That is a genetic impossibility.

Every living thing has a complex genetic code, stored in its DNA—an abbreviation for deoxyribonucleic acid—that determines its fundamental characteristics. The DNA code is analogous to a computer's program. DNA contains the information that enables the organism to reproduce, preserve, and repair itself. The genetic structure of every living organism limits that organism to what it is—no more, and no less. There is no genetic information that can enable an organism to transform itself into something it is not.

Genetics is a fairly recent science. In fact, the father of genetic studies was Darwin contemporary Gregor Mendel. So Darwin was completely unaware of nearly everything modern genetics teaches about reproduction within species. Geneticist Dr. Lane P. Lester has written:

> In the middle 1800s, some scientists believed that variations caused by the environment could be inherited. Charles Darwin accepted this fallacy, and it no doubt made it easier for him to believe that one creature could change into another. He thus explained the origin of the giraffe's long neck in part through 'the inherited effects of the increased use of parts.' In seasons of limited food supply, Darwin reasoned, giraffes would stretch their necks for the high leaves, supposedly resulting in longer necks being passed on to their offspring.[3]

Modern genetics has utterly disproved that hypothesis. The length of a giraffe's neck is determined by its genetic code. There simply is no mechanism that would permit animals to grow longer necks in response to environmental changes. Similarly, breeders have cut the tails off cocker spaniel puppies at birth for generations. This practice will *never* result in puppies being born without tails. The information that determines the length of a giraffe's neck and a cocker spaniel's tail is part of the animal's genetic makeup, and a change in the genetic code would require some form of mutation, which on naturalistic principles could occur only by sheer accident.

Yet that is precisely the scenario the typical evolutionist accepts. According to current evolutionary theory, the millions of species in the world today have adapted to their environment through a series of random, accidental genetic mutations. Evolutionists believe that the giraffe's long neck, like the sea cucumber's ability to generate new organs, the pelican's ability to dive for food from sixty feet in the air, the woodpecker's shock-absorbing head, and the hermit crab's practice of living in other animals' cast-off shells, all are extremely fortuitous accidents. Multiply that times the countless millions of other biological species that are perfectly suited for their environments, and you begin to get an idea of the huge leap of faith—or rather gullibility—that is required to believe in evolution.

The more science discovers about genetics, the more of a problem it poses for the doctrine of evolution. Consider some of the facts of genetics.

Genetic information is carried in DNA, a substance found in the nucleus of every living cell. A DNA molecule—the largest molecule known to science—consists of two long strands twisted into a double helix and joined by hydrogen bonds. If you could unravel and stretch out the DNA in one human cell, it would be more than five feet long and only fifty trillionths of an inch wide. It consists of a string of units called nucleotides, and the nucleotides in the two strands are paired with each other along the length of the strand. Each nucleotide is composed of a phosphate, a sugar (deoxyribose), and a substance known as a base. There are four possible types of bases: *adenine* (A), *thymine* (T), *cytosine* (C), and *guanine* (G). A nucleotide containing adenine will always be paired with a nucleotide containing thymine, and nucleotides containing cytosine are always paired with nucleotides containing guanine. The chemical bond holds the pairs together.

Genes are short sections of the DNA strand. The number of genes in the human genome is uncertain. Some scientists estimate that there may be as many as 120,000, and low-end estimates start at around 35,000. But each gene encompasses some 3,000 nucleotides. The sequence of the nucleotides composes a kind of code. (Scientists attempting to decipher the code signify it with the letters associated with the four bases—A, T, C, and G.) This code contains all the information necessary for every human trait. It is an impressive code, because there are more than three thousand million nucleotides in each molecule of human DNA. The amount of detailed information that can be contained in so small a structure is remarkable—equal to several large libraries.

The number and arrangement of nucleotides is unique for each living species. That means each living organism has been programmed differently, and the genetic program is what determines the appearance, composition, size, and function not only of the creature itself but also of every organ and even every individual cell that makes up the larger organism.

Where did this genetic information come from? It certainly didn't come out of nowhere. It should be obvious to all that it didn't just fall into place by accident or by random chance.

What about mutations? We know that genes sometimes mutate. Changes occur in the DNA structure that cause changes in the appearance of creatures. Could a series of random mutations explain how one species evolves into another?

Certainly not. Mutations can alter or destroy existing information in an organism's genetic code, but they cannot add new information. Mutations are genetic mistakes. They can cause a form of evolution, known as *microevolution*, where the characteristics of a species are slightly altered. Different breeds of dogs and different families of horses are products of microevolution. But genetic mistakes cannot explain *macroevolution*, the theoretical process by which a whole new species is formed. While it is easy to understand how a species of insect might through genetic mutations lose its wings and its ability to fly, there is no known genetic process that might explain how any species of nonflying creatures could develop anything as complex as wings and aerodynamic capabilities.

Scientists have been experimenting with fruit flies for more than a century. Since 1910, when the first mutation was observed, they have logged nearly three thousand random mutations. According to Dr. Lester, "All of the mutations are harmful or harmless; none of them produce a more successful fruit fly."[4]

Genetic information giving a species complex new abilities, such as wings to fly or gills to breathe underwater, would be far too complex to be explained by random mutation. The information would have to come from somewhere. The late Dr. A. E. Wilder Smith, a British chemist who strongly defended biblical creationism, wrote:

> If a primeval kind of amoeba is to develop up to a primate, that primeval cell will have to gather all sorts of new holistic information on how to make

kidneys, livers, four chambered hearts, cerebra and cerebella etc. For the synthesis of such reduced entropy systems, as for example a primate brain, requires all kinds of solid actual holistic information which neither the matter of which the primeval amoeba consisted nor the intact amoeba cell contained. Similarly, inorganic matter will have to assemble huge numbers of bits of holistic information before it can synthesize an amoebae.

Assuming that the original primeval form of life was a kind of an amoeba, where did it obtain the almost infinite number of bits of holistic information required to be stored on its DNA information storage and retrieval system? In order to transform the amoeba type of cell to a mammal, a primate, an octopus or a bee orchid more and new bits of holistic information are required. Neither the primeval amoeba type of cell nor the inorganic matter of which it is constructed, contain such highly specialized holistic information which is necessary to transform the alleged amoeba into say an anthropoid ape. Is it legitimate to assume that such incredible amounts of information arose spontaneously out of thin air, that is, by pure chance?[5]

Coded information such as is found in the genetic structure of every living being does not arise by chance. It is not produced by nothing. It has a source, and that source must be an intelligent Designer.

Random noise could never produce a Bach cantata. Random letters floating in an ocean of alphabet soup will never spell out a chapter from *Moby Dick*. When we hear the music, we know there was a composer. When we read coherent writing, we know there was an author. How much more does this principle apply to the detailed information contained in the DNA of every living creature?

Scientists at this very moment are listening to the random radio waves that constantly bombard the earth from outer space. The Search for Extra-Terrestrial Intelligence (SETI) project has been scanning the skies for years, listening for something, anything, that would indicate the existence of intelligent life on other planets. All they hear is random noise. If they heard a pattern of any kind in that noise—a code that would signify *information*—it would be the lead story on every newscast in the country. They would regard it as proof that intelligent life exists beyond this planet.

And yet multitudes from the scientific community who have studied the DNA code and marveled at the complex efficiency with which it regulates the development of every living thing, nonetheless flatly reject the claim that the DNA code offers any evidence of an intelligent Creator. Why? Because belief in evolution is a spiritual, not a rational, choice they have made. They are blindly devoted to chance because they do not want to be morally accountable to a personal and holy Creator.

Honest scientists must admit that all of life had to be designed by an immensely intelligent mind. The more science looks at life, the more complex it becomes. The human brain is far more complex than NASA's space shuttle. The brain alone is made up of at least six million functioning parts. No one would imagine that the space shuttle evolved by chance from nothing. Why should we have such a view of life itself?

I'm convinced Scripture gives us a reliable and true account of how life on earth was created. From their first appearance on earth at day five, there was a rich variety of living creatures who all reproduced "according to their kind." God had programmed into them all the features they needed to thrive in their environment, and they have thrived ever since. Microevolution, genetic mutation, and other processes may add something to the variety by producing variant families and different breeds within species, but the fundamental differences between creatures were all programmed at creation by an all-wise Creator, who pronounced His work good.

Genesis 1:23 continues the measuring of creation days by the familiar pattern: "So the evening and the morning were the fifth day."

One more day of creation remained before God would rest. Day six would be the most remarkable day of all.

Then God said, "Let the earth bring forth the living creature according to its kind: cattle and creeping thing and beast of the earth, each according to its kind"; and it was so. And God made the beast of the earth according to its kind, cattle according to its kind, and everything that creeps on the earth according to its kind. And God saw that it was good.

—Genesis 1:24–25

7
BEASTS AND CREEPING THINGS
Genesis 1:24–25

WHEN DAY SIX BEGAN, God put a finishing touch on the habitat He had created for man. On day five, He had filled the sea and the skies with life, and now He did the same thing on dry land:

> Then God said, "Let the earth bring forth the living creature according to its kind: cattle and creeping thing and beast of the earth, each according to its kind"; and it was so. And God made the beast of the earth according to its kind, cattle according to its kind, and everything that creeps on the earth according to its kind. And God saw that it was good. (Genesis 1:24–25)

The means of creation is the same as it has been on every previous day: "Then God said . . ." (v. 24); "And God made . . ." (v. 25). Those two expressions constitute a Hebrew parallelism. In other words, they are equivalent expressions, explaining one another and thus sealing the unmistakable clarity of the biblical record. God's creative work was instantaneous, accomplished by nothing more or less than His creative decree. He simply gave the command for things to appear—"and it was so" (v. 24). What He commanded was instantly made complete, fixed, and in place essentially as it has been ever since.

As we have noted previously, day six corresponds with day three of creation in the same way days four and five correspond with days one and two respectively. On day one God created light; on day four He made light bearers. On

141

day two He separated sea from sky; on day five He filled sea and sky with life. On day three he made dry land appear. And now on day six He fills the land with living creatures.

As day six dawns, we have the introduction of all kinds of land animals: "cattle and creeping thing and beast of the earth, each according to its kind" (v. 24). That includes every kind of land-based creature from insects and worms to elephants and giraffes.

Once again, the biblical account makes it unmistakably clear that these creatures did not evolve from lower life-forms, sea life, or birds. All of them were created instantaneously. And to underscore this, Scripture names three categories that God created: "cattle and creeping thing and beast of the earth." All were created simultaneously; one did not evolve from the other.

The threefold division is very simple. Modern biologists classify biological species by a hierarchy of categories called the Linnaean system. Every creature is designated by kingdom, phylum, class, order, family, genus, and species. But the three biblical categories are not meant to give a technical taxonomy of that kind. It's a simple, shorthand way of designating all land-based creatures.

The Hebrew word translated "cattle" is a word that speaks of livestock and animals that are capable of being domesticated. Sheep, goats, and oxen would no doubt be included as well as cattle. "Creeping thing[s]" includes reptiles, insects, and perhaps even small mammals with short legs, such as squirrels and rodents. And "beast[s] of the earth" would include all other kinds of animals. All three categories were made on the same day, by the same creative fiat. The fact that the categories are named again in a different order in verse 25 underscores this point.

In verse 24, God says, *"Let the earth bring forth the living creature according to its kind"* (emphasis added). This is an interesting expression. It doesn't imply any creative forces in the earth itself, or any power in the soil to generate life. It certainly isn't suggesting that these life-forms evolved from inanimate matter. But it reminds us that creatures God made are composed of the very same elements as the earth. Genesis 2:19 affirms this, saying that God formed the living creatures "out of the ground." When they die, their bodies decompose and they go back to the earth. As we shall see in chapter 8, this is true of human beings as well. Adam was formed from the dust of the earth. And when we die, our bodies return to dust (Genesis 3:19). Even this reveals the infinite wisdom of the Creator.

Notice that verses 24 and 25 repeat the phrase "according to its kind" five times. The phrase appears a total of ten times in Genesis 1, repeatedly underscoring the limitations God placed on the variation of species. As we saw in the previous chapter, the genetic code built into each life-form maintains the characteristics of the various types and species. It rules out spontaneous generation, and it rules out macroevolution. Here both Scripture and science agree against the evolutionary doctrine.

As we saw with the creation of the stars, sea creatures, and birds, the variety of what God created is astonishing. It is a world filled with wonders that signify the wisdom of an all-powerful Creator.

CATTLE

Looking at each category individually, we begin with "cattle." Common cattle are remarkable creatures. Their digestive system is a great wonder of creative design. Cows (in common with most ruminants) have four stomachs. Actually, it is probably more accurate to say that their stomach is a complex organ divided into four chambers. When a cow eats grass or hay, the partially chewed fiber passes into the cow's first stomach chamber, called the *rumen*. There it ferments for one to two days. The presence of helpful bacteria in the rumen causes the fermentation, beginning the process of breaking down cellulose and converting it into simple sugars. This first chamber of the cow's stomach is huge—holding the equivalent of nearly fifty gallons.

But when a cow drinks water (typically twenty-five to fifty gallons per day), most of that fluid bypasses the rumen and flows directly into the second chamber, the *reticulum*, where it is mixed with digestive enzymes and more fermentation bacteria. Meanwhile, peristaltic action (muscular movement of the stomach chamber) rolls the fodder in chamber one into little balls, and the partially fermented balls are then passed into the second chamber, where they are infused with the enzyme-saturated liquid.

Later, when the cow has leisure to ruminate, it will regurgitate those soggy balls of fiber from the second stomach chamber and chew them more finely before swallowing again. This is what Scripture speaks of when it designates the cow as one of those animals that chews the cud (cf. Leviticus 11:3). A typical cow spends about six hours per day eating and about eight hours per day chewing its cud.

The cud, after more chewing, is swallowed again, and this time, in a near-liquid state, it passes directly into the second chamber. The construction of the second chamber enables the chewed cud to be filtered. Smaller particles are permitted to pass into a third chamber. The larger particles that remain in the second chamber are regurgitated again for more chewing.

The third chamber is called the *omasum*. There, excess liquid is reabsorbed into the cow's system and the thoroughly chewed cud is compacted while its chemical composition is broken down even more by the digestive process.

The thoroughly refined food then passes from the third chamber into a fourth, called the *abomasum*. This chamber works much like the stomachs of other mammals. It secretes strong acid and digestive enzymes, completing the digestive process. From there, nutrients pass into the cow's blood system, sustaining the cow and providing vital nutrients for milk production.

This remarkable design enables the cow to enjoy a nutritious meal from a simple manger of hay, something that is impossible for mammals not equipped with multichambered stomachs capable of digesting cellulose.

It is a wonderfully efficient design, converting cellulose, which we cannot digest, into edibles—milk, cream, butter, cheese, and a long list of dairy products. The average milk cow produces more than five thousand quarts of milk each year. One cow can therefore supply milk for nearly sixty people. Cows are prodigious eaters, and one cow will also produce up to ten tons of manure in a year, returning vital nutrients to the pasture. In some cultures, the manure is even used as an efficient fuel for cooking food.

Cattle have exceptionally keen hearing and olfactory senses. A cow can smell scent up to five miles. Their cloven hoofs enable them to gallop long distances, even in marshy terrain. They are suited to almost every environment and thrive as well in the cold of Canada as they do in the heat of Florida.

And they are as useful as they are durable. Almost every part of the cow can be used for food, including the cow's bones and hoofs, which can be boiled to extract collagen for making gelatin. The hide makes durable leather.

The cow seems to have been especially designed to serve the needs of humanity. Fully domesticated and easily bred, they can live almost anywhere people can live. They can graze on a wide variety of wild plant life and therefore are relatively inexpensive to feed and maintain. They are God's gracious gift to humanity.

Another animal that seems specially designed for maximum usefulness to man is the sheep. Sheep are also ruminants like cattle and have similar four-chambered stomachs. But they can graze happily on plants other animals won't touch.

Most breeds of sheep do not fare well in the wild. They are passive, timid creatures, easily frightened and virtually defenseless against a host of predators. Unlike most animals, sheep seem to have no instinctive sense of direction and are easily lost. Therefore they hate to be alone and naturally flock together. Their lambs are delicate creatures and in the wild their survival rate is low. That is why flocks of sheep always thrive best when cared for by a shepherd. They are among the most dependent of all animals.

Lack of instinct and self-defense are not the only disadvantages sheep suffer from in the wild. Their thick, lanolin-rich wool is a magnet for dirt. Accumulated mud doesn't turn to powder and flake off, as it does with most animals. Therefore, sheep's wool will become dangerously heavy and occluded if the animal is not kept clean. The wool at the tail end especially must be kept close-cropped to avoid becoming a breeding-place for maggots and other vermin. The normal life expectancy for a sheep is only about eight years.

Yet sheep are vigorous breeders and provide much that is valuable for human life. Their wool makes energy-efficient clothing for both hot and cold weather. It is breathable, fire-resistant, and warm even when wet—superior in many ways to all other fabrics.

Sheep are also raised for their meat and milk. They have been an important part of civilization from the beginning of recorded history. In modern times they have played a crucial role in medical research. Surely one of the Creator's main purposes in creating these gentle animals was for the benefit of the human race.

Camels may also be included in the group of animals classified by Scripture as "cattle." These sturdy creatures are also known chiefly for their usefulness to humanity. Although they were deemed unclean for food under the Mosaic economy (Leviticus 11:4), they are valuable working-beasts, bred and kept in captivity because of their usefulness to humanity. Dromedaries—the single-humped Arabian camels mentioned in Scripture—are not found in the wild today, except in Australia and central Asia, where some feral herds have formed from camels originally imported as domesticated beasts of burden.

Camels are impressive workers, able to carry large loads of a thousand pounds or more in the desert where water is scarce. They are able to do this because of their ability to absorb and retain large quantities of water. Like cattle and sheep, camels are ruminants, but unlike other ruminants they have only three stomach chambers. The second chamber can hold vast quantities of water. It enables a camel to drink nearly thirty gallons of water in ten minutes. So much water would kill most animals, but it can be slowly absorbed into the camel's bloodstream because the camel's blood cells are capable of swelling to more than three times normal size. The camel can then go for days without another drink. Camels have been known to survive for more than two and a half weeks in hot desert climates without drinking any water. The camel's internal water-recycling system is so efficient that they even absorb most of the water from their own dung. Therefore camel droppings can be burned as fuel immediately when they are passed. A camel's urine is also condensed to accommodate extreme desert climates, sometimes becoming syrupy in its consistency and holding twice as much salt as sea water.

Yet with all their amazing ability to retain body fluids, camels can also withstand the effects of dehydration better than any other species. They can lose up to 40 percent of their total body weight and still survive, because their system naturally adapts to the changes in their blood viscosity.

The camel's hump, not primarily a water-storage organ as most people suppose, is a large mass of fat that acts as a food reserve, enabling the camel to live for days in the most extreme desert conditions. The hump also insulates the camel from the heat and other effects of solar radiation. The camel's body temperature can adjust with its environment, enabling it to withstand the heat of the day and then dissipate heat during the cooler nighttime.

Where did the camel acquire such amazing abilities? The answer is clear from Scripture. God made these wonderful animals, as He made other kinds of cattle and creatures capable of being domesticated. And their chief purpose seems to be to render service to humanity.

CREEPING THINGS

Among the "creeping thing[s]" included in Genesis 1:24–25 are countless forms of insects, worms, arachnids, reptiles, small mammals, and other amazing creatures. Living under the curse of sin, we tend to think of many of these creatures as repulsive pests, but they were all created with good purposes, and they reveal the creative diversity, wisdom, and glory of God just as clearly as we see His majesty in the stars. The realm of creeping things is a world of wonders, like every other aspect of God's creation.

Consider the bombardier beetle, for example. This remarkable insect is found mainly in the deserts of New Mexico. It was created with a unique defense mechanism that is impossible to explain by the evolutionary theory. The beetle produces two chemicals in separate reservoirs in its abdomen. The two chemicals, hydraquinone and hydrogen peroxide, are harmless by themselves but potentially explosive when combined. When attacked, the beetle releases the chemicals through a movable jet at the rear tip of its abdomen. Catalytic enzymes in a tiny reaction chamber just inside the expulsion valve set the chemical reaction in motion, and at precisely the right moment, the beetle aims his abdominal turret and releases the explosive mixture in the face of his predator. The combined chemicals instantly reach the temperature of boiling water, creating a surprise and a deterrent that is powerful enough to discourage most predators. The beetle can fire up to five shots in rapid succession, and he instinctively knows how to time the explosion so that it occurs a moment after the chemicals are expelled, never in the reaction chamber where it would destroy the beetle. How does the beetle know how to do this? Could such a complex system possibly have developed through some natural evolutionary process? Consider what all the bombardier beetle's defense system entails: The beetle must be able to produce just the right chemicals, keep them in separate reservoirs, and bring them together at the right time with the necessary catalytic enzymes. He must also possess all the equipment and ability necessary to combine the explosives, aim the mixture accurately, and fire precisely before the moment of explosion. Is it reasonable to think an evolving creature could develop such a system, with so many interdependent parts, through a process of individual, random genetic changes? The answer is clear: The bombardier beetle is the product of intelligent design.

Another amazing creature is the ant. Solomon wrote, "Go to the ant, you sluggard! Consider her ways and be wise, which, having no captain, overseer or ruler, provides her supplies in the summer, and gathers her food in the harvest" (Proverbs 6:6–8). Solomon was right. Ants are some of the hardest workers in the animal kingdom. By most accounts, they are able to lift as much as fifty times their own weight. Ants also have proportionally larger brains than almost any other animal. They work cooperatively without any kind of supervisor. Their short lifetime (as brief as forty-five days in some species) is virtually nonstop work—building their nests, foraging for food, blazing trails, removing obstacles and otherwise maintaining those trails, and carrying food for the queen back to the nest. An ant's life is no picnic. But ants are resilient. They can survive under water, in some cases for days. They can survive being frozen, and they can withstand high temperatures. They adapt quickly to changes in the environment or climate.

The wide variety of ant species is phenomenal. Nearly ten thousand different species of ants have been catalogued, and most entomologists believe there are thousands more species that have not yet been studied. The largest species of ants grow to more than an inch long; the smallest are less than a tenth of a centimeter. And yet ants probably make up more than 10 percent of the earth's total biomass (meaning that ants account for more than a tenth of the world's living tissue by total volume). Experts believe that all the world's ants combined would outweigh all the humans in the world.

Ants live in colonies and are incapable of survival on their own. An ant colony is itself a kind of massive organism, with each individual ant contributing to the welfare of the whole colony. There is an intricate and well-defined hierarchy in every ant colony. At the heart of the colony is the queen—a single queen in some species, multiple queens in others. The queen lays up to two or three thousand eggs per day. Worker ants are infertile females, and they make up the largest number of ants in any colony. Male ants exist primarily to mate with the queen, and they leave the nest and die shortly after mating. If the queen dies, the entire colony will soon die.

After a colony is established and ready to spawn new colonies, the queen lays special eggs that develop into males and young queens. Once they develop into adults, the young queens and males fly off together in swarms and mate in midflight. One mating flight supplies the queen with all the male seed she will need to fertilize every egg she will ever lay. She then flies off to plant a new colony—usually alone. (In some species, however, several tiny workers cling to her legs with their powerful jaws, thus traveling with her to help plant the new colony.)

After this initial flight, the queen loses her wings and will never fly again. She prepares a nest and seals the entrance. In most species, she will stay in the nest for the remainder of her life. Until workers hatch and begin bringing her food, she lives off her own body fat, even consuming the now useless musculature that made her wings work. Her entire life from that point on will consist of laying eggs. (Queens have a much longer life span than worker ants, living as long as ten to twenty years.) She thus populates her entire colony, laying hundreds of thousands of eggs in a lifetime. In order to keep up this prodigious output, she requires massive amounts of food, all brought to her by the worker ants.

Some species of ants actually raid other colonies, take other ants' pupae back to their own nests, and raise them as slaves. Amazon ants, for example, cannot survive without slaves. The shape of their mandibles does not permit them to dig their own nests or feed themselves. So they use other ant species as slaves.

Other species of ants actually cultivate fungus in their nests, fertilize their subterranean gardens with leaves and other organic material, and then harvest the fungus for food. One type of fungus growers are called leaf-cutting ants. They use their sharp mandibles to cut away large leaf-segments and carry them in long single-file lines back to their underground nests, where they chew the leaves and use the pulp as a medium for cultivating an edible fungus. Armies of leaf-cutting ants have been known to strip an entire fruit grove of leaves in a single night.

Dairying ants live off the honeydew left by aphids. They even "milk" the aphids by stroking them to get the aphids to release the honeydew. In return, the ants defend the aphids from predators. In the winter, dairying ants store aphid eggs in their nests and when they hatch in the spring, the ants carry the young aphids out to the plants. Some dairying ants keep permanent "herds" of aphids in their underground nests, where the aphids feed on roots while the ants harvest the honeydew. A queen of this species will carry an egg-laying aphid between her mandibles when she flies off to start a new colony.

Who taught those ants such efficient farming techniques? Clearly God did. He created ants in such abundant variety for a host of purposes that are ultimately beneficial for the whole earth. Ants serve a vital function in the maintenance of earth's soil, aerating and fertilizing the soil, pollinating many plants, and performing a host of other ecological housecleaning services. Ants are so vital to earth's well-being that if all the ants on earth died, the effect would be catastrophic. All earth's land-based ecosystems would quickly collapse.

In fact, ants and plants are so utterly dependent on each other that one could not have possibly evolved before the other. This is further proof that a mere five literal days have elapsed since the beginning of creation. Had these been long eras rather than short days, the plants created on day three would have all perished long before the arrival of the ants on day six. They must have been created together, as Scripture says—in the same week. And the ants are yet another vivid reminder of God's creative ingenuity.

"Creeping thing[s]" would also include reptiles. The reptile world is full of wonders. Chameleons, for example, not only change colors instantly to match their backgrounds, but they also are able to move one eye independently of the other and thus view two scenes at once. Why do chameleons have these abilities, while animals supposedly higher up the evolutionary ladder do not? Science cannot explain such a discrepancy. Scripture says it is because these wonderful animals did not evolve; their incredible abilities are simply the way God designed them.

The basilisk is a lizard that can literally run on water. The toes of his hind feet have flaps that remain furled when he walks on land. But if chased by a predator, he will stand upright and run on his hind legs only, out onto a body of water. The toe-flaps unfurl and in effect his feet become large paddles. By running very fast, he is therefore able to run across the top of the water for a considerable distance. Did the basilisk's amazing foot design evolve by accident? Scripture says he was designed that way by God.

"Creeping thing[s]" includes much, much more. And every species would make a wonderful study. All of them come equipped with remarkable defense mechanisms—built-in camouflage, armor, chemical defenses, and other amazing means of survival. Virtually all of them serve a unique and important function, each doing its own part to maintain the earth's ecosystems. The way it all works together so perfectly is clear evidence of an intelligent Designer.

When you realize the vast numbers of animals, insects, and reptiles and all the various creatures that creep upon the earth, it is mind-boggling to think that God has such a vast creative intellect to design and make so many intricate and interconnected life-forms in a single day. But He did.

BEASTS OF THE EARTH

The final category named in Genesis 1:24–25 embraces all other land creatures: "the beast[s] of the earth." This no doubt would include elephants, lions, tigers, giraffes, bears, wolves, coyotes, and other large and long-legged animals that would not fit the categories of "cattle" or "creeping thing[s]." "The beast of the earth" would also probably include many now-extinct species of dinosaurs.

What happened to the dinosaurs? God in His providence allowed their species to die out—probably about the time of Noah's Flood. Job, possibly the earliest book in all of Scripture, seems to include a description of a sauropod dinosaur. This creature, called the *behemoth*, "eats grass like an ox" (Job 40:15); "his strength is in his hips" (v. 16); and "He moves his tail like a cedar" (v. 17). "His bones are like beams of bronze, His ribs like bars of iron" (v. 18). And he is too large and powerful for any but the Creator to kill him (v. 19).

The dinosaurs may have perished when earth's climate changed severely after the Flood. We know that human life expectancy was severely decreased in the postdiluvean world. Before the Flood it was common for men to live nine hundred years or longer. After that, the human life span decreased notably almost immediately. Severe environmental and atmospheric changes may explain this, and the same types of changes may also explain the extinction of all the dinosaur species.

Today, elephants are earth's largest land species. The elephant's trunk is one of the wonders of the animal kingdom. Strong enough to lift large logs yet sensitive enough to pick up a single peanut, the elephant's trunk is the organ with which he drinks, breathes, and feeds himself. It is also his chief means of feeling objects in order to determine their size, texture, and temperature. The trunk of a typical elephant weighs three hundred pounds, holds up to four gallons of water, is about seven feet long, and comprises the elephant's nose and upper lip. No other animal can grip things or pick up things with its nose. Yet evolutionists believe these remarkable features developed in the elephant by sheer accident.

Bears are fantastic creatures, too—able to hibernate in some climates for up to seven months. But bear hibernation is different from the kind of hibernation observed in other species. When smaller animals (such as squirrels and shrews) hibernate, their body temperature falls to near freezing and their heart rate slows to only one or two beats per minute. They go into a cold, dormant state from which it takes a considerable amount of time for them to be awakened. A bear's hibernation is more like a long and deep nighttime sleep. The bear's body temperature drops no more than ten degrees Fahrenheit. His heart rate slows but maintains a rhythm of at least twelve beats per minute. The bear, if disturbed, can awaken very quickly from this state. Yet while he is asleep, he neither eats nor eliminates food. In most animals, enduring months without elimination would cause a fatal buildup of toxins in the blood. (Other hibernating animals do eliminate during their hibernation.) But the bear's body is designed to accommodate those long months of sleep without any kind of elimination. He burns stored fat for fuel, but it is as if there is no waste produced by the burning of that fat. For reasons biologists cannot yet explain, the level of uric acid and other toxins in the bear's blood remains essentially the same as when he is not hibernating.

Every beast of the earth shows evidence of special design. All of them are born with instinctive intelligence that enables them to survive and thrive in their environments. All of them have remarkable capabilities that set them apart from other beasts. No wonder. All of them were created by an all-wise Creator who endowed them with these extraordinary features. His vast creative wisdom may be clearly seen in all that He has made (Romans 1:20).

If you scan the vastness of the universe at night and contemplate all the wonders it holds, you will be brought face to face with the glory of the Creator. And if you examine a drop of pond water under a microscope, you will see still more evidence of that same glory. His creation is full of wonders, no matter what level you examine it from. Everything in creation reveals the fingerprint of the Creator.

Genesis 1:25 repeats the familiar phrase that gives us God's own assessment of His creation: "And God saw that it was good." This is significant. It rules out the possibility of deformities or mutations prior to Adam's fall into sin. It therefore eliminates the possibility of natural selection and the survival of the fittest. There were no *unfit* animals. They were all good, as God had designed them. There was no imperfection. There was no inferiority. It was all *good*.

Scripture teaches that there was no such thing as death prior to Adam's fall. Death is the result of sin. "Through one man sin entered the world, and death through sin" (Romans 5:12). The curse of sin has adversely affected all of creation. The apostle Paul wrote, "For the creation was subjected to futility, not willingly, but because of Him who subjected it in hope; because the creation itself also will be delivered from the bondage of corruption into the glorious liberty of the children of God. For we know that *the whole creation groans and labors with birth pangs together until now*" (Romans 8:20–22, emphasis added). So all of creation—not merely humanity—was adversely affected by Adam's sin. It brought the introduction of death into the animal kingdom, too.

Of course that means that prior to Adam's fall, none of the animals were carnivores. They did not hunt and kill one another for food. And Scripture affirms this in Genesis 1:30. Furthermore, Scripture teaches that in the millennial kingdom, the whole animal kingdom will return to a herbivorous state. Isaiah prophesied:

> The wolf also shall dwell with the lamb, the leopard shall lie down with the young goat, the calf and the young lion and the fatling together; and a little child shall lead them. The cow and the bear shall graze; their young ones shall lie down together; *and the lion shall eat straw like the ox.* The nursing child shall play by the cobra's hole, and the weaned child shall put his hand in the viper's den. (Isaiah 11:6–8, emphasis added)

Obviously, the animals were designed with instincts and abilities that have served them well even under the curse of sin. But in earth's original, sinless state, they did not use those abilities and instincts for hunting other animals as food. It was a perfect paradise in which there was no death. And thus there was no evolution and no possibility that the survival of the fittest could be any kind of driving force in the development of species.

153

This first act of creation on day six completes the earthly habitat God was making for Adam. Earth was a paradise. Everything was good. And God was now ready for the crowning aspect of His creation: a creature made in His own image.

Then God said, "Let Us make man in Our image, according to Our likeness; let them have dominion over the fish of the sea, over the birds of the air, and over the cattle, over all the earth and over every crreping thing that creeps on the earth." So God created man in His own image; in the image of God He created him; male and female He created them. Then God blessed them, and God said to them, "Be fruitful and multiply; fill the earth and subdue it; have dominion over the fish of the sea, over the birds of the air, and over every living thing that moves on the earth." And God said, "See, I have given you every herb that yields seed which is on the face of all the earth, and every tree whose fruit yields seed; to you it shall be for food. Also, to every beast of the earth, to every bird of the air, and to everything that creeps on the earth, in which there is life, I have given every green herb for food"; and it was so. Then God saw everything that He had made, and indeed it was very good. So the evening and the morning were the sixth day.

—Genesis 1:26–31

8

MAN IN GOD'S IMAGE

Genesis 1:26–31

ALL OF CREATION up to this point has been merely a prelude to what would happen at the end of day six. The creation of the human race was the central object of God's creative purpose from the beginning. In an important sense, everything else was created *for* humanity, and every step of creation up to this point had one main purpose: to prepare a perfect environment for Adam.

The human race is *still* at the center of God's purpose for the entire material universe. We know this because Scripture says everything else will eventually perish. It will all go out of existence. According to Jesus, there is coming a time when even "the sun will be darkened, and the moon will not give its light; the stars of heaven will fall, and the powers in the heavens will be shaken" (Mark 13:24–25). Ultimately, even the heavens will roll up like a scroll (Revelation 6:13–14). "The heavens will pass away with a great noise, and the elements will melt with fervent heat; both the earth and the works that are in it will be burned up" (2 Peter 3:10). In effect, everything that was created will be uncreated. Everything in this universe will cease to exist.

Except humanity. God created man to glorify Him and to enjoy Him *forever.* And when every other element of this universe is long gone, a vast multitude of the redeemed human race will dwell in the presence of the Lord forever.

In other words, the unfolding of creation establishes a theater in which the great redemptive saga can be played out. Man is the main character.

God's own Son even becomes a man at the climax of redemption's drama. This is the purpose for which the entire universe was created: so that God's grace, mercy, and compassion could be lavished on this creature whom God had created in His own image. In the end, the theater is destroyed. It is a profound and humbling thought.

Clearly, the creation of the human race is the main issue in Genesis 1. Everything culminates in this event, and Scripture devotes more space to describing Adam's creation than to any other facet of creation. In fact, because this final act of creation is so crucial, all of Genesis 2 is devoted to an expanded description of it. (Genesis 2 is not a different story or an alternate account; it is an expansion of the description of day six from Genesis 1.) Genesis 1:26–31 simply gives us the basics about day six:

> Then God said, "Let Us make man in Our image, according to Our likeness; let them have dominion over the fish of the sea, over the birds of the air, and over the cattle, over all the earth and over every creeping thing that creeps on the earth." So God created man in His own image; in the image of God He created him; male and female He created them. Then God blessed them, and God said to them, "Be fruitful and multiply; fill the earth and subdue it; have dominion over the fish of the sea, over the birds of the air, and over every living thing that moves on the earth." And God said, "See, I have given you every herb that yields seed which is on the face of all the earth, and every tree whose fruit yields seed; to you it shall be for food. Also, to every beast of the earth, to every bird of the air, and to everything that creeps on the earth, in which there is life, I have given every green herb for food"; and it was so. Then God saw everything that He had made, and indeed it was very good. So the evening and the morning were the sixth day.

Bear in mind that the creation of Adam occurred on the same day all other land animals were created. All of this occurred in one twenty-four-hour period—one revolution of the earth.

Adam, as we see from the text, was specially and personally created by God. There is no way to do justice to the text and maintain the notion that Adam evolved from some already-existing form of animal life. Genesis 2:7 is explicit: "And the Lord God formed man of the dust of the ground, and breathed into his nostrils the breath of life; and man became a living being." Genesis 2 also describes how the first woman, Eve, was made from the rib of her husband (v. 22). So the man and the woman were each created individually—both of them by direct and immediate acts of God.

The genealogies in Genesis begin with a reaffirmation of this truth: "In the day that God created man, He made him in the likeness of God. He created them male and female, and blessed them and called them Mankind in the day they were created" (Genesis 5:1–2). That verse opens and closes with references to a single *day* in which God made humanity. Repeatedly Scripture refers back to that momentous day (cf. Deuteronomy 4:32). It was day six of creation week—and this was God's final, crowning creative act.

A significant change in the creation process occurs at this point. Verse 26 starts with familiar words: "Then God said." That is the same formula used to introduce every previous act of creation (cf. vv. 3, 6, 9, 11, 14, 20, 24). But suddenly there is a major shift in the language. Up to this point, every occurrence of "Then God said" had been followed by the words "Let there be . . ." (vv. 3, 6, 14); "Let the earth bring forth . . ." (11, 24); "let the waters abound . . ." (v. 20); or "Let the waters . . . be gathered together" (v. 9)—always the language of fiat—"let it be done." Those expressions are impersonal in the sense that they are mandates issued to no one in particular. They are sovereign, creative decrees that immediately brought things into existence *ex nihilo*. Never before has God said, "Let Us make" anything.

But now for the first time the expression "Then God said" is followed by personal pronouns: "Let *Us* make man in *Our* image" (v. 26, emphasis added). This speaks of the creation of Adam in terms that are uniquely personal. Scripture deliberately employs such pronouns in order to stress God's intimate connection with this aspect of His creation. It establishes a personal relationship between God and man that does not exist with any other aspect of creation—not with light, not with water, not with the other elements or even the earth itself, not with the sun, the moon, the stars, or the stellar bodies—and not even with the other living creatures He made. He has no personal relationship with any of those things in the same sense He does with humanity. All those things were created by God through His fiat decree, and they began to exist because He ordered them to. But there is never a hint of any intimacy or personal identification between God and those things.

God's relationship with humanity is unique in all of creation. And therefore at every opportunity, Scripture vividly portrays God's personal involvement in the creation of man. "The Lord God formed man of the dust of the ground, and breathed into his nostrils the breath of life; and man became a living being" (2:7).

Here in Genesis 1:26, for the first time in the Bible, God introduces Himself with personal pronouns. Significantly, they are plural pronouns. Not, "Let *Me* . . ."; but, "Let *Us* make man in Our image," and thus we are introduced to a plurality of relationships in the Godhead. Here is the first major, unmistakable evidence of the Trinity. The fact of multiple Persons in the Godhead has been hinted at in the Hebrew word for God that is used in twenty-one of the first twenty-five verses of Scripture, because *elohim* takes the form of a plural noun in Hebrew. But the plural pronouns of verse 26 make the point even more forcefully. It is by no means a full revelation of the doctrine of the Trinity, but it is an unmistakable reference to plurality within the Godhead, and it begins to lay the groundwork for what we later learn of the Trinity from the New Testament.

There was at least one other earlier hint of the Trinity in verse 2, where we were told that the Spirit of God hovered above the face of the waters. But now we see even more clearly that there is a sort of divine executive committee—a council in the Godhead.

The same truth is unfolded with even more clarity in the first chapter of John's Gospel, which begins with an echo of Genesis 1:1: "In the beginning was the Word, and the Word was with God, and the Word was God. He was in the beginning with God. All things were made through Him, and without Him nothing was made that was made" (John 1:1–3). That, of course, refers to the Second Member of the Trinity, Jesus Christ (cf. v. 14)—who was with God at creation and is Himself God.

By putting all those passages together, we see that all three Members of the Trinity were active in creation. The Father was overseeing and decreeing the work. The eternal Word was "with God" and involved in every aspect of the creative process. And the Spirit was brooding over the waters, which also suggests the most intimate kind of hands-on involvement in the process. So with the light of the New Testament shining on this passage, the plural pronouns of Genesis 1:26 take on a rich depth of meaning.

This is one of many Old Testament passages that indicate communication between the members of the Trinity. In Psalm 2:7, for example, we read, "I will declare the decree: The Lord has said to Me, 'You are My Son, today I have begotten You." There the speaker is the Second Member of the Trinity—the Son—and He is quoting words spoken by the First Member of the Trinity—the Father. This is the eternal decree that defines the intra-Trinitarian relationship between Father and Son.

Then in Psalm 45:7 the Father is speaking to the Son: "You love righteousness and hate wickedness; therefore God, Your God, has anointed You with the oil of gladness more than Your companions." (That verse is cited in Hebrews 1:9, where the speaker is clearly identified as the Father, and the one being spoken to is shown to be Christ the Son.)

In Psalm 110:1 the psalmist writes, "The Lord said to my Lord, 'Sit at My right hand, till I make Your enemies Your footstool.'" There again the Father ("the Lord") speaks to the Son ("my Lord") and promises Him eternal dominion.

Isaiah 48 includes an even more remarkable passage. In verse 12 the speaker is plainly identified as "the First, [and] also the Last." (This is a reference to Christ—cf. Revelation 22:13.) And in verse 16, He says, "I have not spoken in secret from the beginning; from the time that it was, I was there. And now the Lord God and His Spirit have sent Me." So the speaker is God the Son, and He quite plainly speaks of "the Lord God and His Spirit" as different Persons in the Godhead.

Such references are found throughout the Old Testament. By themselves, they were not enough to give the typical Old Testament reader a full understanding of Trinitarian doctrine, but they were conspicuous hints of what would later be clearly revealed through the incarnation of Christ and the coming of the Holy Spirit at Pentecost. They were clues showing a plurality in the Godhead.

Here in Genesis 1 the expression suggests both communion and consultation among the Members of the Trinity. "Let Us make man in Our image, according to Our likeness" (v. 26). It also signifies perfect agreement and a clear purpose. It is, as a matter of fact, a crucial step toward the fulfillment of a promise made "before time began" (Titus 1:2)—a promise made in eternity past between the Members of the Trinity. Wrapped up in that promise was the entire redemptive plan of God. In short, the Father had promised the Son a redeemed people for His bride. And the Son had promised to die in order to redeem them. All of this occurred in eternity past, before creation was begun.[1]

"So God created man" (v. 27). Man became "a living being [Hebrew, *nephesh*]" (Genesis 2:7). Like the animals, he moved and breathed and was a conscious life-form. But there the similarity ended. This was a creature who was unlike any other created being. Lower life-forms could never evolve into this. And the distinctiveness of this creature is perfectly reflected in the purposes for which God created him.

TO BEAR THE CREATOR'S IMAGE

First, man was created to bear the likeness of his Maker. "Let Us make man in Our image, according to Our likeness" (v. 26). The two phrases ("in Our image" and "according to Our likeness") are parallel expressions. The second merely repeats the first in different but synonymous terms. Don't imagine that there is a vital distinction between the "image" of God and His "likeness"—as if one expression spoke of spiritual similarities between God and men and the other designated a physical likeness. Some commentators have mistakenly assumed that the coupled expressions have that sort of dual significance, but there is no distinction in the Hebrew language. These are parallel terms. In fact, the repetition is for emphasis. This sort of parallelism is a very common and typical construction in Hebrew. It is used for emphasis, not to make a contrast. And in this case, the parallelism is used to underscore the great importance of this truth: that man was created in the likeness of God.

What does that mean? Before we explore that question, consider the fact that whatever it means, it is something ineffably high and lofty. It is not a state into which lower creatures can evolve. This is not something that can be gained by a random mutation in the genetic code. It is not something that was brought about by a deviation in some higher primate's DNA. It is, after all, the very thing that makes humanity different from every other created animal. It is what defines the human being's unique identity. It is the whole reason God took such a personal interest in the creation of this particular species. It explains why the Bible places so much stress on the fact of God's hands-on creation of Adam. He fashioned this creature in a special way—to bear the stamp of His own likeness. Man was made in the image of God. That sets him apart from every other creature in the physical universe.

What is the image of God? The Hebrew word for "image," *tselem*, comes from a root that speaks of carving. It is the same word used to speak of graven images (Exodus 20:4). It almost seems to convey the idea that man was carved into the shape of God. It suggests that God was, in essence, the pattern for the personhood of man. That is not true of anything else in the space-time universe.[2]

Clearly, because the image of God is unique to humanity, it must describe some aspect of human nature that is not shared by animals. Therefore this cannot speak primarily of man's appearance or biological makeup. We do in fact have many biological features that are common to other animal creatures. Naturally, because we share the same environment, it is reasonable to expect that we would have many of the same biological and physiological characteristics in common with animals. And we do. Our internal organs work in similar ways; in many cases our skeletal structure has strong similarities; and even the way we look on the outside bears a clear similarity to some of the primates. If "the image of God" were a reference to the way we are constructed corporeally— if this meant to suggest that we bear a physical resemblance to the Maker— then it would probably also be accurate to suggest that even chimpanzees have *some* likeness to God.

But this quite clearly is not a reference to the material part of man. It isn't talking about biology or physiology. It certainly isn't a reference to the way we look as creatures made of flesh and bone. After all, "God is Spirit" (John 4:24). And "a spirit does not have flesh and bones" (Luke 24:39).

Clearly this deals primarily with man's spiritual attributes—our self-consciousness, our moral consciousness, and our consciousness of others— especially our consciousness of God Himself. (Animals are conscious, but they are not self-conscious, morally aware, or able to have a truly personal relationship.)

Before the image of God in man was marred by sin, Adam shared in a pure and undefiled way all the communicable attributes of God (those qualities of the divine nature that are capable of being reflected in creatures). These would include holiness, wisdom, goodness, truth, love, grace, mercy, longsuffering, and righteousness. The image of God in man no doubt still includes certain characteristics that mirror some of the virtues of God we learn about through creation—such as an appreciation for beauty, creative abilities, and a love of diversity. Of course, it must therefore include our rational faculties as well. For example, the divine image surely encompasses our ability to understand abstract principles—especially moral concepts like justice, righteousness, holiness, truth, and goodness. And the divine likeness in man therefore seems to include the higher aspects of our intellect and emotions—our ability to reason and solve problems, and emotions such as sorrow, zeal, anger, delight, and joy (all of which can be observed in their perfection in various dispositions Scripture says belong to God).

But above all, the image of God can be summed up by the word *personhood*. We are *persons*. Our lives involve relationships. We are capable of fellowship. We are able to love other persons in a Godlike sense. We understand communion. We have an amazing capacity for language. We have conversations. We know what it is to share thoughts, convey and discern attitudes, give and take friendship, perceive a sense of brotherhood, communicate ideas, and participate in experiences with others. Animals cannot do those things in the same sense people can.

That is why when God created man He immediately said that it was not good for man to be alone. The image of God is personhood, and personhood can function only in the context of relationships. Man's capacity for intimate personal relationships needed fulfillment. Most important, man was designed to have a personal relationship with God.

And this takes us back to the expression in verse 26. When God said, "Let Us make man in Our image, according to Our likeness," He signified that He Himself is a God of relationships. And He created us in His own likeness so that we could enter into a relationship with Him.

Douglas F. Kelly writes:

God Himself has never existed as a single, lonely, solitary, or "cut off" individual. Rather, He has always existed in the fullness of family-like being (cf. Eph. 3:14, 15: "Father . . . of whom the whole family in heaven and earth is named"). Or, as the great St. Athanasius used to say in the fourth century, "the Father has never been without His Son." The amazing mystery of the origin of personality is that the one God exists as three persons in one being or "substance" (or reality"). The one "substance" or being of God inherently involves personhood.[3]

And when God made us in His image, He therefore made us as persons— that is, He made us for having relationships, particularly with Him.

It is impossible to divorce this truth from the fact that man is an ethical creature. All true relationships have ethical ramifications. And it is at this point that God's communicable attributes come into play—marred though our moral and ethical sense may be because of humanity's fall into sin. We still know right from wrong in a basic sense. Even the most determined atheists still understand the *concept* of virtue and the need for morality.[4] In fact, an inherent aspect of true humanity is moral sensibility. We know instinctively that there is a difference between good and evil.

And all of this is what makes us distinct from the rest of creation. It pertains first of all to the invisible part of man—the spirit. It is what makes us spiritual beings. It's the part of our humanness that scientists will never find in our DNA. It is not programmed into our chromosomes. It is spiritual. And it is that true personhood which makes us like God, even in our fallen state.

Physically, we are made of earthly elements—the dust of the earth. And our bodies will eventually return to dust. That is not like God. But our personhood is eternal—and that does make us like God. The seat of God's image is therefore found in our immaterial beings.

That is not to suggest that our bodily form is utterly devoid of anything relevant to the divine image. As John Calvin said, "The image of God extends to everything in which the nature of man surpasses that of all other species of animals. . . . And though the primary seat of the divine image was in the mind and the heart, or in the soul and its powers, there was no part even of the body in which some rays of glory did not shine."[5]

Man's very posture, standing upright, distinguishes him from four-footed beasts and creeping things. The animals' natural posture directs their gaze downward, toward the earth. Man, on the other hand, is naturally positioned to look upward, toward the heavens, where he can contemplate the glory of God displayed there. This is one of many ways the glory of God is displayed even in the physical makeup of our race.

Our tongues, with their ability to form words and speak meaningful language, also reflect our likeness to God.

Even our faces, with their naturally expressive eyes and a host of meaningful expressions, are especially suited for relationships. So while the human body itself is neither the seat nor the primary expression of the image of God in man, even the body is specially made so that it can serve as a vehicle through which that image is manifest.

Henry Morris has written:

> We can only say that, although God Himself may have no physical body, He designed and formed man's body to enable it to function physically in ways in which He Himself could function even without a body. God can see (Genesis 16:13), hear (Psalm 94:9), smell (Genesis 8:21), touch (Genesis 32:32), and speak (2 Peter 1:18), whether or not He has actual physical eyes, ears, nose, hands, and mouth. . . . There is something about the human body, therefore, which is uniquely appropriate to God's manifestation of Himself, and (since God knows all His works from the beginning of the world—Acts 15:18), He must have designed man's body with this in mind. Accordingly, He designed it, not like the animals, but with an erect posture, with an upward gazing countenance, capable of facial expressions corresponding to emotional feelings, and with a brain and a tongue capable of articulate, symbolic speech.
>
> He knew, of course, that in the fullness of time even He would become a man. In that day, He would prepare a human body for His Son (Hebrews 10:5; Luke 1:35) and it would be "made in the likeness of men" (Philippians 2:7), just as man had been made in the likeness of God.[6]

It was not merely Adam who bore the image of God, but the woman did, too—as well as all their offspring. This fact is reflected in verse 26: "Let Us make *man* in Our image . . . ; let *them* have dominion" (emphasis added). The antecedent of the plural "them" is the noun "man," used collectively in this case. It clearly refers not only to Adam, but to all of humanity. And the rest of Scripture affirms this. Genesis 9:6 forbids all acts of murder, "For in the image of God He made man." And James 3:9 forbids us even to curse any fellow human being, because they "have been made in the similitude of God."

The truth that humanity was made in the likeness of God is the starting point for a biblical understanding of the nature of man. It explains our spiritual urges. It helps us make sense of the human conscience. It establishes our moral accountability. It reveals the very essence of the meaning and purpose of human life. It is full of practical and doctrinal significance.

Yet the doctrine of evolution would utterly erase this truth from the collective consciousness of the human race. That is why the battle against evolutionary theory is one Christians cannot afford to abandon.

TO PROPAGATE LIFE

A second purpose for which Adam and Eve were created was to fill the earth. Genesis 1:27–28 says, "Male and female He created them. Then God blessed them, and God said to them, 'Be fruitful and multiply; fill the earth.'" Here we see God's perfect plan for marriage and procreation. From the beginning, God's design was for permanent monogamous relationships between men and women. Genesis 2:24 makes this plain: "Therefore a man shall leave his father and mother and be joined to his wife, and they shall become one flesh."

The evolutionary lie has brought even this under attack, as society now seeks to justify and legitimize fornication, easy divorce, homosexual relationships, and other perversions that undermine the sanctity and uniqueness of the marriage relationship.

In our study of creation, we have seen throughout the plant and animal kingdoms that God produced all living species to procreate. But with the human race this takes on an especially sacred meaning. Keep in mind that of all earthly creatures, only man is created in the image of God—and the very essence of that image is the ability to have relationships. The marriage relationship is here established as the first and most intimate of all relationships between humans. The two "become one flesh," uniting in a bond that is designed to supersede every other relationship, no matter how close ("a man shall leave his father and mother"). The bond between husband and wife is also designed to be lasting, unbreakable, and inexpressibly intimate ("a man shall . . . be joined to his wife, and they shall become one flesh").

So an interesting and ironic feature in Adam's creation is the fact that he was first created alone. It appears from the language of Genesis that when God created other living species, he created them all in abundance. The sea swarmed with sea life and the skies were filled with birds. Although Scripture doesn't expressly say how many He created of each species, the language suggests that there must have been multiple pairs of each.

But when it comes to the creation of human beings, Scripture is clear that He made only one pair. In fact, He began by making just one—Adam.

Of course it was God's plan from the beginning that Adam would have a mate. ("Known to God from eternity are all His works"—Acts 15:18.) Don't get the impression that Eve was an afterthought or a modification of the divine plan. Some people misread the account of Eve's creation in Genesis 2 and imagine that she was tacked onto creation as an addendum to God's original plan. That is not what the text means. It is true that Eve was not created until *after* God had instructed Adam to name the animals and given him time to begin the process. (One preacher suggested that God held off creating Eve so that Adam wouldn't have to deal with a second opinion every time he named an animal. I doubt that.) But Eve was part of God's plan from the beginning. Her separate creation merely stresses the fact of how special she was—and how uniquely suited she was for compatibility with Adam.

One thing stands out clearly. After each stage of creation, God pronounced His work *good*. "God saw that it was good" is the constant refrain of the creation narrative (Genesis 1:4, 10, 12, 18, 21, 25, 31). The only time God pronounced anything not good was when He said, "It is not good that man should be alone" (2:18). Again, this is not to suggest that God had discovered a flaw in His original plan. Rather, the point is that the original plan was not yet complete with Adam alone. Man had been created for relationships, and he still needed a perfect mate for the marriage relationship.

So Scripture says, "The Lord God caused a deep sleep to fall on Adam, and he slept; and He took one of his ribs, and closed up the flesh in its place. Then the rib which the Lord God had taken from man He made into a woman, and He brought her to the man" (2:21–22).

Adam, of course, was delighted. "And Adam said: 'This is now bone of my bones and flesh of my flesh; she shall be called Woman, because she was taken out of Man'" (v. 23).

Eve was made to be a *helper* for Adam (vv. 18, 20). This is not talking about domestic help—someone to do his dishes, take out his trash, or make his bed. Adam *could* have managed such duties without a wife. But he had a more important duty for which he needed her help. He was to procreate, propagate the human race, and populate the earth with people. Obviously, he needed a partner for that.

As God brought animals to Adam and he went through the process of naming them each, he began to see that he was alone in all of creation. "For Adam there was not found a helper comparable to him" (v. 20). He must have known that he was not merely a glorified animal. He was made in the Creator's image, and he needed a partner who was also made in the same image. So God made him a partner from his own rib. In other words, Eve's genetic structure was derived from and therefore perfectly harmonious with Adam's.

Genetic research has shown that one pair of human chromosomes, labeled X and Y, determine the gender of our offspring. All males have both X and Y chromosomes; all females have only a pair of X chromosomes. From a purely biological point of view, therefore, the Y chromosome is what determines maleness. If the offspring inherits an X chromosome from the father, it will be female. If the chromosome is Y, the offspring will be male. The father's seed is the determining factor.

Genetically therefore, it is possible to create a female from a male. It would not be possible to extract a male's genetic code from a female, however, because the female has no Y chromosome. That is perfectly harmonious with what God did here. Science, when it deals with facts rather than theories, always agrees with the biblical account.

The command, "Be fruitful and multiply; fill the earth" (1:28) echoes throughout Genesis. It is repeated in Genesis 9:1, after the Flood. It also lay at the heart of God's promise to Abraham (22:17–18). It is a unique and beautiful expression of God's love for humanity, that He created us with the ability to procreate and thus produce more creatures made in His image. And not only did He want a world full of them, but He also designed men and women to partake in the joy of fulfilling that purpose. Children themselves are therefore a blessing from the Lord (Psalm 127:3). This is, in fact, one of the main ways God designed to bring gladness and enjoyment to the human race—which brings up yet another reason why humanity was such a special part of creation.

TO RECEIVE DIVINE BLESSING

Here is a third purpose for which God created the human race: We were created to be the recipients of joy and blessing from the hand of God. He made our race so that He could pour out His goodness on us. Genesis 1:28 says that after Adam and Eve were created, "Then God blessed them."

"Blessed" here speaks of something more than a ceremonial consecration. God did not merely invoke some verbal formula of blessing. What this suggests is that He conferred well-being on them. He caused them to prosper. He made them happy.

That is still God's design for the human race. He wants us to enjoy Him and to enjoy the rich goodness of His creation. The apostle Paul said God "gives us richly all things to enjoy" (1 Timothy 6:17). The Old Testament sage wrote, "It is good and fitting for one to eat and drink, and to enjoy the good of all his labor in which he toils under the sun all the days of his life which God gives him; for it is his heritage" (Ecclesiastes 5:18).

And in Adam's case, all the enjoyment and blessing in the world were his in a paradise untainted by sin or evil. He had all he could ever want, in a perfect environment, with a perfect climate, with an ideal partner, and with a mandate from God to enjoy and use everything (with just one restriction) freely. "And God said, 'See, I have given you every herb that yields seed which is on the face of all the earth, and every tree whose fruit yields seed; to you it shall be for food. Also, to every beast of the earth, to every bird of the air, and to everything that creeps on the earth, in which there is life, I have given every green herb for food'; and it was so." (Genesis 1:29–30).

Notice that Adam, as well as every other creature in the animal kingdom, was a vegetarian at this point. There was no sin, and therefore there was no death. There could therefore be no carnivores. All the animals were tame, and even those species that are now carnivores were once pure vegetarians. But the world was filled with abundant food, and vast varieties of it.

Everywhere Adam looked, food was literally hanging on trees. The whole world reflected the abundant goodness and generosity of God. After all, God could have made a brown sky, brown water, and a colorless world—with nothing to eat but plain rice. But instead, He filled the world with a vast array of wonderful fruits and vegetables. He created all these things for us to enjoy.

And he gave us senses to enjoy them with. Imagine how bland all life would become if we lost the ability to taste and smell. God has given us those capabilities to bless us—to enable us to enjoy to the fullest everything He made. And Adam and Eve were given full and unfettered freedom to enjoy anything they wanted in the garden of God.

Again, however, there was one significant exception. In all the vast array of fruits and vegetables God had created, just one tree was declared off limits. "The Lord God commanded the man, saying, 'Of every tree of the garden you may freely eat; but of the tree of the knowledge of good and evil you shall not eat, for in the day that you eat of it you shall surely die'" (2:17). They were free to eat all they wanted from any other tree—including the tree of life. But they were forbidden to eat from the tree of the knowledge of good and evil. To eat what was forbidden would bring on them the judgment of God, resulting in their death.

As we shall see in chapter 10, they did exactly what God had forbidden. They not only brought judgment on themselves and the whole human race, but they also brought a curse on all creation. That which God had made for their pure enjoyment was spoiled by sin. Death entered the world, and along with death, sickness, weeds, hard work, and difficulties of all kinds (Genesis 3:17–19). Sin spoiled that perfect paradise.

But God had originally made it good. He had made it to bless humanity. That was one of His purposes in creation. And even in this sin-spoiled world, He still fulfills that purpose. His creation, even in its fallen state, is filled with blessings for us.

TO RULE CREATION

Finally, the human race was designed for and given a mandate to exercise dominion over the rest of creation. Immediately after saying "Let Us make man in Our image, according to Our likeness," God said, "let them have dominion over the fish of the sea, over the birds of the air, and over the cattle, over all the earth and over every creeping thing that creeps on the earth." In verse 28, God reiterates this purpose in His instructions to Adam: "Fill the earth and subdue it; have dominion over the fish of the sea, over the birds of the air, and over every living thing that moves on the earth." Man was intended by God to be the sovereign of the planet. He was literally instructed to subdue the planet, take dominion, and rule over everything God had placed on earth.

Of course this speaks collectively of the whole human race—not just Adam. This is made clear by the plural pronoun in verse 26: "Let them have dominion." And the scope of humanity's dominion over the earth was very broad, too. It was to include every living creature. God's mandate to Adam expressly listed the creatures in the order of their creation: "the fish of the sea . . . the birds of the air . . . the cattle . . . [and] every creeping thing" (v. 26).

The first step of this dominion involved something very practical. Genesis 2:19 records this: "Out of the ground the Lord God formed every beast of the field and every bird of the air, and brought them to Adam to see what he would call them. And whatever Adam called each living creature, that was its name." That was Adam's first task. He had to look at the characteristics of each creature and give it a fitting name.

Man was made in God's image, so it was appropriate that God would delegate to man something of His own sovereign prerogative. Notice that God Himself had already named day and night (v. 5), heaven (v. 8), and the earth and the seas (v. 10). It is the Creator's privilege to name what He creates, but in this case He delegated that task to Adam. It became Adam's first duty as ruler of the world.

Another responsibility was assigned to Adam. He was made the gardener in Eden. Genesis 2:15 says "Then the Lord God took the man and put him in the garden of Eden to tend and keep it." Of course, this task was given to him before he fell into sin. That means there was no curse yet, so there were no weeds, and the environment was perfect. This was an easy and pleasant assignment for Adam. No doubt it was a source of great joy. And it was the only work he was given to do—if such an occupation can even be called "work" in a sweatless, weedless, curse-free environment. The garden was filled with every kind of fruit tree God had made. Water for the garden was readily available from a river that ran through it. And Adam's only responsibility was to make sure that the trees and plants in this perfect environment had appropriate care. It was the most pleasant vocation any person could ever have.

Adam's responsibility to subdue the earth and rule over it was perfectly complemented by his duty to tend the garden. In Douglas F. Kelly's words:

> The call to tend the garden and classify the animals provides a fine and fruitful balance in the relationship of mankind to the environment which God has placed under his derived authority. This healthy balance is not to be found outside the biblical faith. Eastern religions, such as Hinduism and Buddhism, for instance, tend to neglect developing "the garden" (viewing it as a sort of God, not to be tampered with), as do some forms of Christian mysticism; materialist, technological industrialism tends to destroy "the garden" for short-sighted economic purposes, whether in the strip mines of West Virginia, the slag heaps of the English Midlands, or the dead rivers of Romania; and the ultra-environmentalists or "Greens" tend to elevate it above the legitimate needs and purposes of human society, thus losing their own significance and failing to bring to fruition what man could accomplish with the remarkable capacities of the created order. But the dominion of Genesis teaches man both to respect and to subdue nature, so as to shape it in a direction that will reflect the beauty, order and glory of its Creator.[7]

So Adam was given both dominion over God's creation and the responsibility to care for it.

Unfortunately, when he fell, Adam abdicated some of his God-given authority. When he yielded to Satan, he forfeited the absolute dominion God had given him over the earth. It is interesting that Jesus repeatedly referred to Satan as "the ruler of this world" (John 12:31; 14:30; 16:11). That was supposed to be man's role. But Adam's willful sin in effect forfeited dominion to the devil.

Christ Himself will return to regain that dominion and establish Himself as the ruler of this world. He has already defeated the powers of evil at the cross: "Having disarmed principalities and powers, He made a public spectacle of them, triumphing over them in it" (Colossians 2:15). And upon His return to earth, He will receive His kingdom and establish it worldwide, reigning on an earthly throne in His glorified human body. And thus in the Person of Christ, humanity will finally have the full dominion God planned from the start—and more. Hebrews 2:8 celebrates this certainty: "'You have put all things in subjection under his feet.' For in that He put all in subjection under him, He left nothing that is not put under him."

The writer of Hebrews continues, "But now we do not yet see all things put under him." We still live in a world that is under the curse of sin, so we cannot subdue the garden of God as we would like. Weeds, pests, harmful bacteria, harmful viruses, and other effects of the curse—not to mention fallen human nature—keep the task of subduing the earth constantly out of reach. It is ironic that man was originally given dominion over all of creation, and yet in his fallen state, even the tiniest microbes can bring him low.

And yet even fallen humanity *has* managed to take dominion over creation to an amazing degree, devising technology that allows us to cultivate only a fraction of the earth's potential farmland and still grow enough crops to feed the world. Technology has permitted us to travel to the moon, develop amazing communications networks, travel across vast continents by air in a few hours, build dams to create large reservoirs, devise power systems that harness the energy in the universe and put it to humanity's benefit, and develop medical technology that prolongs life. Even in his fallen state, the human being is a wonderful creature, still endued with the image of his Maker.

But we do not yet see all things subjected to him. There is still war and disease and poverty. Most of the technology humanity has developed has created new problems while attempting to solve old ones. Man sometimes has a destructive effect on his own environment. Above all, man is unable to subdue his own sinful tendencies.

Christ, the perfect Man, will do what fallen man has been unable to do. He will destroy all the works of the devil (1 John 3:8)—and even destroy the devil himself (Hebrews 2:14). That victory was already sealed when Christ rose from the dead. We are now simply awaiting its culmination. And that will occur at the end of the age. "Then comes the end, when He delivers the kingdom to God the Father, when He puts an end to all rule and all authority and power. For He must reign till He has put all enemies under His feet.

The last enemy that will be destroyed is death. For 'He has put all things under His feet'" (1 Corinthians 15:24–27).

Scripture says the redeemed will reign with Christ in an earthly kingdom for a thousand years (Revelation 20:4). The earth will be restored as a paradise. Major elements of the curse will be reversed. "The wilderness and the wasteland shall be glad for them, and the desert shall rejoice and blossom as the rose; it shall blossom abundantly and rejoice" (Isaiah 35:1–2). The animals will revert to their pre-fall state, so that none will be carnivorous, and even the most fearsome predators will pose no danger to humanity or to other species (Isaiah 11:6–9).

Even sin and death will be mitigated in the millennial kingdom. "No more shall an infant from there live but a few days, nor an old man who has not fulfilled his days; for the child shall die one hundred years old, but the sinner being one hundred years old shall be accursed" (Isaiah 65:20–21). In other words, infant mortality will be eliminated and life expectancy greatly extended. (It seems reasonable to think that many who enter into the kingdom alive might survive through the entire millennium.) Since those born in the earthly kingdom do inherit a sin nature, the effects of sin will not be entirely erased. Most people, it appears, will be redeemed. But those who persist in sin and unbelief will be judged with death. And humanity's normal life expectancy will be such that if someone dies at one hundred years old (because of willful sin and persistent unbelief), he will be regarded as someone who died tragically young—as if he died in childhood.

During that millennial kingdom, humanity will finally get a taste of what life in Eden could have been. With Christ reigning and the effects of sin mitigated, earthly life will be as close to paradise as a world tainted with sin could ever know.

And finally, when the millennial kingdom is complete, the heavens and earth will pass away and be replaced by a new creation (Revelation 21:1). That world, untainted with sin or sorrow of any kind, will even surpass Eden in its delights. And a Man—the man Christ Jesus—will have dominion over it, with His saints finally sharing the perfect dominion man was originally created to enjoy.

Thus the heavens and the earth, and all the host of them, were fin-ished. And on the seventh day God ended His work which He had done, and He rested on the seventh day from all His work which He had done. Then God blessed the seventh day and sanctified it, because in it He rested from all His work which God had created and made.

—Genesis 2:1–3

9

THE REST OF CREATION

Genesis 2:1–3

CREATION IS NOW COMPLETE. Additional details about the creation of Adam and Eve fill most of Genesis 2. But Genesis 2 begins with an account of day seven, bringing creation week to a close: "Thus the heavens and the earth, and all the host of them, were finished. And on the seventh day God ended His work which He had done, and He rested on the seventh day from all His work which He had done. Then God blessed the seventh day and sanctified it, because in it He rested from all His work which God had created and made" (vv. 1–3).

The seventh day is unique. It is an exalted day, because God blessed it and sanctified it. The Hebrew word translated "sanctified" in verse 3 is *qedesh*. Its root meaning is "holy," and it conveys the idea of being set apart. This is the first time in Scripture anything is said to be holy.

Douglas F. Kelly writes, "Grammatical considerations indicate that two things are implied by the clause: 'he hallowed it': on the one hand, He made it holy (the *Piel* stem of the verb here implies causation), and on the other hand, He declared it to be holy, or consecrated it (for this form of the verb also carries here a declarative sense)."[1] In other words, God's cessation of activity on the seventh day naturally made that day holy, and this is reinforced by the fact that He expressly declared it to be a special day. It was a day set apart. It was elevated above the other days and deemed holy.

There are three reasons this day was unique, and those three reasons are indicated by three verbs in the passage. The first verb is "finished" (v. 1). The same Hebrew word (*kalah*) is used again in verse 2, where it is translated "ended." The second verb in verse 2 is "rested" (Hebrew, *shabath*), and it appears again in verse 3. The third verb is in verse 3: "blessed" (Hebrew, *barak*). Each of those verbs is associated with the seventh day explicitly: "on the seventh day God ended His work" (v. 2); "He rested on the seventh day" (v. 2); and "God blessed the seventh day" (v. 3). Furthermore, in each case, God is the grammatical subject in the clause: "God ended. . . . He rested. . . . God blessed."

So the structure of this passage is simple, and its significance is unfolded in the verbs it employs.

HE FINISHED HIS WORK

Genesis 2:1–2 indicates that the uniqueness of the seventh day stems first of all from the fact that God had ended the work of creation. "Thus the heavens and the earth, and all the host of them, were *finished*. . . and He rested on the seventh day from *all His work which He had done*." The entire work of creation was complete. There were no loose ends to tie up. There were no problems to fix. No modifications to the original plan were required. Everything was completed in six days, just as God had planned. And with the dawn of the seventh day, God ceased from creating. Four times in the first three verses of Genesis 2, the text emphatically states that God had finished *all* the work of creation.

This argues powerfully against the evolutionary doctrine, which suggests that creation is a work still in process. The biblical emphasis is on the utter perfection of everything God created and the wondrously brief time in which He accomplished it all. The clear statement of Scripture is that "the heavens and the earth, and all the host of them, were *finished*" (v. 1, emphasis added). Interestingly, science itself offers evidence that Genesis 2:1 is true. The first law of thermodynamics rules out the possibility of ongoing creation, and the second law of thermodynamics eliminates the possibility that an ordered universe evolved naturally from chaos.

The first law of thermodynamics deals with the conservation of energy. This principle means simply that energy cannot be destroyed; neither is it being created. Systems that use energy do not use it up; they merely convert it to different forms of energy—heat, motion, sound, light, or chemical or electromagnetic energy. (Remember also that Einstein's famous theorem, $E=MC^2$—energy equals mass times the speed of light squared—teaches that matter is simply another form of energy. That means matter, like energy, cannot be destroyed; it can only be converted to another form.)

The amount of energy within any system remains constant unless outside forces interact with the system. The only way to *increase* the energy in an energy-using system is for an external force to do work on that system—adding heat, fuel, or kinetic energy to it. Likewise, energy will *decrease* in a system only if it is transferred out of the system as heat, light, or some other form of energy. That means in a closed system (one not subject to any outside force or external exchange of energy), the sum of all forms of energy always remains constant.

The natural universe itself is such a closed system. The universe by definition includes all the matter and energy that exist. There is no natural energy outside the universe that can be added to it; and there is no place outside the universe where energy may be dissipated to. Therefore, as far as science can determine, the amount of energy and matter in the universe must remain constant. In other words, energy in the natural universe is not being created or destroyed. Indeed, there absolutely is no evidence of any ongoing creation.

But where did all the matter and energy in the universe come from in the first place? If the natural universe is a closed system, its matter and energy must have come from a supernatural source, just as Scripture teaches.

Couldn't matter and energy be eternal? Is it possible that the universe is just an immense perpetual-motion machine, always evolving? No. That possibility is eliminated by the second law of thermodynamics.

The second law of thermodynamics states that the total amount of entropy in nature is increasing. *Entropy* is a measure of the randomness and disorder in a system. Put simply, the second law of thermodynamics means that things run down. They wear out. Systems left to run on their own always evolve from order to chaos, and never the other way around.

What does this have to do with thermodynamics? In nontechnical terms, entropy measures the amount of "wasted" energy in a system. Although energy is not destroyed when it is converted from one form to another, it becomes less useful as it is converted. For example, heat is generated and dissipated when a car engine runs. That heat performs no work, and the measure of that nonproductive energy is the measure of the system's entropy. All systems, even closed ones, are subject to the second law of thermodynamics. Entropy applies to everything in nature.

The second law means, for example, that heat never passes naturally from a cooler to a hotter body. Heat transfer is always one way, and the process is irreversible. So in a closed system, heat will move from warmer bodies to cooler ones, lowering the temperatures of the former and raising the temperatures of the latter, until exact equilibrium is reached and the system becomes inert.

All working systems result in a decreasing availability of useful energy. *Everything* will run down, wear out, and become disorderly if some external force doesn't keep it running and ordered. This very principle rules out any kind of perpetual-motion machine—even on a cosmic scale. In other words, matter and energy cannot be eternal. All things in the material universe decay (Hebrews 1:10–12; Matthew 6:19). Everything dissipates and disintegrates. If the universe were infinitely old, it would be wound down already. So the processes we observe all clearly point to a beginning. It is a beginning that must have been set in motion by supernatural causes—precisely what Scripture teaches.

The Bible consistently says that God created it all in six days, and Genesis 2:2 says that on the seventh day He ceased His creative work. There is no ongoing creation of matter or energy; in His perfect wisdom God designed the universe so that what He created would be complete and will remain functioning as long as it serves His purposes. It is neither eternal nor self-sufficient. It is the product of God's creative genius.

And God's own verdict on His creative work, at the end of day six, is stated in Genesis 1:31: "Then God saw everything that He had made, and indeed it was very good." Throughout the entire process, when each stage of the process was completed, God's appraisal of His work was the same: "God saw . . . that it was good" (1:4, 10, 12, 18, 21, 25). Now the text adds for emphasis, "*Indeed* it was *very* good." There were no flaws or omissions. The work was complete in every sense. God was pleased with it. As Solomon wrote, "I know that whatever God does, it shall be forever. Nothing can be added to it, and nothing taken from it. God does it, that men should fear before Him" (Ecclesiastes 3:14).

The words of Psalm 104:24 are a fitting description of this moment: "O LORD, how manifold are thy works! in wisdom hast thou made them all: the earth is full of thy riches" (KJV). The heavens and the earth were now complete. A whole universe now existed where nothing had existed only a week earlier. It was a vast cosmos full of countless wonders, each of which displayed the glory and wisdom of a good and perfect Creator. As Paul wrote Timothy, "Every creature of God is good." The heavens were declaring His glory and the firmament displayed His handiwork (Psalm 19:1). And He was pleased. "May the glory of the Lord endure forever; may the Lord rejoice in His works" (Psalm 104:31).

On each day of creation week, God had wrought a plethora of wonders, and each day's work perfectly complemented the others. This is the whole thrust of the biblical creation account: God created the entire universe with all its untold marvels out of nothing, bringing it to utter perfection in six days. The time frame is neither figurative nor incidental to the point Scripture aims to make. God accomplished the whole of His creative work in one week—not six long geological ages.

The amazing excellence revealed in the creative work of God is forfeited to a very large degree if we abandon the days of creation in favor of an ages-long evolutionary process.

Moreover, the emphasis that is given to this seventh day throughout Scripture is especially significant in establishing the time frame for creation. That first week determined the periods of labor and rest God would later require of His covenant people. And the truth of a literal six-day creation week was therefore written into the Ten Commandments: "Six days you shall labor and do all your work but the seventh day is the Sabbath of the Lord your God. . . . For in six days the Lord made the heavens and the earth, the sea, and all that is in them, and rested the seventh day" (Exodus 20:9–11).

God reiterated the same truth again when he set forth the specific Sabbath requirements: "The children of Israel shall keep the Sabbath. . . . It is a sign between me and the children of Israel forever: for in six days the Lord made the heavens and earth, and on the seventh day He rested, and was refreshed" (Exodus 31:16–17). The whole point is nullified if the days can be turned into time periods of indefinite duration.

HE RESTED

God's rest on day seven is another major reason why this day was an especially hallowed one. Verse 2 says, "And on the seventh day God ended His
work which He had done, and He rested on the seventh day from all His
work which He had done." Notice again the double emphasis on the utter
completion of God's work, signified by the repetition of the phrase "His work
which He *had done.*"

Having finished His work in consummate perfection, God rested. Don't
get the notion that God was weary or needed to recoup His strength. As
Isaiah 40:28, says, "The Creator of the ends of the earth, neither faints nor is
weary." When God works there is no dissipation of His energy. He cannot be
fatigued, and He doesn't need rejuvenation. "Behold, He who keeps Israel
shall neither slumber nor sleep" (Psalm 121:4).

The Hebrew word translated "rested" in Genesis 2:2 (*shabat*) simply
means that He abstained from creative work. He had completed all creation,
so there was nothing more for Him to create. Therefore, He ceased His work.

Look again at Exodus 31:17, which established the weekly Sabbath as a
sign between God and Israel forever: "For in six days the Lord made the
heavens and the earth, and on the seventh day He rested and was
refreshed." To say that God was "refreshed" does not imply that He was reju-
venated by regaining lost energy. Rather, the sense of it is that He paused to
delight in His works. He was "refreshed" by delight and satisfaction in what
He had done. The "rest" and "refreshment" of which this speaks is figurative, describing God's cessation of work and His repose for the sole purpose
of enjoying what He had made. The imagery is like that of a master artisan
who, having completed a masterpiece, pauses to admire and reflect on his
finished work.

Specifically, God ceased His *creative activity.* This doesn't mean that God
withdrew His providential working or that He ceased working altogether. He
continued to sustain and govern His creation, just as He sustains it and prov-
identially rules over it even today. Jesus told the Jewish leaders, "My Father
has been working until now, and I have been working." He was speaking
specifically of good works, works of charity, and acts of kindness toward people in need, which according to Jesus have always been permissible on the

Sabbath (Mark 3:4). He was underscoring the fact that God Himself did not utterly cease work altogether on the seventh day. In other words, God did not withdraw from the universe and leave it to run on its own, as deism would suggest. He merely "rested" from the work of creation, permanently ending that aspect of His work.

God's cessation from His creative works is seen even in the current functioning of the universe. Henry Morris writes:

> The present processes of the universe are, without exception, processes of *conservation* and *disintegration*, as formulated in the two universal laws of thermodynamics. The processes of the creation period, on the other hand, were processes of *innovation* and *integration* (or "creating" and "making"), which are exactly opposite.[2]

This is precisely why science can never speak with any real authority when it comes to the question of the origin of the universe:

> Science can deal only with present processes, to which alone it has access. It should be completely clear to all who are not willfully ignorant that universal processes of conservation and disintegration could never produce a universe requiring almost infinite processes of innovation and integration for its production. Therefore, if we really want to *know* anything about this creation period (other than the fact that there must have been such a period, to produce the universe, a fact certainly required by the two laws of thermodynamics), then such knowledge can be acquired only by divine revelation.[3]

Scripture *is* that revelation, and from it we learn that God created everything in six days; then He rested from creation on the seventh day.

It is worth noting that in the context of the Genesis creation account, no mention is made of any rest for Adam. In fact, man is not even mentioned in connection with this seventh-day creation rest. Above all, no ordinance *mandating* Sabbath rest and worship is expressly instituted here. There were no restrictions governing what Adam could and could not do on the seventh day of the week. All of that came later, with the giving of the law to Israel.

(The word *Sabbath* doesn't even appear in Scripture until Exodus 16:23.) The ceremonial Sabbath restrictions therefore pertained to national Israel in a particular way.

Indeed, there was no need for Sabbath restrictions to be imposed on Adam. In fact, the specific ceremonial requirements outlined in the Mosaic Sabbath laws would have been totally superfluous in Eden.

For example, the Israelites were commanded to remain in their dwelling places on the Sabbath (Exodus 16:29). But Adam's dwelling place was all of Eden, and he did not leave it until God drove him out after he sinned (Genesis 3:24).

The Israelites were forbidden to kindle fires on the Sabbath (Exodus 35:3); they were also instructed not to cook food on that day (Exodus 16:23). But Adam needed no fire for warmth in Eden (he didn't even need clothing in that perfect environment—Genesis 2:25); and his food was fresh fruit, which he could pluck from the trees all around him and eat freely without cooking (Genesis 2:16).

The Israelites were prohibited from doing any work or carrying any burdens on the Sabbath (Exodus 20:10; Jeremiah 17:27). Adam, however, lived in a paradise where no toil (as we know it) was ever necessary and the carrying of any load would be utterly unnecessary as well. There was no need to store food or build shelter, so what heavy load would he ever need to carry?

The Israelites were not supposed to buy or sell anything on the Sabbath (Nehemiah 10:31). Of course, there was nothing to buy or sell in Eden; all Adam's needs were supplied in that perfect paradise.

And the Israelites were to set aside the Sabbath to delight in the Lord (Isaiah 58:13–14). But prior to his fall, Adam's whole existence was given to perfect fellowship with and delight in his Creator.

So everything about Adam's life before he sinned was precisely what the Sabbath laws pictured. In a sense, Israel's Sabbath observances were designed to show in microcosm what life in Eden was designed to be. And this aspect of Moses' law was merely a ceremonial reminder of what God's original design for human life involved.

Since the Sabbath restrictions were ceremonial in nature, they were abolished under the New Covenant along with the rest of the Old Covenant's priestly and ceremonial commandments (Colossians 2:16–17). Christ has restored in a more perfect way the *spiritual* Sabbath rest of Eden (Hebrews 4:10), so Christians are no longer bound by the ceremonial aspects of the Sabbath laws that were instituted at Sinai. Those things pertained only to national Israel: "Therefore the children of Israel shall keep the Sabbath, to observe the Sabbath throughout their generations as a perpetual covenant. It is a sign between Me and the children of Israel forever" (Exodus 31:16–17).

Nonetheless, the creation week did establish a permanent pattern for the rhythm of all human life. God made us in His image, and He programmed us so that we thrive best under a pattern of work and rest that closely parallels His activities during creation week. One day of rest in seven is an ideal ratio. People quickly show signs of fatigue when they miss that one day of rest per week, and productivity suffers when the work week is shortened.

In any case, humanity has always numbered the passing of time in seven-day units, and it is obvious that this pattern began at creation. Of course, prior to Adam's fall, there was little if any distinction between labor and leisure, so the pattern of six days' work and one day's rest would have had little significance anyway until after Adam sinned. Again, that is why there is no record that God required of His people any ceremonial Sabbath observance until the law was given at Sinai.

Notice, too, that there is a significant omission in the biblical record of day seven. Every other day's record ends with similar words: "And the evening and the morning were the [nth] day" (cf. vv. 5, 8, 13, 19, 23, 31). But no such formula is used to close the seventh day. This does not suggest, as some have asserted, that day seven was a long era that covers all of human history. The omission is by no means an indication that the days of creation were really long epochs. As we have seen repeatedly, the sequence of creation, the language of Genesis, and the clear statements found in such passages as Exodus 20:11 and 31:17 make clear that these were normal twenty-four-hour days. Another day certainly followed this seventh day. But the omission of the formula on day seven suggests that the rest God entered into was a *permanent* rest from His creative works. He ceased creating and was completely satisfied with what He had created.

In other words, the rest that commenced on day seven could have continued indefinitely if it had not been interrupted by Adam's sin. Everything was in a state of pristine perfection. There was no decay. There was no sickness or pain or death. There was no labor, in the sense we think of labor in a fallen world. Adam would have lived in a perpetual Sabbath rest, if he had not fallen into sin. Everything in creation was perfectly delightful, and God was enjoying it—as were all His creatures. What a paradise it must have been!

Only sin could have interrupted such a rest, and as we shall see in the following chapter, that is precisely what happened. We don't know how long the paradise lasted, because we don't know how long it was until man sinned. But Scripture seems to suggest that the Fall came almost immediately after creation—before Adam and Eve had conceived any children. God then interrupted His rest to undertake the work of redemption.

To summarize what Scripture says about God's rest, then, it was a rest from the work of creation while God delighted in the goodness of everything He had made. It was characterized by divine delight and satisfaction. He was pleased and refreshed by the excellence of His work. He enjoyed perfect fellowship with Adam and Eve—and they with Him. He had ceased from His creative work, and He was perfectly satisfied with it. That first Sabbath was the most delightful day in the history of the universe.

HE BLESSED THE DAY

That brings us to the third verb in this passage: "God blessed the seventh day, and sanctified it" (v. 3). He hallowed the day. In other words, set it aside as a memorial. He made it a permanent reminder of the glory of creation and the surpassing glory of the Creator.

Again, there is no rational reason, no cosmic reason, no philosophical reason, no mathematical reason, and no scientific reason for seven-day weeks. There is frankly no other explanation for why the 365 days of our solar years were divided into sevens. The year doesn't even divide neatly that way. So why are our calendars ordered by weeks? There is only one reason: God Himself established that order in the pattern of His creation. Every week of our lives we go through a cycle that is intended by God to remind us that He created the world in six days and rested on the seventh. The seventh day is a reminder that God is our Creator. It is a memorial to a completed creation.

To reject a six-day creation is to unbless the seventh day. It robs God of the glory that is due His name. If everything evolved from nothing, or if creation was spread over eons of time, there was no seventh day. Thus any view of this passage other than a literal six-day creation totally confounds the blessing of the seventh day.

On the other hand, if we believe what the Bible says, then every seventh day is a memorial and a reminder that God created the entire universe in one week. And for that glorious accomplishment He deserves our praise.

What does this mean in practical terms? It suggests that Saturday should be identified in our minds with the completion of creation. Each week thus ends with a perpetual reminder that God created everything in six days' time. It is a day to remember the glory of the Creator. In Western society, where Saturday often means a day off work, it is an ideal day for enjoying His creation and delighting with Him in the goodness of His work. Just as Sunday is set aside for celebrating the finished work of the Savior, Saturday ought to be a remembrance of the finished work of the Creator.

This is not to suggest that we are bound by the ceremonial requirements of the Mosaic law with regard to the Sabbath. Again, nothing in Genesis suggests that Adam—or anyone else from Adam to Moses—was given any ceremonial restrictions that forbid any kind of activity on Saturday. But the text simply says that God hallowed the day. He set it apart as a memorial. And the seventh day is still a reminder and a perpetual witness that God finished the work of creation. Likewise, Sunday is a perpetual witness that He has finished the work of redemption.

God's blessing of the seventh day consummates His blessing on all of creation. Remember, at the end of Genesis 1, God surveyed everything He had made and saw that it was *very good*. There's a wealth of theology in that simple blessing. It testifies that God is not the author of evil. When He ceased creating, everything was good. Evil was not to be found anywhere.

Philosophers struggle to explain the origin of evil. One thing is certain: God is not its author, creator, or efficient cause. Everything He created was *good*. Evil was no part of His creation.

Who then created evil? No one. Evil is neither substance, being, spirit, nor matter. It is not a created thing. It is simply a want of moral perfection in moral agents who were originally created sinless. Evil has no existence apart from fallen creatures.

How could creatures made sinless fall into sin? John Calvin dealt with that very question:

> The Lord had declared that "everything that he had made . . . was exceedingly good" [Gen. 1:31]. Whence, then comes this wickedness to man, that he should fall away from his God? Lest we should think it comes from creation, God had put His stamp of approval on what had come forth from himself. By his own evil intention, then, man corrupted the pure nature he had received from the Lord; and by his fall drew all his posterity with him into destruction. *Accordingly, we should contemplate the evident cause of condemnation in the corrupt nature of humanity—which is closer to us—rather than seek a hidden and utterly incomprehensible cause in God's predestination.*[4]

God, although absolutely sovereign over all things, is not the author or instigator of sin. He did not concoct sin, encourage it, sanction it, condone it, approve it, or otherwise countenance it. But He created moral agents with a capacity to make moral choices, and they fell (in Calvin's words) by their own evil intention.

Although sin is no part of creation, neither is it something that sneaked in and caught God by surprise. Sin was not something that thwarted the plan of God; rather, it was part of God's plan from the beginning. He had a *good* purpose in allowing it, but still He was neither the instigator nor the author of His creatures' evil deeds. Rather, He made them moral agents and gave them freedom to act, and they fell into sin by their own choice. (We will examine how that came to pass in chapter 10.)

In other words, God is sovereign over all, and evil was in no sense a breach of His absolute sovereignty. But He did not take the same active role in the devising of evil that He did in the creation of good. Fallen creatures themselves bear full responsibility for their sin. God's creation at its completion was impeccably flawless. Evil spoiled its perfect goodness *after* God had finished creating.

God's sovereign purpose from the beginning was to overrule His creatures' evil deeds and destroy evil forever, restoring His creation to a glory that surpasses even the glory and perfection of Eden.

Consider this: The glory of God's *original* creative work is diminished by any theory that stretches creation out over long ages of time, because the evolutionary process would mean that God spent ages tinkering with creation before He got it right. In other words, evolution at any stage of the creative process overturns the biblical assertion that everything God created was "very good." Instead, it suggests that He created things in an unfinished state and then brought them to completion through natural processes. That is not what Scripture teaches.

You simply will not find evolution anywhere in Genesis. It isn't there. The whole of the biblical account, from the first day through the seventh, underscores the truth of an immediate, direct creation, fully accomplished and completed to perfection in a week. Any other interpretation simply doesn't do justice to the plain language of Scripture. And until Adam sinned, all creation remained a perfect paradise. How that paradise was lost is the focus of Genesis 3.

Now the serpent was more cunning than any beast of the field which the Lord God had made. And he said to the woman, "Has God indeed said, 'You shall not eat of every tree of the garden'?" And the woman said to the serpent, "We may eat the fruit of the trees of the garden; but of the fruit of the tree which is in the midst of the garden, God has said, 'You shall not eat it, nor shall you touch it, lest you die.'" Then the serpent said to the woman, "You will not surely die. For God knows that in the day you eat of it your eyes will be opened, and you will be like God, knowing good and evil." So when the woman saw that the tree was good for food, that it was pleasant to the eyes, and a tree desirable to make one wise, she took of its fruit and ate. She also gave to her husband with her, and he ate. Then the eyes of both of them were opened, and they knew that they were naked; and they sewed fig leaves together and made themselves coverings. And they heard the sound of the Lord God walking in the garden in the cool of the day, and Adam and his wife hid themselves from the presence of the Lord God among the trees of the garden. Then the Lord God called to Adam and said to him, "Where are you?" So he said, I heard your voice in the garden, and I was afraid because I was naked; and I hid myself." And He said, "Who told you that you were naked? Have you eaten from the tree of which I commanded that you should not eat?" Then the man said, "The woman whom You gave to be with me, she gave me of the tree, and I ate." And the Lord God said to the woman, "What is this you have done?" The woman said, "The serpent deceived me, and I ate." So the Lord God said to the serpent: "Because you have done this, You are cursed more than all cattle, and more than every beast of the field; on your belly you shall go, and you shall eat dust all the days of your life. And I will put enmity between you and the woman, and between your seed and her Seed; He shall bruise your head, and you shall bruise His heel." To the woman he said: "I will greatly multiply your sorrow and your conception; in pain you shall bring forth children; your desire shall be for your husband, and he shall rule over you." Then to

Adam He said, "Because you have heeded the voice of your wife, and have eaten from the tree of which I commanded you, saying, 'You shall not eat of it': Cursed is the ground for your sake; in toil you shall eat of it all the days of your life. Both thorns and thistles it shall bring forth for you, and you shall eat the herb of the field. In the sweat of your face you shall eat bread till you return to the ground, for out of it you were taken; for dust you are and to dust you shall return." And Adam called his wife's name Eve, because she was the mother of all living. Also for Adam and his wife the Lord God made tunics of skin, and clothed them. Then the Lord God said, "Behold, the man has become like one of Us, to know good and evil. And now, lest he put out his hand and take also of the tree of life, and eat, and live forever"—therefore the Lord God sent him out of the Garden of Eden to till the ground from which he was taken. So He drove out the man; and He placed cherubim at the east of the garden of Eden, and a flaming sword which turned every way, to guard the way to the tree of life.

—*Genesis 3:1–24*

10
PARADISE LOST

Genesis 3:1–24

GENESIS 3 is one of the most vitally important chapters in all the Bible. It is the foundation of everything that comes after it. Without it, little else in Scripture or in life itself would make sense. Genesis 3 explains the condition of the universe and the state of humanity. It explains why the world has so many problems. It explains the human dilemma. It explains why we need a Savior. And it explains what God is doing in history.

In other words, the truth revealed in Genesis 3 is the necessary foundation for a true and accurate world-view. Every world-view that lacks this foundation is utterly and hopelessly wrong.

When God completed His perfect creation, there was no disorder, no chaos, no conflict, no struggle, no pain, no discord, no deterioration, and no death. Yet our lives today are filled with all those things all the time. Frankly, we find it hard to imagine what a perfect world would have been like. Genesis 3 explains how we got from that paradise of unimaginable perfection to where we are today.

Evolution offers no explanation for the human dilemma, much less any solution to it. Why is human existence fraught with so many moral and spiritual problems? Evolution will never be able to answer that question. In fact, pure naturalistic evolution cannot account for *anything* that is moral or spiritual.

Yet we are clearly moral and spiritual creatures, and we all know this. The concepts of good and evil are innate in the human psyche. (Even the most atheistic evolutionists have consciences.) We know from bitter experience that we cannot keep ourselves from evil. We find the pull of sin irresistible. We *cannot* do everything we know we ought to do. Worse, we cannot reform ourselves. Evolution offers no explanation for this dilemma and no hope for a solution.

Instead, the doctrine of evolution (if followed consistently) ends with a denial of the reality of evil. If naturalistic evolution is correct and there is no God, neither can there be any inviolable moral principles that govern the universe. And therefore there is no moral accountability of any kind. In fact, if evolution is true, things are the way they are by sheer chance, for no transcendent reason. Nothing under such a system could ever have any real moral significance. The very notions of good and evil would be meaningless concepts. There would be no reason to condemn a Hitler or applaud a good Samaritan.

Who wired us to distinguish between good and evil? Where did the human conscience come from? And why is human nature universally drawn to evil? Evolutionists are clueless.

Scripture says we were made in the image of God but are fallen creatures, born with an inclination to sin. We inherited our sinfulness from Adam. When he sinned, he plunged the whole race into a helplessly fallen state of bondage to evil. That, in a nutshell, is the doctrine known as "original sin."

The biblical description of humanity's fall into sin refutes the fundamental idea of evolution. Instead of teaching that man began at the bottom of the moral ladder and slowly rose higher by social and psychological evolution, Genesis 3 teaches us the opposite. Man began at the pinnacle of the created order and because of Adam's sin, the history of humanity is the story of a disgraceful moral and spiritual decline (cf. Romans 1:21–32). Humanity today is *worse* than ever before (2 Timothy 3:13).

Who can deny that evil is pervasive in this world? Evidence of it is all around us. And in particular, the universal moral depravity of human beings is abundantly clear. G. K. Chesterton wryly referred to the doctrine of original sin as "the only part of Christian theology which can really be proved." He goaded modernist theologians who "in their almost too fastidious spirituality, admit divine sinlessness, which they cannot see even in their dreams. But they essentially deny human sin, which they can see in the street."[1]

Evidence of the sinfulness of our race is all around us. It is published in the daily newspapers, it is shown to us on the evening news, and it is writ large in human history. No one in all our acquaintance is sin-free. Most of all, if we're honest with ourselves, some of the most persuasive proofs of our hopeless depravity are presented to us by our own consciences.

How did we get in this state? Genesis 3 answers that question with clarity and simplicity. Our first ancestor, Adam, deliberately disobeyed God. Somehow his sin defiled the whole race, and now every one of his natural offspring has inherited a love for sin and a contempt for true righteousness. And this manifests itself in our behavior.

According to Romans 5:12 and 1 Corinthians 15:22, when Adam sinned, he brought death and judgment not only upon himself, but upon the whole human race. Every one of us inherits sin and guilt from Adam. And that is what is wrong with us. That is why we have a vile, rebellious, corrupt, destructive nature—a sinful heart that corrupts all our thoughts, emotions, and will. "Because the carnal mind is enmity against God; for it is not subject to the law of God, nor indeed can be. So then, those who are in the flesh cannot please God" (Romans 8:7–8).

That inability to love, obey, or please God is the very essence of human depravity. And the only solution to that predicament is the re-creative work of God (2 Corinthians 5:17). That is why Jesus told Nicodemus, "You must be born again" (John 3:7). "Unless one is born again, he cannot see the kingdom of God" (v. 3). This is what salvation is all about: God miraculously changes the nature of those whom He redeems, so that they are drawn to the very same righteousness they formerly hated. This was the central promise of the New Covenant:

> I will sprinkle clean water on you, and you shall be clean; I will cleanse you from all your filthiness and from all your idols. I will give you a new heart and put a new spirit within you; I will take the heart of stone out of your flesh and give you a heart of flesh. I will put My Spirit within you and cause you to walk in My statutes, and you will keep My judgments and do them. (Ezekiel 36:25–27)

So, nothing we can do for ourselves will free us from the bondage of sin. Adam's transgression had a catastrophic effect, not only on him and his environment, but also on his progeny, including you and me. And we cannot make sense of our moral plight until we come to grips with where it all began.

Romans 8:20–22 says, "The creation was subjected to futility, not willingly, but because of Him who subjected it in hope; because the creation itself also will be delivered from the bondage of corruption into the glorious liberty of the children of God. For we know that the whole creation groans and labors with birth pangs together until now." In other words, because of sin, no part of creation now exists as God originally made it. It "was subjected to futility," meaning that it was rendered unable to achieve the purpose for which it was originally designed. It was spoiled—defiled by sin, and thus subject to God's curse instead of His blessing. It was enslaved to corruption and placed in bondage to the debasing effects of sin—including decay, degradation, and death. All creation now "groans and labors with birth pangs"—picturesque language depicting the suffering and pain caused by sin's defilement. All these things, according to Scripture, are the effects of Adam's disobedience.

This clearly argues against evolution. If God used evolutionary processes or "natural selection" to create the world in the first place, then death, decay, mutation, and corruption were part of creation from the beginning. If death and natural selection were part of the means God used to create the world, then nothing was actually created perfect; everything had defects built in. But Scripture plainly attributes all such things to Adam's sin. They are the consequences of the curse that came after that first act of disobedience.

Deliverance from this state will not come from any process of evolution, either. In fact, the whole of creation—including the human race—is now subject to a kind of *devolution,* which no amount of education, enlightenment, environmentalism, psychology, civilization, or technology will ever be able to reverse. What is needed is *redemption* (Romans 8:23).

The remainder of Genesis is filled with evidence of humanity's downward spiral into utter moral degradation. Genesis 3 is the turning point. Before that, God looked at creation and pronounced everything "very good" (1:31). But after Genesis 3, all human history has been colored by that which is very *bad.* (The only exceptions are examples of God's redemptive work; they are not examples of human nobility.)

Genesis 4 records the first murder, a case of fratricide. Genesis 4:19 contains the first mention of polygamy. Verse 23 tells of another act of murder. And from there the human race declines so grievously that by Genesis 6:5, "The Lord saw that the wickedness of man was great in the earth, and that every intent of the thoughts of his heart was only evil continually." So God destroyed the entire race, except for one family.

Genesis also records the beginnings of such evils as homosexuality (19:1–5), incest (19:30–38), idolatry (31:30–35), rape (34:1–2), mass murder (34:25–29), harlotry (38:14–19), and numerous other forms of wickedness.

All of this stemmed from Adam's one act of disobedience (Romans 5:19). Adam's sin poisoned not only his offspring, but also the rest of creation. How did this evil come about? Genesis 3:1–7 gives a clear answer:

> Now the serpent was more cunning than any beast of the field which the Lord God had made. And he said to the woman, "Has God indeed said, 'You shall not eat of every tree of the garden'?" And the woman said to the serpent, "We may eat the fruit of the trees of the garden; but of the fruit of the tree which is in the midst of the garden, God has said, 'You shall not eat it, nor shall you touch it, lest you die.'" Then the serpent said to the woman, "You will not surely die. For God knows that in the day you eat of it your eyes will be opened, and you will be like God, knowing good and evil." So when the woman saw that the tree was good for food, that it was pleasant to the eyes, and a tree desirable to make one wise, she took of its fruit and ate. She also gave to her husband with her, and he ate. Then the eyes of both of them were opened, and they knew that they were naked; and they sewed fig leaves together and made themselves coverings.

This is not a fable or a myth. It is presented as history, and it is treated as history throughout the remainder of Scripture (cf. Romans 5:12–19; 1 Timothy 2:13–14; 2 Corinthians 11:3; Revelation 12:9; 20:2).

THE SOLICITOR

Many would point to the talking serpent as evidence that this account is mythical. Yet Jesus Himself alluded to this account as real and historical when He referred to the devil as a murderer and a liar and the father of lying (John 8:44).

According to Genesis 3:1, "The serpent was more cunning than any beast of the field which the Lord God had made." We are not to think God created reptiles with the ability to talk and reason. The "cunning" this particular serpent displayed is not a characteristic of serpents in general. What is described here is something more than a mere animal; he is a being who knew God, a personality who spoke with great intelligence and shrewdness. He was a being who was opposed to God. He was deceptive, hostile, and bent on destroying the moral innocence of the first couple.

We learn by comparing Scripture with Scripture that this serpent was really Satan, masquerading as an animal (cf. Revelation 12:9; 2 Corinthians 11:3). Satan, master of disguises, who even has the power to transform himself into an angel of light (2 Corinthians 11:14), had apparently either taken the physical form of a serpent or somehow possessed the body of one of the creatures in the garden.

The name *Satan* is a transliteration of the Hebrew word for "adversary." In its Old Testament occurrences, the word is often used with a definite article, suggesting that it was not originally a proper name but a descriptive expression ("the adversary"). The technical meaning of the Hebrew term conveys a legal nuance that speaks of one's adversary—the one who brings an accusation—in a legal context. And of course, this is perfectly descriptive of Satan's role. He is the accuser of the brethren (Revelation 12:10). In the Old Testament Book of Job we see him working behind the scenes to discredit and ruin Job. And in the New Testament, he seeks power over Peter, so that he can sift him like wheat at the hour of Peter's greatest vulnerability (Luke 22:31). So his behavior and his activity are always consistent with what we see in Genesis 3.

Where did Satan himself come from, and how are we to understand his character and work, in light of the fact that God had declared all His creation good?

God did not make Satan evil. As we saw at the end of the previous chapter, everything God made was good, and evil did not exist in His creation. In Genesis 1:31, God emphatically declared everything He had made "very good." Satan appears suddenly and unexpectedly in Genesis 3:1. That means Satan's fall must have occurred sometime between the end of creation (marked by that glorious day of rest on day seven) and the events described in Genesis 3—which appear to have come very soon after the creation of Adam and Eve, before they had conceived any offspring.

Genesis, maintaining an earthly perspective on the creation story, is silent about the fall of Satan, which occurred in heaven. From elsewhere in Scripture, however, we learn that Satan was an angel who fell when he was lifted up with pride. Perhaps the clearest account of Satan's rebellion is given in Ezekiel 28:11–19:

> The word of the Lord came to me, saying, "Son of man, take up a lamentation for the king of Tyre, and say to him, 'Thus says the Lord God: "You were the seal of perfection, full of wisdom and perfect in beauty. You were in Eden, the garden of God; every precious stone was your covering: the sardius, topaz, and diamond, beryl, onyx, and jasper, sapphire, turquoise, and emerald with gold. The workmanship of your timbrels and pipes was prepared for you on the day you were created. You were the anointed cherub who covers; I established you; you were on the holy mountain of God; you walked back and forth in the midst of fiery stones. You were perfect in your ways from the day you were created, till iniquity was found in you. By the abundance of your trading you became filled with violence within, and you sinned; therefore I cast you as a profane thing out of the mountain of God; and I destroyed you, O covering cherub, from the midst of the fiery stones. Your heart was lifted up because of your beauty; you corrupted your wisdom for the sake of your splendor; I cast you to the ground, I laid you before kings, that they might gaze at you. You defiled your sanctuaries by the multitude of your iniquities, by the iniquity of your trading; therefore I brought fire from your midst; it devoured you, and I turned you to ashes upon the earth in the sight of all who saw you. All who knew you among the peoples are astonished at you; you have become a horror, and shall be no more forever."'"

Although this is addressed as a prophetic word against the king of Tyre, the context makes clear that its message reached beyond that earthly king to the supernatural source of his wickedness, pride, and corrupted authority. This was a prophetic message from God to Satan.

The text clearly identifies the object of those words of condemnation by saying "You were in Eden, the garden of God" (v. 13). The words were addressed to no mere man, but to an angelic being, "the anointed cherub who covers" (v. 14). He was the very epitome of created perfection, "the seal of perfection, full of wisdom and perfect in beauty" (v. 12). The Lord says to him, "You were perfect in your ways from the day you were created, till iniquity was found in you." (v. 15). This can be none other than the fallen creature who masqueraded as a serpent in Eden. It is that fallen angelic creature known to us as Satan.

The passage in Ezekiel clearly states that this creature was once an angel, one of the cherubim whose role was heavenly worship. That explains the reference in verse 13 to "the workmanship of your timbrels and pipes . . . prepared for you on the day you were created." In fact, he seems to have been the highest-ranking cherub ("the anointed cherub who covers"), a creature whose beauty and majesty were unsurpassed. He may have been the highest of all archangels.

How sin arose in him is not explained, but *where* that sin originated is clear: "iniquity was found *in you*" (v. 15, emphasis added). It was not a defect in the way he was made ("You were perfect in your ways from the day you were created"). The evil did not come from his Maker; and yet it did not arise from outside the creature; it was found *in* him. And as a result, the Lord says, "You became filled with violence within, and you sinned" (v. 16).

How could this creature have been unsatisfied with his perfection? What could have provoked him to rebel against his Creator? The text offers no explanation, except to underscore the truth that the fault arose within the creature himself and in no sense was the result of any imperfection in the way he was created. Nor was his fallenness a state that was imposed on him against his will. It was a choice he made for himself.

Isaiah 14 sheds even more light on Satan's fall. Like the passage in Ezekiel, it is a prophetic condemnation addressed to an earthly king, the king of Babylon (v. 4). But like the Ezekiel passage, it contains expressions that seem to look beyond any earthly ruler and address Satan himself. Verses 12–15 say,

> How you are fallen from heaven, O Lucifer, son of the morning! How you are cut down to the ground, you who weakened the nations! For you have said in your heart: "I will ascend into heaven, I will exalt my throne above the stars of God; I will also sit on the mount of the congregation

on the farthest sides of the north; I will ascend above the heights of the clouds, I will be like the Most High." Yet you shall be brought down to Sheol, to the lowest depths of the Pit.

Lucifer means "shining one," a fitting name for the anointed cherub who covers. And the sin for which he is condemned is a sin that arose from his own heart. It is the sin of pride. He wanted to exalt his throne above all others and "be like the Most High" (v. 14). He literally intended to usurp the throne of God. All of that supports the notion that the creature in view here is Satan. We know from 1 Timothy 3:6, for example, that this very attitude of pride was the reason for Satan's downfall and condemnation.

And the moment he was lifted up with pride, he fell. Jesus said, "I saw Satan fall like lightning from heaven" (Luke 10:18). As quickly as he sought to go up, he went down. Though his desire was to be like God, he instantly became as much *unlike* God as possible.

He did not fall alone. According to Revelation 12:4, a third of the angels in heaven went with him. They evidently became demons, ministers of Satan, and deceivers like him (2 Corinthians 11:15–16). According to Matthew 25:41, everlasting fire is prepared for them. Their ultimate doom is as certain as the unchanging faithfulness of God.

Why did God not consign them all to the eternal flames the moment they fell? Scripture does not explicitly answer that question, but it is clear that Satan and the demons have been given opportunity to exploit every avenue of their power until God destroys them at the end of human history. Despite their evil influence and the utter incorrigibility of their wickedness, they somehow fit into God's plan to show grace and mercy and provide salvation for fallen humans. The time for their destruction is set (Matthew 8:29). Their doom is absolutely certain, but until God's purposes are fulfilled, they have a measure of freedom to advance their evil agenda—perhaps to prove in the end that there is no conceivable evil that God cannot triumph over.

Remember that salvation for the human race was planned and promised before Satan ever fell—before the foundation of the world (Ephesians 1:4; Titus 1:1–2; 2 Timothy 1:9; Revelation 13:8). So even Satan's fall and his deception in Eden fit into the eternal plan of God.

In other words, God *allowed* Satan to confront Eve. This encounter in the garden was not an unexpected event that somehow derailed the plan of God. God had planned for it from the beginning.

THE STRATEGY

Satan's strategy in tempting Eve is the same strategy he always uses. He is a liar and the father of lying (John 8:44). But he comes disguised as one who brings the truth—"an angel of light" (2 Corinthians 11:14).

Only in lying is Satan consistent. Everything from him is deceptive. "There is no truth in him. When he speaks a lie, he speaks from his own resources" (John 8:44). But here he begins with what sounds like a very innocent question from an interested observer concerned about Eve's well-being. "Has God indeed said, 'You shall not eat of every tree of the garden'?" (Genesis 3:1).

"Has God indeed said . . . ?" That is the first question in Scripture. Before this, there were only answers; no dilemmas. But his question was wickedly designed to start Eve on the path of doubting and distrusting what God had said. That sort of doubt is the very essence of all sin. The gist of *all* temptation is to cast doubt on God's Word and to subject it to human judgment. That is what the serpent was doing here.

In fact, notice how Satan cunningly twisted and misrepresented the Word of God. God had said, "Of every tree of the garden you may freely eat; but of the tree of the knowledge of good and evil you shall not eat" (Genesis 2:16–17). God's emphasis had been on their perfect freedom to eat from all the trees except one. Satan's question turned the emphasis around and stressed the negative, implying that God was fencing them in with restrictions. Notice also how starkly the serpent's words contrast with God's actual command. God had said, "Of every tree of the garden *you may freely eat*" (emphasis added). The emphasis was on their freedom to eat. Satan's version negated the whole point: *"You shall not eat* of every tree of the garden" (emphasis added). In this way he focused her attention on the prohibition and set her up for the main assault on God's Word.

Satan's motive was the utter destruction of the first couple, even though he was pretending to have their best interests at heart. That's why Jesus said, "He was a murderer from the beginning" (John 8:44). The serpent had deliberately confronted Eve when she was isolated from Adam and most vulnerable. He aimed his initial attack at her alone ("the weaker vessel"—1 Peter 3:7). Clearly, his aim was to deceive her by his craftiness (2 Corinthians 11:3) while she was unprotected by Adam.

If Eve was surprised to hear a serpent speak, Scripture does not say so. After all, Eden was new and undoubtedly filled with many wonders, and the first couple were still just discovering all the marvels of creation. In that paradise, Eve had never known fear or encountered danger of any kind. So she conversed with the serpent as if this were nothing extraordinary. She had no reason to be suspicious. She herself was innocent, having never before encountered "the wiles of the devil" (Ephesians 6:11).

Satan's strategy was to portray God as narrow, strict, uncharitable, and too restrictive—as if He wanted to limit human freedom and deprive Adam and Eve of enjoyment and pleasure. He was implying that evil and untruthfulness were part of God's character. He was hinting to Eve that God might be cruel and uncaring.

Moreover, the reptile Satan slyly insinuates that *he* is more devoted to Eve's well-being than God is. He implies that he is for freedom while God is restrictive. The fact that God gave Adam and Eve *everything* else to eat is set aside as negligible. Thus he casts suspicion on God's goodness.

Eve was unaware of Satan's strategies, so she replies naively—defending God to some degree: "We may eat the fruit of the trees of the garden" (Genesis 3:2). Evidently she did not know that this was God's supernatural foe. Scripture says she was "deceived" (2 Corinthians 11:3; 1 Timothy 2:14). Satan beguiled her by taking advantage of her innocence.

But even though she did not know her enemy, she should have been able to thwart this attack. She had sufficient advantage to do so. She knew God. She knew God's character as good—and only good. She had experienced nothing but abundant blessing and unrestrained generosity from His hand. She was surrounded by all of creation, which abundantly displayed God's good will. She also had a clear, unambiguous command from God. And even that command not to eat of one tree was a gracious restriction for her own good.

Eve should have been suspicious of the talking reptile. She should have found out more about her tempter before she yielded to his enticements. Above all, she should have made a strong and emphatic disavowal of the suspicion that God had withheld some goodness from her and her husband.

Instead, her reply was only a partial refutation of the reptile's allegations. She said, "We may eat the fruit of the trees of the garden; but of the fruit of the tree which is in the midst of the garden, God has said, 'You shall not eat it, nor shall you touch it, lest you die'" (vv. 2–3).

Let's analyze her response. Notice first that she omitted the word *all* when she said, "We may eat the fruit of the trees of the garden"—suggesting that she was already beginning to lose sight of the vast goodness of God. Then she moved further, recounting the restriction God had imposed on them, and not defending His goodness. And worst of all, she added something to the words of the command, claiming God had said, "nor shall you touch it, lest you die." Apparently beginning to feel the restriction was harsh, she added to the harshness of it.

Her heart had already set its course. She was not defending God and His goodness. She was not affirming His glorious majesty and holy perfection. She ignored the fact that God's desire was only for her good. She did not take offense at the serpent's insult against God's character. And so she played right into his hands. She was already starting to believe Satan rather than God.

The fall was inevitable from the instant Eve began to doubt. The course for her subsequent action was set by that wavering in her heart. What followed was merely the evidence that wickedness had entered her heart already.

At this point, Satan knew he had succeeded and he pushed for total victory. Immediately, he suggests that he knows more than God. His next statement is an assertion that flatly contradicts the Word of God and impugns the motives of God: "You will not surely die. For God knows that in the day you eat of it your eyes will be opened, and you will be like God, knowing good and evil" (vv. 4–5). This bold denial stated definitely what Satan had merely implied before. Now he openly slanders not only the goodness of God, but also God's truthfulness.

Suspicion had already found root in Eve's mind. God's majesty had been insulted; His goodness had been maligned; His trustworthiness had been defamed. And she had not responded in faith. So Satan moved in for the kill.

"God is a liar," he says. "He has deceived you, taken your freedom, and restricted your joy." Satan's lie is still the same today: "You can be free. Do whatever you want. It is your life. There are no divine laws; no absolute authority; and above all, no judgment. You will not surely die."

At this point, Eve was faced with a clear choice. She could either believe God or believe the devil. That is the same choice that has confronted humanity ever since. Who is telling the truth? God or Satan? Does God want to place undue restrictions on you? Does He want to cramp your freedom and minimize your joy? If God is like that, Satan implies, He doesn't love you. He is not to be trusted.

The lie is the same today. God's authority is often portrayed as too restrictive, destructive of human freedom, and detrimental to our well-being. In the words of E. J. Young:

> Modern psychology, we can hear the tempter saying, has brought to light the deep recesses of the human soul. That soul is a very tender thing, and to restrain and bind it by the imposition of categorical law is to harm it. The soul should be free to develop and to express itself, and this it can do only through freedom and love. Narrowness and restriction, such as absolute authority impose, must be abandoned, if there is to be any development of the personality. Would you be warped in your personality? If so, then continue submitting to God and His commandments.[2]

Satan was suggesting to Eve that the only reason God could be so restrictive, forbidding them to eat from that tree, was because there was a flaw in His character. His love must be defective. He wanted to keep them from being all they could be, lest they rival His greatness.

And thus what Satan pretended to offer them was precisely what he himself tried to obtain but could not: "you will be like God" (v. 5).

Satan knew from personal experience that God tolerates no rivals. God said through Isaiah, "I am the Lord, that is My name; and My glory I will not give to another, nor My praise to carved images" (Isaiah 42:8). God yields His rightful place to no one. That is what makes Him God. His glory outshines the glory of all others. He has no equals and therefore all who pretend equality with Him or seek recognition as His equal, He must reject. That is because He is holy, not because He is selfish.

Satan, however, implied that this was some kind of petty jealousy on God's part. As if God must keep Adam and Eve from becoming all they could be lest they become a threat to the Almighty. The suggestion is absurd, but for Eve it was an intoxicating thought. Perhaps she thought it a noble aspiration to be like God. She may have convinced herself it was an honorable desire.

The reptile's false promise ("you will be like God") is the seed of all false religion. Numerous cults, ranging from Buddhism to Mormonism, are based on the same lie. It is a twisting of the truth. God wants us to be like Him, in the sense that we share His communicable attributes—holiness, love, mercy, truthfulness, and other expressions of His righteousness. But what Satan tried to do—and what he tempted Eve to try doing—was to intrude into a realm that belongs to God alone and usurp His power, His sovereignty, and His right to be worshiped. And those things are forbidden to any creature.

Notice how *Satan* characterized equality with God: "you will be like God, knowing good and evil" (v. 5). It was a dangerous half-truth. If they ate the fruit, they would indeed know evil, but not as God knows it. They would know it experientially. What Satan held out to them as the highroad to fulfillment and truth was in reality a back alley to destruction. "There is a way that seems right to a man, but its end is the way of death" (Proverbs 14:12).

THE SEDUCTION

James 1:13–15 says, "God cannot be tempted by evil, nor does He Himself tempt anyone. But each one is tempted when he is drawn away by his own desires and enticed. Then, when desire has conceived, it gives birth to sin; and sin, when it is full-grown, brings forth death." That process was already underway in Eve.

Sin in the mind goes to work in the emotions. That incites the will, which yields the act.

Genesis 3:6 says, "When the woman saw that the tree was good for food, that it was pleasant to the eyes, and a tree desirable to make one wise, she took of its fruit and ate. She also gave to her husband with her, and he ate." Self-fulfillment has become Eve's goal, and for the first time ever, her own self-interest and self-satisfaction are what drive her. *Sin has already been conceived in her heart.* Now, that sin was beginning to work in her to bring about the evil act. But she was guilty already, for she had sinned in her heart. Jesus illustrated this principle when he said, "Whoever looks at a woman to lust for her has already committed adultery with her in his heart" (Matthew 5:28).

Eve saw three features of the forbidden fruit that seduced her. First, "the tree was good for food." We have no idea what kind of fruit it was. It is often portrayed as an apple, but the text does not say it was an apple. The specific variety of fruit is not important. What is important is that Eve was seduced by her *physical appetite*. This was not a legitimate hunger. There was plenty of food in the garden if Eve had been hungry. It was an illicit appetite. It was a fleshly lust provoked by a selfish discontent and a distrust in God—as if He were keeping something good from her.

Second, she saw "that it was pleasant to the eyes." This seduction appealed to her *emotional appetite*. The fruit excited her sense of beauty and other passions. Not that there wasn't plenty of other attractive fruit in the garden. There was a rich variety of colors, shapes, and sizes, and it all looked good. But Eve was focused on *this* fruit, because Satan had planted the idea in her mind that it represented something good that God was keeping from her. As covetousness grew in her heart, the forbidden fruit looked better and better.

Third, she saw "a tree desirable to make one wise." This was an appeal to her *intellectual appetite*. Incipient pride caused her to fancy the "wisdom" that would come with knowing good and evil. She desired that knowledge and was tempted by the false promise that it would make her like God.

Thus she was seduced by "the lust of the flesh, the lust of the eyes, and the pride of life"—everything evil in this world (1 John 2:16–17). Temptation always comes in one or more of these three categories. When Satan tempted Christ, he urged Him to turn stones to bread (Matthew 4:3). That was an appeal to the lust of the flesh. The devil also showed Him all the kingdoms of the world and their glory, promising Him authority over them (vv. 8–9). That was an appeal to the lust of the eyes. And he set Him on the pinnacle of the temple (v. 5), appealing to the pride of life. That's why Hebrews 4:15 says, "[He] was in all points tempted as we are, yet without sin."

THE SIN

Ultimately, predictably, the doubt and covetousness in Eve's head gave way to evil behavior. When sin penetrates the mind, emotions, and will, it will *always* be manifest in sinful actions.

Genesis 3:6 says, "she took of its fruit and ate." It was a simple act with a massive impact. Emboldened by her own misdeed—perhaps relieved by the fact that she had not been instantly struck dead, "She also gave to her husband with her, and he ate."

Adam appears, from where we are not told, and discovering that his wife had already disobeyed the Lord's command, he partook with her. There is no record of how Adam was enticed to do this. We could surmise that Eve related the words of the serpent to him. She may have also enticed him with a recounting of how pleasurable the forbidden fruit was. (Scripture acknowledges that there is pleasure in sin for a season—Hebrews 11:25). In any case, Adam doesn't appear to have needed much convincing. It is ironic that the one whom God had given to Adam to be his *helper* became the instrument of disaster and death to him.

But Adam's guilt was greater, not less, than Eve's. And throughout Scripture, Adam is the one who is indicted for the fall (cf. Romans 5:12–19; 1 Corinthians 15:22). Eve was immensely guilty, of course. But she was deceived; Adam disobeyed deliberately (1 Timothy 2:14). As the representative head of the human race, he bore the ultimate responsibility for the fall, and his actions were determinative for all his offspring.

How was Adam's guilt and the corruption caused by his sin passed to his progeny? Scripture does not expressly say. But it is enough for us to know that it happened. Once Adam ate the fruit, the principle of decay and death began to rule creation. And the whole human race was plunged into evil. God Himself would have to become a man and die in order to undo it.

Adam and Eve could never have known the impact of their sin. Perhaps Satan had some grasp of it, and he reveled in it. Certainly God knew, and yet He allowed it so that He could display His glory in destroying evil.

THE SHAME

Now that Adam and Eve knew evil by personal experience, their minds were open to a whole new way of thinking. They were susceptible to evil thoughts. They were drawn by evil desires. They no longer desired fellowship with God as they had before. And above all, they were conscious of their own guilt.

The serpent had promised them enlightenment—"Your eyes will be opened" (Genesis 3:5). What they actually received was a hideously twisted caricature of enlightenment. It was eye-opening only in a negative sense. It opened their eyes to the meaning of guilt, but it made them want to hide their eyes in shame. And in reality, it brought them into a state of spiritual blindness from which they could never recover without a divinely wrought miracle of regeneration.

Their knowledge of evil was real, too—but it was nothing like God's. A healthy oncologist "knows" cancer, and with an expertise and objectivity that surpasses his patients' experiential knowledge. But the person who is dying of cancer also "knows" cancer in an intimate way—but in a way that is also destructive. Adam and Eve now had a knowledge of evil that was like the terminal cancer patient's knowledge of carcinoma. It was not the kind of enlightenment Satan had led Eve to believe she would obtain. She and Adam did *not* become like God, but the opposite.

Sin instantly destroyed their innocence. They felt it strongly. They suddenly were self-conscious about their guilt. They felt exposed. This manifests itself in shame about their nakedness. Even the holy gift of their physical relationship was polluted with a sense of shame. Gone was the purity of it. Now present were wicked and impure thoughts they had never known before.

And in that state of self-conscious shame, "They sewed fig leaves together and made themselves coverings" (v. 7). This was a noble effort to cover their sin and mask their shame. Ever since then, clothing has been a universal expression of human modesty. It is fitting and right that fallen man should want to cover his shame. Naturists and anthropologists are wrong when they try to portray public nudity as a return to innocence and nobility. Nudity does not recover fallen man's innocence; it only displays a denial of the shame we ought to feel. It is appropriate that those bearing the guilt of sin should cover themselves. And God Himself demonstrated this when He killed animals to use their skins as a covering for the fallen couple (vs. 21).

In fact, this was a graphic object lesson showing that *only* God can provide a suitable covering for sin, and the shedding of blood is a necessary part of the process (Hebrews 9:22).

Like Lucifer, Adam and Eve fell so far that now there was nothing good in them (cf. Genesis 6:5; Job 15:14–16; Ephesians 2:1–3; Romans 7:18; 8:7–8). Nothing in life or in the world would ever be the same. God Himself cursed the earth, so that thorns now grew naturally, and fruit trees had to be cultivated. A multitude of woes, including increased pain in childbearing, sorrow, toil, distress, disease, and death would now plague all of creation. An avalanche of sin was loosed and could never stop.

EPILOGUE: BLESSINGS FROM THE CURSE

Genesis 3:8–21

IT WOULD BE EASY to see Adam's fall as a bitterly disappointing ending for the creation story. The perfection of God's glorious creation is destroyed. Humanity, created in God's image, is fallen. Death and decay now infect all of life. At the end of Genesis 3, Adam and Eve are driven out of paradise and sent forth into a hostile, sin-cursed world.

But Genesis 3 isn't merely a sad ending to the creation story; it is also the glorious beginning of the redemptive saga that fills the rest of Scripture. Genesis 3 contains the first promise of a Deliverer, and the remainder of the Bible is devoted to telling the story of how God, by that Deliverer, ultimately redeems fallen humanity and the rest of creation from the cursed state into which Adam's sin had plunged everything. The chronicle of redemption therefore becomes the true closing chapter of the creation account—giving it a more glorious and uplifting finale than any merely human mind could ever have invented.

In fact, the story of God's New Creation is more glorious than all the combined glories of the original creation. It is a triumphant story of divine grace—God's free and unmerited mercy and kindness to sinners who deserve nothing but condemnation.

God had no obligation to redeem Adam or any of his offspring. It is significant that when Satan led the rebellion of angels, those who sinned were summarily cast out of heaven and immediately condemned to eternal punishment. No provision was made for their redemption. No appeal for repentance was ever issued to them. No redeemer was sent to save them. They were instantly and irremediably sentenced to hell.

God could have done that with humanity, and no one could ever have faulted His justice. He owes no one mercy. In fact, justice calls for the punishment of sinners, not for their redemption.

But Scripture teaches that God is "ready to pardon, gracious and merciful, slow to anger, [and] abundant in kindness" (Nehemiah 9:17). And in His grace, He had planned before the foundation of the world to redeem an innumerable host of humanity from their own sin (Ephesians 1:4–5; 2 Timothy 1:9–10). The outworking of that plan begins in Genesis 3, when God confronted Adam for the first time after Adam sinned.

From the moment of their sin, Adam and Eve were conscious that something was now seriously wrong. They were feeling guilt and shame. That's why they tried so desperately to cover their nakedness by sewing makeshift clothing out of fig leaves. Scripture also adds, "They heard the sound of the Lord God walking in the garden in the cool of the day, and Adam and his wife hid themselves from the presence of the Lord God among the trees of the garden" (Genesis 3:8). They now feared the very thing they had previously delighted in the most: "the presence of the Lord." Sinners always despise His presence, because they know they cannot stand in the face of such holiness.

But while they were hiding, God was already seeking them, with a merciful intent. "The Lord God called to Adam and said to him, 'Where are you?'" (v. 9). It was not that God did not know where they were. There is nothing He does not know. He certainly knows what is in the heart of man. "For He knows the secrets of the heart" (Psalm 44:21). "There is no creature hidden from His sight, but all things are naked and open to the eyes of Him to whom we must give account" (Hebrews 4:13).

The Lord's question to Adam was therefore not designed to elicit information; it was designed to probe the conscience of Adam for Adam's sake—to elicit a confession.

"So [Adam] said, 'I heard Your voice in the garden, and I was afraid because I was naked; and I hid myself.'" It is significant that by Adam's own admission, the reason for his fear lay in himself, not in God. Notice that God came to the garden as He had always come before—not with a burning fury, but gently, with kindness, walking in the cool of the day, eager to share His goodness with His creatures and enjoy fellowship with them.

But the possibility for fellowship was now broken by sin, and God's questions to Adam were designed to get Adam to confess what had happened. "He said, 'Who told you that you were naked? Have you eaten from the tree of which I commanded you that you should not eat?'" (Genesis 3:11).

Adam's reply attempts to shift blame: "Then the man said, 'The woman whom You gave to be with me, she gave me of the tree, and I ate'" (v. 12). Notice the not-so-subtle accusation against God. Adam implied that God was at least partly to blame because, after all, it was He who created Eve. And Eve was to blame for coaxing Adam into the deed. Only after he had established such a bogus hierarchy of blame did Adam finally say, "I ate."

It was a pitiful attempt to evade responsibility for his own sin, but it is typical of the sinner when confronted with his guilt. Adam had sinned deliberately. Unlike Eve, he was not deceived (1 Timothy 2:14). He should have acknowledged his guilt and confessed what he had done, but instead, he tried every way he could find to mitigate his culpability.

"And the Lord God said to the woman, 'What is this you have done?' The woman said, 'The serpent deceived me, and I ate'" (Genesis 3:13). Strictly speaking, Eve's confession was true, but the facts did not acquit her from guilt. The serpent had deceived her. But she had willfully and selfishly disobeyed a clear commandment of God.

God's reply to the sin of Adam and Eve was a threefold curse. He spoke first to the serpent, then to the woman, and finally to the man. He outlined the consequences of their sin to each in turn:

> So the Lord God said to the serpent: "Because you have done this, you are cursed more than all cattle, and more than every beast of the field; on your belly you shall go, and you shall eat dust all the days of your life. And I will put enmity between you and the woman, and between your seed and her Seed; He shall bruise your head, and you shall bruise His heel." To the woman He said: "I will greatly multiply your sorrow and your conception; in pain you shall bring forth children; your desire shall be for your husband, and he shall rule over you." Then to Adam He said, "Because you have heeded the voice of your wife, and have eaten from

the tree of which I commanded you, saying, 'You shall not eat of it': Cursed is the ground for your sake; in toil you shall eat of it all the days of your life. Both thorns and thistles it shall bring forth for you, And you shall eat the herb of the field. In the sweat of your face you shall eat bread till you return to the ground, For out of it you were taken; for dust you are, and to dust you shall return" (Genesis 3:14–19).

Included in that curse are a number of significant features. The serpent was condemned to crawl on his belly in the dust. Apparently, prior to the curse, serpents had legs like other reptiles. Now they would be slithering creatures, symbolic of all that is loathsome, feared, and avoided by humans, "cursed more than all cattle, and more than every beast of the field."

Notice the subtle implication: cattle and other beasts of the field were cursed too. In fact, all creation was affected by Adam's sin—"subjected to futility" (Romans 8:20). Weeds and thorns would henceforth infest the ground. Pain, weariness, and sweat would make life difficult. And that is by no means an exhaustive list of the negative effects of the curse. In addition to the troubles expressly named in Genesis 3, a number of other woes have made human life difficult from that point on. For example, harmful germs and viruses, disease, disaster, and decay of all kinds also stem from the divine curse. Calamity, sorrow, strife, and other difficulties have become an unavoidable part of human life. Insects and other creatures have overstepped their original beneficial purposes and become annoying pests. Nature itself often becomes destructive, with floods, earthquakes, droughts, famines, and other natural disasters. That is why all creation "groans and labors with birth pangs" (Romans 8:22), waiting for the consummation of God's redemptive work.

The woman would be afflicted with pain in childbirth. That pain would be a perpetual reminder that the woman helped conceive sin in the human race and passes it on to her children. The Lord also told her that she would from now on chafe under her husband's authority.

And then the Lord told Adam he was condemned to a life of labor and sweat, tilling the cursed earth, to which he would one day return in death.

So Adam and Eve were disgraced and shamed and their lives were made difficult. More significantly, they were condemned to die, just as God had forewarned them.

And yet even in the midst of all this, we see clear evidence of divine grace toward Adam and Eve. The very words of the curse actually gave the fallen couple much reason for hope. Consider some of the blessings that flow from the curse.

THE ASSURANCE OF HUMANITY'S SURVIVAL

First of all, God's words to Eve clearly imply that humanity as a race would survive. Eve would give birth to Adam's offspring. Even though pain would accompany childbirth, the very mention of childbirth proved that God was not going to destroy Adam and Eve and the future of the human race along with them.

This was a remarkable assurance. Remember, God's original warning to Adam and Eve seemed to suggest that they would die instantly if they ate the fruit of the tree of the knowledge of good and evil: "In the day that you eat of it you shall surely die" (Genesis 2:17). As always, God's Word to Adam was perfectly fulfilled. Spiritually, our first parents did die in the very same day they partook of the forbidden fruit. But physically, their lives were graciously prolonged.

God could have justly executed the couple instantly and summarily the very moment they sinned. Instead, He spared the race from utter annihilation. In a sense, human life itself became a process of dying. But Adam and Eve did not suffer instant destruction. (As a matter of fact, Adam lived 930 years—Genesis 5:5). And as a result, they and their offspring were graciously given an opportunity for repentance and salvation.

So even as Adam and Eve listened to the grim words of the curse, a tremendous wave of relief and gratitude must have swept over them. Although they now knew toil and sorrow and woe would permeate their whole existence, they nonetheless had the promise of a posterity for their race.

In fact, immediately after recording the words of the curse, Scripture says, "Adam called his wife's name Eve, because she was the mother of all living" (Genesis 3:20). Obviously, Adam drew from God's words large expectations for the future of his race. He had clearly found reason for hope, even in the curse.

THE GUARANTEE OF SATAN'S DESTRUCTION

A second reason for hope is found in God's words to the serpent. The curse God pronounced against the reptile included a prophecy that the woman's Seed would crush the serpent's head. "Seed" could not be a reference to her offspring in general, because the expression translated "He shall bruise your head" in Genesis 3:15 clearly refers to a specific individual. We know from the rest of Scripture—and the fulfillment of the promise itself—that this can only be a reference to Christ, the incarnate Son of God. He was the promised Seed of the woman. And although the serpent would bruise His heel (causing suffering and pain), He would crush the serpent's head (signifying a fatal blow).

The true meaning of the prophecy looks beyond the actual reptile to the spirit-being who indwelt the serpent. In other words, this was a guarantee of Satan's ultimate destruction. It spoke of the final triumph of God over all that is evil. It was another reason for Adam and Eve to hope. The one who had destroyed paradise would himself be destroyed.

The prophecy is echoed in Paul's words of encouragement to the church at Rome: "The God of peace will crush Satan under your feet shortly" (Romans 16:20). Satan's destruction gives all believers reason to hope. His downfall not only signifies God's final triumph over all the devil's works, but in particular it represents the full reversal of Adam's fall. In other words, the promise of salvation from the curse of sin was implied in the prophecy about the serpent's destruction.

Hebrews 2:14 says this is the very reason Christ became human: "That through death He might destroy him who had the power of death, that is, the devil." First John 3:8 says, "For this purpose the Son of God was manifested, that He might destroy the works of the devil." And at the very end of redemptive history, Satan himself will be "cast into the lake of fire and brimstone," where he "will be tormented day and night forever and ever" (Revelation 20:10).

All of that was implicit in the curse, and it gave Adam and Eve another firm anchor for their hopes.

THE FIRST PROMISE OF A REDEEMER

But the greatest blessing that is bound up in the curse is the promise of Christ, the Redeemer, the Seed of the woman—the One who would crush the serpent's head. Consider what is revealed about Him here.

First, He would be the Seed of *the woman*. This is significant language, because normally, offspring are spoken of as the seed of their fathers. This seems to be a subtle reference to Christ's virgin birth. He was the offspring of a woman in a particular sense, but God was His only Father (Luke 1:34–35).

Second, there would be enmity between Him and the serpent. "I will put enmity between you and the woman, and between your seed and her Seed" (Genesis 3:15). This signifies the continuous conflict between Satan and Christ. Satan, the destroyer of men's souls, opposes Christ, the Savior of the world. The evil one hates the Holy One and has therefore set himself and "his seed"—all those who belong to his kingdom (both demons and humans)—against the Seed of the woman.

Third, the Seed of the woman would suffer. Satan would bruise His heel. This speaks of Christ's suffering on the cross. "He was wounded for our transgressions, He was bruised for our iniquities; the chastisement for our peace was upon Him, and by His stripes we are healed" (Isaiah 53:5).

Fourth, the Savior would triumph. He would end the enmity forever by crushing the serpent's head. Satan, the serpent, did his best to destroy Christ, but in the end it left only a bruise that would heal. Christ rose from the dead in triumph, gaining redemption for Adam's fallen race, while destroying the works of the devil. And in that act he sealed Satan's final defeat, crushing the serpent's head as promised.

Remember, the first glimmer of hope that all this would occur shone forth, of all places, in the curse God pronounced after Adam sinned! And the rest of Scripture, from this point on, merely fills in the gaps in the drama of redemption.

How did Christ redeem sinners from their sin? In the first place, He bore their sin. He took the guilt of sin upon Himself and was punished for it. That is why Satan was permitted to "bruise" Him. Peter wrote, "[He] bore our sins in His own body on the tree" (1 Peter 2:24). Isaiah the prophet, foreseeing the crucifixion of Christ, wrote, "Surely He has borne our griefs and carried our sorrows; yet we esteemed Him stricken, smitten by God, and afflicted. But He was wounded for our transgressions, He was bruised for our iniquities; the chastisement for our peace was upon Him, and by His stripes we are healed" (Isaiah 53:4–5). The writer of Hebrews says, "Christ was offered once to bear the sins of many" (Hebrews 9:28).

The apostle Paul, in shocking language, says, "[God] made Him who knew no sin to be sin for us" (2 Corinthians 5:21). God took His own spotless, sinless Son, imputed to Him the guilt of our sin, and then punished Him for it! Isaiah wrote, "It pleased the Lord to bruise Him; He has put Him to grief" (Isaiah 53:10).

So it was not only the serpent who bruised the Seed of the woman, but God Himself dealt Christ a dreadful blow, pouring out His full wrath against sin upon the person of His own innocent Son, who bore a world of guilt that didn't even belong to Him.

That is the gospel. It is good news, and God began to unveil it to fallen humanity before He had even finished His initial curse against their sin!

That is not all. Because Christ has paid the debt of sin on behalf of those who believe, their sins are forgiven them, and more: The very righteousness of Christ—all the full merit of that spotless, sinless life—is imputed to them. They lay hold of it by faith. This is the other side of 2 Corinthians 5:21: "[God] made Him who knew no sin to be sin for us, that we might *become the righteousness of God in Him*" (emphasis added). Thus He fully reverses the results of Adam's fall. "For as by one man's disobedience many were made sinners, so also by one Man's obedience many will be made righteous" (Romans 5:19).

In other words, we are clothed in the righteousness of Christ. There is a beautiful picture of this in Genesis 3, where, after pronouncing the curse, God graciously gave Adam and Eve more suitable clothing than the fig leaves they had stitched together. Genesis 3:21 says, "Also for Adam and his wife the Lord God made tunics of skin, and clothed them." In other words, God slew an animal—the first blood sacrifice, symbolizing the bloody cost of atonement—and covered their shame with the skin taken from that sacrifice.

In a similar way, Christ, whose atoning blood was shed for us on the cross, provides His own righteousness as a garment that covers all those who trust Him as Savior.

Again, that pure and perfect righteousness of Christ is laid hold of by faith. That means it cannot be earned through human merit: "To him who does not work but believes on Him who justifies the ungodly, his faith is accounted for righteousness. . . . God imputes [this] righteousness apart from works" (Romans 4:5–6). To try to earn righteousness through our own merit is the spiritual equivalent of making clothing from fig leaves. Our own "righteousness" is a tawdry, ineffectual covering for sin. Such self-righteousness is like dressing in the filthiest imaginable rags rather than a clean garment (Isaiah 64:6).

Those who remain in unbelief, as well as those who insist on trying to earn merit with God through their own works, will find no redemption from the effects of Adam's fall. "Nor is there salvation in any other, for there is no other name under heaven given among men by which we must be saved" (Acts 4:12). Jesus said, "I am the way, the truth, and the life. No one comes to the Father except through Me" (John 14:6).

Dear Reader,

I must not close this book without challenging you to examine yourself to see whether you are in the faith (2 Corinthians 13:5)—clothed with Christ's righteousness. And if you are not resting in Christ alone for salvation, I urge you to set aside your unbelief and self-effort and humbly receive the salvation that is freely offered in Him.

Creation and the fall are merely the prelude to redemption. Redemption is the real heart of the biblical message. Even if you originally picked this book up out of idle curiosity about biblical creationism, I believe God has brought you this far in your study for a reason. He is giving you an opportunity to be reconciled to Him (2 Corinthians 5:18–20), and as an ambassador of Christ, I implore you to respond to Him with repentant faith and with your whole heart.

Simply call on Him where you are. Ask Him to forgive your sins, give you a clean heart, and clothe you in His own righteousness. You don't even have to speak aloud to do it, for He knows your heart. And Scripture promises that "whoever calls on the name of the Lord shall be saved" (Romans 10:13). If you call on Him in faith, with a broken, yielded heart and will, He promises to hear and perform a creative miracle: "If anyone is in Christ, he is a new creation; old things have passed away; behold, all things have become new" (2 Corinthians 5:17). My prayer for you is that you will know the reality of that New Creation.

ENDNOTES

Introduction

1. Michael Ruse is an evolutionist who testified in the 1980s at the infa-
   mous Arkansas creationism trial *(McLean v. Arkansas)*. During the trial,
   he claimed that creationism is a religion because it is grounded in
   unproven philosophical assumptions. But Darwinism is a science, he said,
   because it requires no philosophical or religious presuppositions. Ruse has
   since admitted that he was wrong, and he now acknowledges that evolution "is metaphysically based"—grounded in unproven beliefs that are no
   more "scientific" than the set of beliefs on which creationism is based.
   See Tom Woodward, "Ruse Gives Away the Store: Admits Evolution Is a
   Philosophy." Found at http://www.origins.org/real/ri9404/ruse.html.

2. Carl Sagan, *ABC News Nightline*, 4 December 1996.

3. Carl Sagan, *Pale Blue Dot* (New York: Random House, 1994), 9.

4. Thomas Huxley, "Evolution and Ethics," The Romanes Lecture, 1893.
   Huxley nonetheless went on to try to justify ethics as a positive result of
   humanity's higher rational functions, and he called upon his audience
   neither to imitate "the cosmic process" nor to run away from it, but rather
   to combat it—ostensibly by maintaining some semblance of morality and
   ethics. But what he could not do—what he and other philosophers of his
   era did not even bother attempting to do—was offer any justification for
   assuming the validity of morality and ethics per se on purely naturalistic

principles. Huxley and his fellow naturalists could offer no moral compass other than their own personal preferences, and predictably, their philosophies all opened the door wide for complete moral subjectivity and ultimately amorality.

5. Stephen Jay Gould, *Ever Since Darwin* (New York: Norton, 1977), 26.

6. Edward J. Young, *Studies in Genesis One* (Phillipsburg, N.J.: Presbyterian & Reformed, n.d.), 99.

7. Ibid.

8. Marvin L. Lubenow, *Bones of Contention: A Creationist Assessment of Human Fossils* (Grand Rapids: Baker, 1992), 188–89.

9. Douglas F. Kelly, *Creation and Change* (Fearn, Ross-shire, U.K.: Christian Focus, 1997).

10. John Ankerberg and John Weldon, *Darwin's Leap of Faith* (Eugene, Oreg.: Harvest House, 1998).

11. Phillip E. Johnson, *Reason in the Balance: The Case against Naturalism in Science, Law, and Education* (Downers Grove, Ill.: InterVarsity, 1995).

12. Henry Morris, *The Genesis Record* (Grand Rapids: Baker, 1976).

13. Ken Ham, *Creation Evangelism for the New Millennium* (Green Forest, Ark.: Master Books, 1999).

Chapter 1—Creation: Believe It or Not

1. Ingrid Newkirk, cited in Katie McCabe, "Who Will Live and Who Will Die?" *The Washingtonian*, August 1986, 114.

2. Ingrid Newkirk, cited in Chip Brown, "She's a Portrait of Zealotry in Plastic Shoes," *Washington Post*, 13 November 1983, B-10.

3. Ibid.

4. Les U. Knight [pseud.], "Voluntary Human Extinction," *Wild Earth* 1, 2, (summer 1991), 72.

5. They "advocate" cannibalism, for example, with the slogan, "Eat people, not animals"—to make the point that in their view the act of eating any animal is the moral equivalent of cannibalism.

6. The fact that we can carry on this rational dialogue and animals can't is itself reason to believe man is far above animals—possessing sensibility and personhood, which are totally absent in the animal realm. See

chapter 8 for a thorough discussion of this point.

7. Jacques Monod, *Chance and Necessity* (New York: A. A. Knopf, 1971), 112–13, cited in Ankerberg and Weldon, *Darwin's Leap of Faith*, 21.

8. Scripture teaches that such "random" events are actually governed by God's sovereign providence (Proverbs 16:33; Matthew 10:30). God Himself ultimately controls all the factors that determine the flip of the coin. Nothing whatsoever happens by "chance."

9. George Wald, "The Origin of Life," *Scientific American*, May 1954, 46.

10. Ibid., 48.

11. Herbert Spencer, *First Principles* (London: Williams and Norgate, 1862), chapter 3.

12. Spencer maintained that human consciousness is a manifestation of an infinite and eternal cosmic energy; hence even consciousness is ultimately a material, rather than a spiritual, reality. Many modern evolutionists still hold such a view.

13. Spencer's "solution" to this dilemma was to regard force as eternal.

14. Interestingly, Spencer spoke of force as "the ultimate of ultimates" (Ibid., paragraph 50).

15. Morris, *The Genesis Record *, 18.

16. Ankerberg and Weldon include a long section documenting evolutionists' attempts to silence and marginalize their colleagues who do not toe the naturalist line. See *Darwin's Leap*, chapter 6, "Professional Objectivity and the Politics of Prejudice," 93–111.

17. Douglas F. Kelly, *Creation and Change*, 15–16.

18. Francis Schaeffer, cited in Kelly, *Creation and Change*, 17.

Chapter 2—How Did Creation Happen?

1. *Fiat* is a Latin word meaning, "let it be done."

2. A full discussion of the geological evidences for creation and the Flood is far beyond the scope of this book. But many fine resources outlining those evidences in detail are available from The Institute for Creation Research (http://www.icr.org) and Answers in Genesis (http://www.answersingenesis.org). See also John Woodmorappe, *Studies in Flood Geology* (Santee, Calif.: Institute for Creation Research, 1999); John C. Whitcomb and

Henry M. Morris, *The Genesis Flood* (Grand Rapids: Baker, 1961); and John C. Whitcomb, *The World that Perished* (Grand Rapids: Baker, 1990).

3. See Rebecca Gibson, "Canyon Creation," *Creation Ex Nihilo* (Sep–Nov 2000), 46–48.

4. Douglas F. Kelly, *Creation and Change*, 164–65.

5. Ken Ham, *Did Adam Have a Belly Button?* (Green Forest, Ark.: Masta Books, 1999). See also Gary Parker, "Did Adam have a belly button?" Found at http://www.answersingenesis.org/docs/1260.asp.

6. Hugh Ross, *The Fingerprint of God* (New Kensington, Pa.: Whitaker House, 1989), 96.

7. Mark Van Bebber and Paul S. Taylor, *Creation and Time: A Report on the Progressive Creationist Book by Hugh Ross* (Gilbert, Ariz.: Eden Communications, [year]), 86–89.

8. Ross, *The Fingerprint of God*, 160.

9. Van Bebber and Taylor, *Creation and Time*, 105–110. See also Danny Faulkner, "The Dubious Apologetics of Hugh Ross," found at http://www.answersingenesis.or/docs/4149.asp and Dr. Bolton Davidheiser, "A Statement Concerning the Ministry of Dr. Hugh Ross," found at http://www.ldolphin.org/bolton.html.

10. Hugh Ross, *Creation and Time* (Colorado Springs: NavPress, 1994), 56 (emphasis added).

11. Ibid., 57.

12. Ross, *The Fingerprint of God*, 145.

13. Ibid., 56.

14. Ibid., 143.

15. Ibid., 159.

16. Morris, *The Genesis Record*, 45.

17. Young, *Studies in Genesis One*, 53.

18. Ross, *The Fingerprint of God*, 160.

Chapter 3—Light on Day One

1. Ross, *The Fingerprint of God*, 141.

2. Augustine, *The City of God*, 11:6.

3. Ibid.
4. Ibid., 12:10.
5. Ross, *The Fingerprint of God*, 160.
6. Morris, *The Genesis Record*, 41.
7. Ibid., 52.
8. Kelly, *Creation and Change*, 83.
9. Ibid., 85.
10. Novation, cited in Kelly, *Creation and Change*, 88.

Chapter 4—When He Marked Out the Foundations of the Earth

1. Gregg Easterbrook, "Science and Religion: Academics Ponder the Ties Between Faith and Fact," *Los Angeles Times*, 14 March 1999, 1.
2. Michael Behe, *Darwin's Black Box: The Biochemical Challenge to Evolution* (New York: Free Press, 1996), 39.
3. For an interesting discussion of this problem see Don Batten, "Ligers and wholphins? What next?" Found at http://www.answersingenesis.org/home/area/magazines/docs/v22n3_liger.asp.
4. Morris, *The Genesis Record*, 64.
5. Ibid.

Chapter 5—Lights in the Heavens

1. Richard Stenger, "Sun aims powerful flares at Earth" (1 March 2000). Found at http:www.cnn.com/2000/TECH/space/03/01/sunspots/.
2. Ken Ham, "How can we see distant stars in a young Universe?" Found at http://www.answersingenesis.org/docs/405.asp.
3. Easterbrook, "Science and Religion" 1.
4. C. S. Lewis, *God in the Dock* (Grand Rapids: Eerdmans, 1970), 52–53.
5. C. S. Lewis, *Miracles* (New York: MacMillan, 1947), 21.

Chapter 6—An Abundance of Living Creatures

1. Kelly, *Creation and Change*, 208.
2. Someone might raise the question of how hermit crabs obtained their

borrowed homes prior to the fall of Adam, when there was no death and hence no discarded gastropod shells. In such an environment, of course, the crab would have no need of any protection from predators. So the crabs no doubt lived very well without shells. But the all-knowing Creator had built into their species the ability to acquire the ideal form of protection when it was needed.

3. Lane P. Lester, "Genetics: No Friend of Evolution." Found at http://www.answersingenesis.org/docs/1356.asp.

4. Ibid.

5. A. E. Wilder Smith, *The Scientific Alternative to Neo-Darwinian Evolutionary Theory* (Costa Mesa, Calif.: Word For Today, 1987), 14–15.

Chapter 8—Man in God's Image

1. For a fuller discussion of this eternal promise between the members of the Godhead, see my book *The Murder of Jesus* (Nashville: Word, 2000), 78–80.

2. Angels may also share something of the image of God, for Scripture says that redeemed people in their glorified state will be "like angels in heaven" (Mark 12:25). Angels are also sometimes referred to in Scripture as "sons of God" (e.g. Job 1:6), suggesting that they, too, bear God's likeness. But in the material universe, humanity alone bears this distinction.

3. Kelly, *Creation and Change*, 220.

4. The reference in the text is to the issue covered in footnote 4 in the Introduction—the lack of any ground for morality under naturalism.

5. John Calvin, *Institutes of the Christian Religion* Henry Beveridge, trans. (Grand Rapids: Eerdmans, n.d.), 1.15.3, p. 164.

6. Morris, *The Genesis Record*, 74–75.

7. Kelly, *Creation and Change*, 224.

Chapter 9—The Rest of Creation

1. Kelly, *Creation and Change*, 237.
2. Morris, *The Genesis Record*, 80–81.
3. Ibid., 81.
4. John Calvin, *Institutes of the Christian Religion*. Ford Lewis Battles, trans. (Philadelphia: Westminster, 1940), 3.23.8, p. 957.

Chapter 10—Paradise Lost

1. G. K. Chesterton, *Orthodoxy* (London: Lane, 1909), 22.
2. Edward J. Young, *Genesis 3* (Edinburgh: Banner of Truth, 1966), 34–35.

SUBJECT INDEX